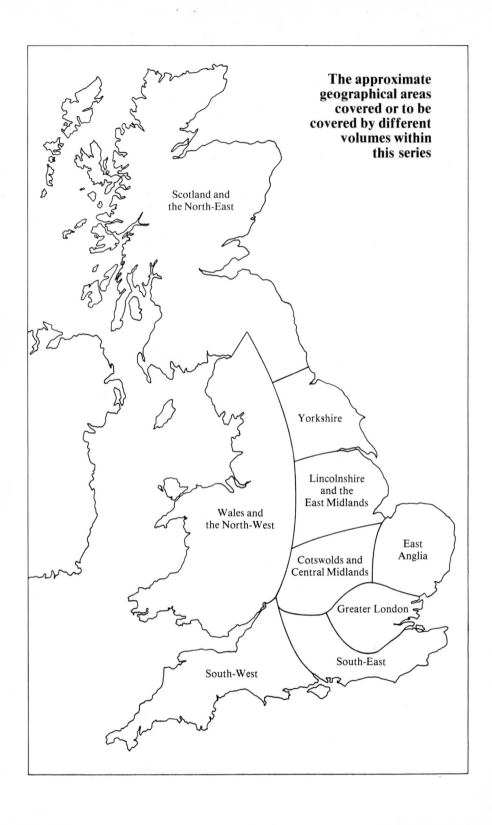

The approximate
geographical areas
covered or to be
covered by different
volumes within
this series

Scotland and
the North-East

Yorkshire

Lincolnshire
and the
East Midlands

Wales and
the North-West

East
Anglia

Cotswolds and
Central Midlands

Greater London

South-East

South-West

ACTION STATIONS

2. Military airfields of Lincolnshire and the East Midlands

Bruce Barrymore Halpenny

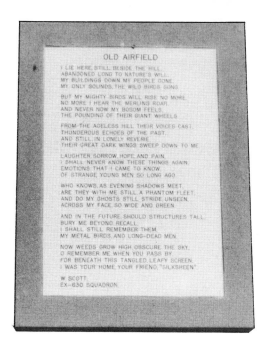

OLD AIRFIELD

I LIE HERE STILL, BESIDE THE HILL,
ABANDONED LONG TO NATURE'S WILL,
MY BUILDINGS DOWN, MY PEOPLE GONE,
MY ONLY SOUNDS THE WILD BIRDS SONG.

BUT MY MIGHTY BIRDS WILL RISE NO MORE,
NO MORE I HEAR THE MERLINS ROAR.
AND NEVER NOW MY BOSOM FEELS,
THE POUNDING OF THEIR GIANT WHEELS.

FROM THE AGELESS HILL THEIR VOICES CAST,
THUNDEROUS ECHOES OF THE PAST,
AND STILL IN LONELY REVERIE,
THEIR GREAT DARK WINGS SWEEP DOWN TO ME.

LAUGHTER, SORROW, HOPE AND PAIN,
I SHALL NEVER KNOW THESE THINGS AGAIN,
EMOTIONS THAT I CAME TO KNOW,
OF STRANGE YOUNG MEN SO LONG AGO.

WHO KNOWS, AS EVENING SHADOWS MEET,
ARE THEY WITH ME STILL A PHANTOM FLEET,
AND DO MY GHOSTS STILL STRIDE UNSEEN,
ACROSS MY FACE SO WIDE AND GREEN.

AND IN THE FUTURE SHOULD STRUCTURES TALL,
BURY ME BEYOND RECALL,
I SHALL STILL REMEMBER THEM,
MY METAL BIRDS AND LONG-DEAD MEN.

NOW WEEDS GROW HIGH OBSCURE THE SKY,
O REMEMBER ME WHEN YOU PASS BY,
FOR BENEATH THIS TANGLED LEAFY SCREEN,
I WAS YOUR HOME, YOUR FRIEND, "SILKSHEEN"

W SCOTT,
EX—630 SQUADRON.

PSL Patrick Stephens, Cambridge

Title page *From the East Kirkby memorial—see page 90.*

*This book is dedicated to the memory of
Leanda (Wibby) Woods*

© Bruce Barrymore Halpenny

First published in 1981

British Library Cataloguing in Publication Data

Action stations.
  2: Military airfields of Lincolnshire and the
East Midlands
  1. World War, 1939-1945—Aerial operations, British
  2. Air bases—England—History
  I. Halpenny, Bruce Barrymore
  II. Military airfields of Lincolnshire and the
East Midlands
  940.54'43'42   D786

ISBN 0-85059-484-7

Photoset in 9pt and 10 on 11pt English Times by
Manuset Limited, Baldock, Herts. Printed in Great Britain
on 100 gsm Fineblade coated cartridge by
The Garden City Press, Letchworth, Herts,
and bound by Norton Bridge Bookbinders Limited, Stotfold,
Herts, for the publishers, Patrick Stephens Limited, Bar Hill,
Cambridge, CB3 8EL, England.

Contents

Introduction

In both the First and Second World Wars the vast open flat Lincolnshire countryside has been home to many military airfields and the woods and fields occasionally reveal their wartime inheritance. Lincolnshire is the renowned bomber county and it has been my privilege to do research and to interview many of the bomber crews and fighter pilots. My mandate was to produce a factual but readable account of the history of the airfields and the men and aircraft that used them. It cannot be definitive for how can history covering thousands of men, women and aircraft ever be so?

During the late 1930s it was a public relations practice for towns and cities to 'adopt' an RAF squadron; for example, Sheffield linked with No 49, then at Scampton, which thereafter took the name 'Sheffield's Own'. With war declared and the sudden expansion of airfields, everyone became involved in one way or another.

The early bombing raids of World War 2 quickly pointed the needs for further technical improvements and this caused RAF Bomber Command to switch predominantly to night operations for the duration of the war. Further development culminated in such equipment as the H2S radar that was carried on board the new generation of four-engined bombers. These brought even greater bombs and bomb loads. At the outbreak of war, bombs normally weighed up to 1,000 lb. The Lancaster was able to carry bombs of up to 4,000 lb and was adapted progressively to accommodate bombs weighing 8,000, 12,000 and, finally, the 22,000 lb 'Grand Slam', the largest conventional high explosive bomb dropped in World War 2.

Night after night the bombers took off while the fighters defended our shores. The bomber crews had many problems to face; apart from the flak and German night fighters, they also had to contend with frost-bite, frozen guns, icing, over-heating engines, oxygen failures, lack of fuel and a deadly enemy on their return—fog.

It is not possible to mention the role of every unit on every airfield. A unit and its role has been selected at different airfields and one can then obtain an overall picture of specialist squadrons, training units, operational training units, defence of airfields, etc. The combats of one squadron or person, however outstanding and heroic, form only the general pattern. From Wickenby, a full raid report, recorded at the time on 'K' report No. 1G/K19, is shown and, even though it was not a Canadian squadron, five out of the seven-man crew were Canadians.

To give the atmosphere of the station and those wartime days which were a sense of shared effort and responsibility, sadly now missing from our self-oriented society, I have injected interviews of those who were there, and many recalled those wartime days as if they were only yesterday. Let us remember the deeds that were carried out from these airfields and the whys and wherefores that made Great Britain, Great.

It is deplorable that such a man as Duncan Sandys, Minister of Defence in the infamous 1957 White Paper, should forecast the end of manned aircraft and their replacement by guided missiles. The passage of two decades proves which end he was talking through but, this meant the run-down and eventual closure of many airfields. In the early and mid-1970s there were further closures due to the streamlining of the RAF's command structure, Manby being one of the victims.

Over the years nothing has been done to prevent demolition of the airfields and as these are part of the nation's heritage they should not be bulldozed away or left to die. All wartime airfields, whether operational or training, are memorials to great men and should have a small inscribed monument as they fade into history. A few memorials have been erected but these do not record the function or period of service of the station.

Airfield buildings have architectural and civil engineering interest and it is an everlasting credit to their builders that many of them remain almost intact today. Who could have known that their material efforts would be forever in the memories of men in the four corners of the earth? The RAF wartime station was a principality of its own and the airfields have a great historical value, yet there are few official listings of World War 2 airfield structures for airfield conservation. A few organisations are now working to conserve a few items, but it needs to be done with those in power. The City of Lincoln wants the glory of the last flying Lancaster but is not interested in the airfields. A few airfields should have been preserved intact as working museums with aircraft being housed in the hangars. At the end of the war there were 721 Lancasters in Lincolnshire, but how many survive?

I trust this book will make one ponder awhile and reminisce the wartime role of the airfields for there is a sad and strange fascination about them as they crumble into oblivion. Left to die, many are desolate, bleak, windswept sites and even on those devoid of hangars and main buildings there is a strange silent atmosphere that can be felt; Kelstern is an example. A few buildings remain on many of the sites, standing more like the vanquished than the victor and in the evening mist, like ghosts from the past.

Bruce Barrymore Halpenny
Grantham, June 1980

Acknowledgements

The material for this book comes from my years of researching and writing about military aviation. Over the years hundreds of people have assisted me and to everyone—thank you. A special mention must be made for a number of individuals for a variety of reasons:

Major The Earl of Ancaster, KCVO. Angela and Jane for keeping me mobile. Anglia Aeropics.

Bill Baguley, for his outside research and photography work on the airfields. Mrs Ruth Bell, Quebec, Canada. Dave Benfield for some research material and photographs. Ken Border for assistance with the research material.

Flight Lieutenant G.R. Carter—CRO, RAF Coningsby. Harry Coulby, a very loyal friend over the years, for his ever-readiness to help. Fred Cubberley for photographs and details of present day airfields. L.D. Cowell. Edward H. Currotte, ARW, New Brunswick, Canada, for his collection of RAF terminology and his weekly letters. These were most welcome not only for the information and photographs but, the weekly PS—my favourite: Typing getting poor . . . Oh for the days of a good looking WAAF secretary complete with lisle stockings, 'airwoman for the use of'. Alan Cutherbertson, Manitoba, Canada.

A.F. Dales, Indian Head, Canada. Hon Walter Dinsdale, MP, Ottawa, Canada. Elsie Dodd, (née Williams) for her wartime photographs and material. Ex-Sergeant Jack Dunn. Eric C. Dyer, Airport Director—East Midlands Airport, for photographs and material. *Edmonton Journal*, Canada. Stephen Elliott, for assisting with outside photography work. Ted Evans, a very special friend.

Neville Franklin—his help with photographs, material and general assistance whenever needed. Mick Fisher.

Flight Lieutenant J.D. Hamlyn, RAF Cottesmore, for the first Tornado photograph. Harold Hamnett, British Columbia, Canada. Joan Hatfield. Heathrow Airport. George Henry. Mr E. Hine, Imperial War Museum, London. Rodney Houldsworth, for his assistance with printing some of the many photographs.

Flight Lieutenant David A. Ingham BSc, RAF, Royal Air Force College, Cranwell, and Mrs J.M. King, the College Librarian. Ken Irlam, Canada (ex-410 Squadron).

Squadron Leader Jacko Jackson and crew for giving me a 'buzz' in the Lancaster on June 15 1980 to keep me at it. To hear those Merlins was a great injection.

Major Paul K. Kahl, Sr, USAF, Department of Defence, Texas. Major A.R. Kingsford, New Zealand, for photographs and information regarding World War 1 airfields and aircraft.

H.J. Lazenby. Lillian for her understanding and her permission to read her wartime letters, photographs and poem.

Flight Lieutenant I.B. Medhurst, RAF Waddington. C.V. Middleton & Son, Lincoln, for bringing out the best in many old prints and negatives. A. Millns, Manitoba, Canada. Robert E. Morrow, QC, Canada, for his outstanding photographs and material—and patience.

George Penfold, Canada. Ex-Flight Sergeant A. Perry. Air Commodore H.A. Probert MBE, MA, RAF (Rt'd), Head of Air Historical Branch (RAF).

J.E. Raw-Rees, DFC, JP, DL—photographs. Frank and John Richardson, two very good friends who supplied me with a mountain of much needed scrap paper. Nick Roberts and his time with the airfield plans and crash information.

Nancy Shenker, Christchurch, New Zealand. General Sikorski Museum. R. Simpson, Department of Aviation Records, RAF Museum, Hendon. Group Captain Chris Sprent, RAF, Coningsby, for his immediate action with my requests, and for his excellent display in the Hurricane. Bud Stevenson, Ontario, Canada. Commander G.N.P. Stringer OBE, DFC, RN (Rt'd).

Bill Taylor, Reginald Trueman.

Les Wallace, Ontario. Wing Commander Ken Wallis, CEng, FRAeS, RAF (Rt'd). Squadron Leader Tom Wardle, RAF (Rt'd). Flight Lieutenant R.M. Wright, RAF Scampton. Flight Lieutenant D.T. Wynne, RAF Newton.

The many libraries, in particular: Miss N.A. Harper, FLA, Oakham Library. Mrs Judith Flint, Melton Mowbray. Miss Lorna Rattray, Loughborough. Hucknall Library. Mr A.W. Stevenson, Leicester. Mr Stephen Best, Nottingham.

Many newspapers and magazines who published my request letters over the years: *Daily Express*, London. *News of the World*, London. *Toronto Star*, Canada. *The Press*, New Zealand. *London Free Press*, Canada.

A very special thank you to Mrs Margaret Morris who deciphered my appalling scribble and transferred it into a legible manuscript after many hours of typing and re-typing. A most loyal friend who made sure it was produced on time.

Last but not least my wife Marion for the hours of proof reading and my son Baron who had to do without me for many months.

My special thanks for all those who loaned me material and photographs, with apologies to any that I might have forgotten.

The author would be interested to receive any new facts, photographs or other material for incorporation in future publications.

Glossary

AAC Army Air Corps.
AAF Auxiliary Air Force.
ACHU Aircrew Holding Unit.
ADF Air Defence Squadron.
AFTCC Air Force Troop Carrier Command.
AOP Air Observation Post.
ASC Air Support Command.
ASR Air Sea Rescue.
B&GF Bombing & Gunnery Flight.
BATF Beam Approach Training Flight.
BC Bomber Command.
Bde Brigade.
BDTF Bomber Defence Training Flight.
Bf Bayerische Flugzeugwerke (Messerschmitt).
BoB Battle of Britain.
Bn Battalion.
CFE Central Fighter Establishment.
CFS Central Flying School.
CGM Conspicuous Gallantry Medal.
CGS Central Gunnery School.
Chastise Code name for the attack on the Ruhr dams by No 617 Squadron on May 16/17 1943.
C&M Care and Maintenance.
CO Commanding Officer.
Comm Communications (Flight)
'Cookie' Name given to a 4,000 lb High-Capacity bomb.
Con Conversion (Flight).
CU Conversion Unit.
DFC Distinguished Flying Cross.
DFM Distinguished Flying Medal.
Div Division.
DSO Distinguished Service Order.
DZ Dropping Zone.
E/A Enemy aircraft.
EFTS Elementary Flying Training School.
EGS Elementary Glider School.
FAA Fleet Air Arm.
FC Fighter Command.
FIS Flying Instructors' School.

F/O Flying Officer.
FPP Ferry Pilots Pool.
FTC Flying Training Command.
FTR Failed to return.
FTS Flying Training School.
Fw Focke-Wulf.
Gardening Code name for sea mine-laying by aircraft.
GEE Medium-range radio aid to navigation and target identification with ground transmitters and airborne receiver.
Gp Group.
Group Pool Squadron Training Unit.
HCU Heavy Conversion Unit.
HGCU Heavy Glider Conversion Unit.
HGMU Heavy Glider Maintenance Unit.
HFF Heavy Freight Flight.
ICBM Inter-Continental Ballistic Missile.
IFF Identification Friend or Foe.
Inf Infantry.
LAC Leading Aircraftsman.
LFS Lancaster Finishing School.
LRDF Long Range Development Flight.
MAN Maschinenfabrik Augsburg-Nürnberg Aktiengesellschaft.
MAP Ministry of Aircraft Production
Me Messerschmitt.
MT Motor Transport.
MU Maintenance Unit.
MUG Mid-Upper Gunner.
NAAFI Navy, Army, Air Force Institute.
NATO North Atlantic Treaty Organisation.
'Nickel' Leaflets, usually propaganda.
OCU Operational Conversion Unit.
Operation 'Bellicose' First 'shuttle bombing' raid by Bomber Command on June 20/21 1943. Aircraft landed at Algiers and bombed Spezia on their return to the UK.

Operation 'Dodge'   Ferrying troops home from Italy. Many 8th Army 'Desert Rats', etc, by air.

Operation 'Exodus'   Repatriation by air of British ex-PoWs from the continent.

Operation 'Manna'   Dropping of food to the starving Dutch people.

Operation 'Millennium'   Code name for first 1,000-bomber raid on Cologne, May 30/31 1942.

Operation 'Robinson'   Lancaster raid on Le Creusot on October 17 1942.

Operation 'Varsity'   Airborne landings on March 24 1945.

OTU   Operational Training Unit.

'Overlord'   Code name for D-Day, June 6 1944, the Allied invasion of France.

(P)AFU   (Pilot) Advance Flying Unit.

PFF   Pathfinder Force.

'Post Mortem'   Evaluation of German early warning radar system in June and July 1945 by Bomber Command.

PoW   Prisoner of War.

RAAF   Royal Australian Air Force.

RAFC   Royal Artillery Flying Club.

RCAF   Royal Canadian Air Force.

RDF   Radio Direction Finding.

RF   Reserve Flight.

RFC   Royal Flying Corps.

Rgt   Regiment.

RLG   Relief Landing Ground.

RNZAF   Royal New Zealand Air Force.

ROC   Royal Observer Corps.

SAM   Surface to Air Missile.

SC   Strike Command.

Scramble   An immediate operational take-off.

SD   Special Duties.

SF   Servicing Flight.

SFTS   Service Flying Training School.

S/Ldr   Squadron Leader.

SLG   Satellite Landing Ground.

Sortie   Operational mission by a single aircraft.

STT   School of Technical Training.

SU   Signals Unit.

TCU   Transport Conversion Unit.

TCW   Troop Carrier Wing.

TDS   Training Depot Station.

TF   Training Flight.

Tng   Training.

TS   Training Squadron.

TTC   Technical Training Command.

TTF   Target Towing Flight.

TTTE   Tri-national Tornado Training Establishment.

u/s   Unserviceable.

USAF   United States Air Force.

USAAF   United States Army Air Force.

VC   Victoria Cross.

W/Cdr   Wing Commander.

W/T   Wireless Telegraphy.

Airfield history

An aerodrome is described by the International Civil Aviation Organisation as a definite area on land or water normally used for the take-off and landing of aircraft. This includes any buildings and installations and covers satellite aerodromes, emergency and relief landing grounds.

During the early part of the First World War there was a need for airfields and a large number were established to cope with the vast increase of aircraft. At the end of 1914 there were about 300 or so aircraft in service, of which the RNAS had 50 seaplanes and six airships and the RFC had 63, front line strength. By November 30 1918 the Royal Air Force had 22,647. A typical training airfield was a grass square with 2,000-ft sides. Facilities included three pairs of hangars, either of brick of wood and possibly an additional single hangar, plus up to 12 canvas Bessoneaux hangars. Aircraft were at this period very susceptible to weather damage and had to remain under cover, hence the need for all the hangars. Accommodation was mainly in wooden huts and tents. Therefore, it did not take long to dismantle them and, after the war, the majority of these buildings soon disappeared from the landscape.

During the 'Expansion Period' of the Royal Air Force in the mid-1930s, a standard pattern was devised for the airfield which would now have permanent hangars and accommodation. With the aircraft then available it was decided an airfield should have a main landing strip 1,300 yards long by 400 yards wide and two subsidiaries 1,000 yards by 200 yards. Up to the outbreak of the Second World War several stations had a dual purpose and housed Flying Training Schools (FTS) and Maintenance Units (MU), but the difficulties soon became obvious and, although the dual role continued in some instances, various kinds of improvised landing fields came into being during the 1939-1945 war.

It was decided that the eastern side of the country, Yorkshire, Lincolnshire and East Anglia, should house the operational bomber airfields, the Midlands the Operational Training Units, the majority of the fighter airfields being in the south.

At the beginning of World War 2 the cost of building a bomber station was £550,000 but by 1945 this figure had risen to £1,000,000. Military airfields usually kept to the triangular pattern and needed an area of between 700 and 1,000 acres. The tangential pattern was put forward to the service authorities but was abandoned.

Beginning as nothing more than a stabilisation of the topsoil, all airfields were grass covered at the outset; at the outbreak of war in September 1939 only nine airfields had runways and by March 1941 a mere three operational bomber stations were equipped with concrete runways. However, with the coming of the large four-engined bomber, with aircraft of 70,000 lb weight, paved runways were needed at least 3,350 yards in length and at least 40 yards in width. Aircraft weights and wing loadings rose rapidly and went from the 10 to 15 lb per square foot of the First World War to over 50 lb per square foot and this meant not only extended paved runways but also extended cleared areas beyond the ends of the runways. For the bomber station the changes were not just on runways but also dispersal areas for the bigger and heavier four-engined bombers. The big change with the operational airfield meant that aircraft were only taken into hangars for major servicing. Aircraft were now sited around the perimeter at dispersal points. Thus, servicing bays were also needed for fighters. These being concrete standings, walled in on three sides.

Extensive servicing equipment and personnel are needed for operating and maintaining a large bomber station. A force of 3,000 officers and men during the Second World War could attain a movement rate of 30 aircraft per hour.

Originally, fighter stations did not need the larger runways or have to be paved and continued with grass surface. At a later date many were fitted with prefabricated runways of which there were about ten or more types, the main one being pierced steel planking. A perimeter track and some hardstandings were also added at some fighter airfields. The specification drawn in March 1941 stated that a fighter airfield should have one 1,300-yard runway and two of 1,100 yards.

Construction reached its peak in 1942 with a labour force of some 60,000 men employed solely on airfield construction. This was the largest construction programme in English history and a new airfield was being started every three days. When the USAAF began to arrive in the middle of 1942 it meant a further requirement of 50 airfields for the USAAF's VIIIth and IXth Air Forces. From September 1938 to September 1946 there were 560 military airfields constructed in the UK and Northern Ireland. This included airfields taken over and extended. A total of 167 airfields had grass runways.

Class A-type airfield

This became the Air Ministry Directorate—General of Works standard for heavy bomber stations, bomber OTUs and transport stations. It is the Class A-type airfield that concerns us mostly in this volume, and was the ultimate standard that remained for the duration of the war. All airfields that were extended were brought up to Class A standard. The recommended requirements were three intersecting runways, the main one being 2,000 yards in length with the two subsidiaries being 1,400 yards each. The width of all the runways was theoretically standardised at 50 yards and the main one had the lighting equipment. The main runway should have been aligned to the prevailing winds, but this was not always the case as it depended more on being able to fit the airfield into the land available as well as avoiding population centres and obstructions.

A perimeter track, 50 ft wide, encircled the airfield and averaged some three miles in length. Branching off from the perimeter track were the dispersal points for the aircraft that sometimes led off into the surrounding fields or woodland. The main type of hardstandings were the 'frying pan' type, which aptly

From these two examples of the same airfield one can see the wartime pattern and the jet age requirement of a single runway of about 9,000 ft in length which became the norm for V-bomber stations and civil aerodromes. **Left** *An RAF photograph of the deserted airfield taken on March 1 1950 which shows Castle Donington in its wartime configuration* (Crown copyright). **Right** *East Midlands Airport, ex-Castle Donington, as at March 1972. Modern day layout of a single main runway, but its former outlines can still be made out.*

describes their shape, these being either 125 ft or 150 ft circular aprons that were linked to the perimeter by a taxiway. The other type was the 'spectacle' loop concrete hardstanding and these were found to be better for manoeuvring aircraft. On the early airfields there were 30 such hardstandings, but this was later increased to 36. For the American stations 50 hardstandings were needed and on the airfields they took over it was raised to this number.

Relief Landing Ground (RLG)
After the outbreak of war the Flying Training Schools were brought up to their wartime establishment and as the number of courses increased pressure was put on the grass airfields. So, the Relief Landing Ground, sometimes referred to as a satellite landing ground, was put into service. These were usually flat areas of land that offered a single landing strip of about 1,000 yards arranged in the direction of the prevailing wind and were in many cases parks and other open spaces that gave natural camouflage. Some RLGs were fitted with Pierced Steel Planking (PSP) and the earlier Somerfeld Tracking. The RLGs were as close as possible to the parent station and were without any permanent buildings or pavement. The reasoning behind the RLG was that it increased the parent station facilities as aircraft strength increased yet did not demand a lot of the agricultural land. Draining was often the problem and as the permanent satellite airfields came into being the RLGs were handed over to MUs for storage; some

were never used at all and all had been derequisitioned by mid-1946. Only the expert could ever find any trace of the RLGs today.

Emergency airfields (ELG)

Emergency landing grounds were built on the same lines as the RLGs but were single hard-surface runways over 200 ft wide and 3,000 yards long with overshooting surfaces at each end. These strips were sited near the coast, examples being Carnaby in Yorkshire, Woodbridge in Suffolk and Manston in Kent. These stations could deal with any kind of emergency and were maintained by a minimum of personnel, only those needed for the key equipment, firefighting appliances, radio, ambulances and heavy lifting equipment. They had very little other equipment or buildings, for their purpose was to provide an emergency landing ground for the aircraft, not house or repair them.

The ELGs used in the First World War were very primitive and were called forced landing ground illuminations. These consisted of petrol tins in the form of a letter 'L'—on the long arm there were six tins and on the short, two tins. Old cotton waste was burnt in them. Three such ELGs were sited in Lincolnshire.

Aerodrome buildings

These were kept to a minimum and on the standard World War 2 airfield were always well dispersed for obvious reasons. Usually on pre-war bases there were up to five hangars which were only used for major overhauls, these being adjacent to the technical site. Each airfield had ten or more sites dispersed through the countryside around the airfield which included the sick quarters, domestic and sewage sites, etc. The aerodrome was completely self-contained with its own electrical generator, fuel in underground tanks and water that was stored in the familiar water towers perched high above the ground. The bomb dump and ammunition buildings were usually constructed in remote areas on the opposite side of the airfield to the domestic site.

FIDO

Fog had always been a problem, very much so in the First World War, and was the greatest worry for the pilots. Fog would suddenly come in from the North Sea and blot out all the landmarks leaving the aircrew hopelessly lost and many either crashed or wandered out to sea, ran out of fuel, and were never heard of again.

During fog or other difficult weather conditions a pilot would try to land with the help of a parachute flare. This was a stick of magnesium in a tube, approximately 12 × 4 in, and was released by pressing a button on the dashboard. It was ignited by a battery as it was released and a parachute opened on descent. The magnesium burned for two to three minutes, illuminating the ground. The pilot also had two wing-tip flares that he released as he neared terra-firma; control staff also had a signal mortar which, in the words of one witness, 'seemed to light the whole country'.

Fog had caused many casualties, the greatest World War 2 disaster occurring on the night of December 16-17 1943. A total of 492 bombers had been despatched and 450 had attacked Berlin, their target. 25 aircraft were shot down. However, on their return the Lancaster crews found their bases covered in fog which caused 29 aircraft to crash with a loss of 131 lives. A total of 54 aircraft lost and over half because of fog.

Fortunately help was at hand for Churchill had seen the danger in fog and the results it has on tired aircrews, so he had instructed Geoffrey Lloyd, the Minister in charge of the Petroleum Warfare Department, to find means of dissipating fog at airfields. The result was the successful device known as FIDO (Fog Investigation Dispersal Operation). The first airfield to have it installed was Graveley, near Huntingdon, in 1943, and it enclosed 1,200 yards of runway. The first emergency use of FIDO was made there on November 19/20 1943 when four Halifaxes of No 35 Squadron landed. Six further airfields were then equipped with FIDO and in all 15 UK airfields eventually were equipped with it, of which four come within the scope of this volume—Fiskerton, Ludford Magna, Metheringham and Sturgate. In all 2,486 aircraft were landed with the help of FIDO in conditions of fog during the war.

Post-war

Immediately after the Second World War there was a rapid demob of airmen and disbandment of squadrons whose strength was reduced to an average of eight aircraft. In August 1945 the official strength of the Royal Air Force was 1,079,835 men and women in addition to which 70,253 had been killed in action and 13,115 were Prisoners of War. This rapid reduction meant it was now possible to house several squadrons on one airfield, an example being Waddington which housed Nos 50, 57, 61 and 100 Squadrons. This also meant that there were now hundreds of redundant airfields and the obvious ones to retain were the mid-1930s Expansion ones with brick-built accommodation.

With the jet age and the new V-bombers, longer runways were required, a single one of 9,000 ft becoming the standard size for these airfields. By way of comparison, the longest runway in the UK is 10L/28R at Heathrow with a length of approximately 12,000 ft.

Many disused airfields have taken on a variety of uses and markets have been held at Langar, Melton Mowbray, Sturgate and Hibaldstow. Also, several County Constabularies have made skid pans on airfields for training purposes. And the disused airfield has become a firm favourite for the learner-driver, negotiating the piles of concrete, pot holes and oil drums. However, a few of the wartime airfields have retained some flying connection even if it is only the occasional light aircraft that flutters around on a fine summer's day.

Airfield architecture

Control towers

Webster's Third *New International Dictionary* defines 'control tower' as: 'an elevated glass-enclosed structure which has an unobstructed view of a landing field and from which air traffic may be controlled, usually by radio.'

America was first to use the centralised control building during the 1930s and this then spread to Britain, but did not catch on so quickly with the Royal Air Force. The early buildings were known as watch offices and served as a centre for pilots to 'book in and out'. With the type and volume of air traffic there was no need for them to be in a central position and the early watch offices were either small wooden huts or bungalows. These gave way to various constructions until they were standardised with the coming of World War 2. The main one used between the wars was the 'Fort' type as seen at Digby on page 83. The Air Ministry now referred to it as a 'watch tower' but it was soon to become best known by its American terminology—a control tower. Radio was the method for enabling aircraft to land and by the time the war ended instrument approach and landing systems were becoming familiar at the larger bomber stations.

During World War 1 and the early part of the Second World War air traffic control was very primitive and it was not until 1940 that development increased in this field. With the vast increase in air traffic and the coming of paved runways the control tower became a prominent feature with a standard design. This was a box-like structure and the distinguishing marks were a projecting balcony and external staircase. The brickwork was normally rendered with concrete and sometimes the building had an observation office on the roof.

Usually, the control tower was sited inside the perimeter track and was not far from the technical site. In front of the tower was the signals square, outlined in whitewashed concrete, which was used for non-radio aircraft. The same system is still in use today at smaller airfields. In front of the square would be the aerodrome identification ('Pundit') letters. Behind the tower there were often other buildings, possibly a Nissen hut for flying gear, or briefing rooms which were usually not far away, nor were the duty crash vehicles.

Redundant after the war, they were left to decay but in some cases they were brought into a variety of uses, stores for farm goods or animals, and even turned into a house, good examples being Hibaldstow and Gamston. Those that remain in service on airfields in use today are almost as they were, an example being Wickenby which remains with only slight modifications. The big changes came with the airport control towers, now known as Visual Control Rooms.

Top *An early austerity type control tower at Saltby, which was superseded by an improved type* (**above**) *but still with a poor view. This was standard for all airfields built during 1943. Sadly both these control towers have now been demolished.* **Below** *Blyton— same austere style of wartime architecture but with a building at each end and a small observation office on the top.*

Above *Coleby Grange—same uncomplicated austere style but with larger windows and observation office on the roof.* **Below** *Langar—showing well the buildings often attached to or near the tower. It also features the rooftop observation room which was a later addition, probably during the Canadian period, and is on the lines of the modern day tower.* **Bottom** *Strubby—another example of the post-war observation room added to the wartime tower.*

Above *Swinderby—with post-war type visual observation room on the top of World War 2 style tower.* **Below** *Barkston Heath—Post-war control tower has the same style observation room as Swinderby and Cranwell.* **Bottom** *Skellingthorpe—a rather unusual design with the windows to the roof and no corner pillars. Sadly, it has been demolished.*

Manby. **Top** *A fine example of an original control tower on the main site and* **(above)** *the control tower built in the 1960s. Both photographed in June 1980.* **Below** *Wigsley—a substantial brick-built three-storey tower (May 1980).*

Top *Ingham—this must be the most unusual of all the wartime control towers. Two-storey construction, having concrete floors upstairs and down. The stairs to the upper floor are wood which again is unusual. The upper floor is one complete room. The downstairs is divided into three rooms, the one at the rear being the operations room (June 1980).* **Above** *Newton—retaining the wartime box appearance and the balcony but has increased the frontal vision with large areas of glass. Between the powered glider and the control tower can be seen the signals square.*

Hangars

These have been the dominating feature of all airfields. During the First World War hangars were built in a cluster on one side of the aerodrome, a good example of which can be seen from the aerial photograph of Harlaxton aerodrome on page 107. This shows a group of six 1917-style hangars, but it soon became apparent what a target they offered an enemy bomber and this way of siting hangars was quickly abandoned with the growth of the new airfields.

Up to 1941 the type of hangars varied with each new airfield, the most common being the Bellman (8349/37), the curved roof 'J' and 'K' types and the 'C' type Hipped, which were built in varying lengths; then the 'T2' emerged as the main hangar and is the one most common on the airfields in this volume. There were many kinds of 'T2' as can be seen in the elevations on page 21, but the commonest built during the war was the 'T2' (Home), 3653/42, with a length of 239 ft 7 in. These prefabricated 'T' hangars, built by the Tee-Side Bridge & Engineering Company, could be erected quickly and, with the right engineer, in double quick time. Ted Stone, who worked on airfield construction throughout the East of England, was one such engineer.

William Arrol and Company Limited, Dunn Street, Glasgow, had the contract to build the structural steelwork on four of the hangars at Scampton, and the assistant engineer was Ted Stone. The steelwork on the first hangar had to be erected in as short a time as possible in order to allow other contractors to start work on the floors, walls, roofing, etc, but the time limit of eight weeks set by the Air Ministry was a near impossibility.

However, Ted Stone was not a man to be beaten and he successfully devised a workable plan, which was to split the work force into three gangs. The hangars consisted of the usual stanchions, the main boom girders (17 tons each) and the boom girders 'filled in' by 12 northern light trusses in each bay or from boom girder to boom girder. Because of the size of the boom girders all steelwork had to be assembled on site and it was this assembly work that was going to take the time. Ted Stone's plan was to cut the work force down from 20 men to 12: four men to build the main boom girders on the ground; four men erecting the booms and trusses (as the main girders took little or no time to sling lift and erect, the same four erectors helped the other four to build the trusses); and to complete the team four labourers moving and levelling the crane tracks. The first two hangars took just 20 days to build and to achieve this the contract men worked non-stop in atrocious conditions. Ted Stone did manage to get his men ten hours' extra pay each week but the £500 'backhander' from Dorman Longs that was paid for this particular job did not find its way into Ted Stone's pocket.

During 1941 the Blister hangar began to appear and was most common on the satellite fighter airfields. Today very few remain in their wartime positions, the only ones in the area covered by this volume being at Wellingore and Caistor.

Up to mid 1942 all hangars were painted in camouflage colours but after that date all new hangars were finished in black bitumen.

After the war many hangars were dismantled when the airfields closed. Some were left to die and now house only the birds as they rot away. Others that were retained by the Government on some of the vacant airfields were, and still are, used for storing certain commodities and equipment. One example was the 'Ground Nut Scheme' when all the hangars at Ludford Magna were filled with peanuts. A useful scheme that gave the locals some windy mice for many months!

Hangar elevations

The following pages list some of the main hangar elevations that will enable the reader to trace the main type of hangars. This is by no means a complete list for that would be a book in its own right. During the 1930s there were the Bellman Balloon Sheds, 7697/37, length 87 ft 6 in and door clearance of 65 ft that I have not been able to show, nor the earlier Hinaidi, 1136/27 with a length of 240 ft in 18 bays at 13 ft 4 in and with a door clearance of 100 ft. A 'T3' (Home) 3505/42 followed on the 'T' hangars and was a scaled-down version of the 'T2' for it only had a door clearance of 66 ft and a length of 75 ft in six bays at 12 ft 6 in.

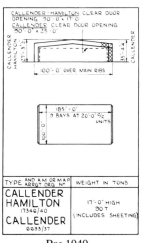

TYPE	AND A M OR MAP ARRGT DRG N°	WEIGHT IN TONS
CALLENDER HAMILTON 1734G/40 CALLENDER GG33/37		17'-0" HIGH 90 T (INCLUDES SHEETING)

Pre 1940

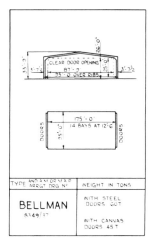

TYPE	AND A M OR MAP ARRGT DRG N°	WEIGHT IN TONS
BELLMAN 8349/37		WITH STEEL DOORS 50T WITH CANVAS DOORS 45 T

Pre 1940

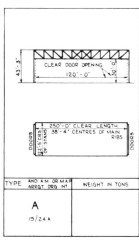

TYPE	AND A M OR MAP ARRGT DRG N°	WEIGHT IN TONS
A 19/24 A		

Pre 1940

TYPE	AND A M OR MAP ARRGT DRG N°	WEIGHT IN TONS
D 2312 2313 /36		WT STEEL RUNWAYS DOORS 205 T

Pre 1940

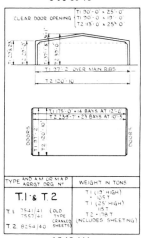

TYPE	AND A M OR MAP ARRGT DRG N°	WEIGHT IN TONS
T.1 & T.2 T.1. 7541/41 (OLD 7557/41 TYPE CRANKED T.2. 8254/40 SHEETS)		T.1 (19' HIGH) 105 T T.1 (25' HIGH) 115 T T.2 178 T (INCLUDES SHEETING)

1940/41

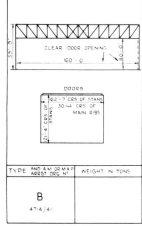

TYPE	AND A M OR MAP ARRGT DRG N°	WEIGHT IN TONS
B 4714/41		

1940/41

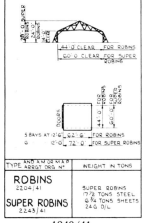

TYPE	AND A M OR MAP ARRGT DRG N°	WEIGHT IN TONS
ROBINS 2204/41 SUPER ROBINS 2243/41		SUPER ROBINS 17½ TONS STEEL 6¾ TONS SHEETS 24 G D/L

1940/41

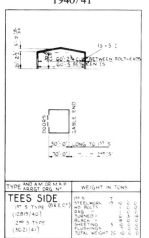

TYPE	AND A M OR MAP ARRGT DRG N°	WEIGHT IN TONS
TEES SIDE 1ST S TYPE (B&E C) (12819/40) 2ND S TYPE (3G21/41)		1ST S STEELWORK 15 10 0 0 H.D. BOLTS 3 0 0 RAG " 5 0 0 TURNED " 3 0 0 BLACK " 3 0 0 SHEETING 5 0 0 FLUSHINGS 5 0 0 TOTAL WEIGHT 20 10 0 0

1940/41

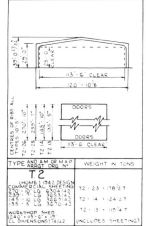

TYPE	AND A M OR MAP ARRGT DRG N°	WEIGHT IN TONS
T2 (HOME) 1943 DESIGN COMMERCIAL SHEETING 270' - 10' LG 6304/42 239' - 7' LG 6305/42 145' - 10' LG 6306/42 135' - 5' LG 3G01/42 WORKSHOP SHED (240'×113'-6' × 19' CL DIMENSIONS)74/42		T2-23 + 178½ T T2-14 + 124/2 T T2-13 + 119¼ T (INCLUDES SHEETING)

1942

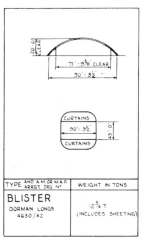

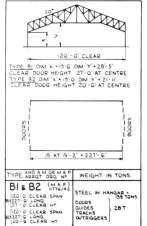

TYPE	AND A.M. OR M.A.P ARRGT. ORG. N°	WEIGHT IN TONS
BLISTER DORMAN LONGS 4G30/42		12¾ T (INCLUDES SHEETING)

TYPE	AND A.M. OR M.A.P ARRGT. ORG. N°		WEIGHT IN TONS
B1 & B2 (M.A.P) 1176/42	B1 {120'-0" CLEAR SPAN / 227'-6" LONG / 27'-0" CLEAR HT	STEEL IN HANGAR - 135 TONS	
	B2 {120'-0" CLEAR SPAN / 227'-6" LONG / 20'-6" CLEAR HT	DOORS GUIDES TRACKS OUTRIGGERS } 28 T	

Left *Hangar designs and elevations 1942.*

Below *Blister hangar at Caistor.*

Bottom *'B1' at Wickenby.*

Right *'J' at Goxhill.*

Below right *Group of three 'J' hangars at Swinderby, the Chipmunk giving some idea of size.*

Bottom right *'C' Hipped, ten-bay at Hemswell.*

Top *'T2' at Bottesford.* **Above** *Inside 'T2'.* **Below** *'T2' with 'B1' in the background. Note sharp contrast of roof angle. Photographed at Barkston Heath in June 1980.*

Airfield names

It is widely thought that the naming of RAF stations is something of a mystery and that they were sometimes called after a village some distance away in order to confuse the enemy. Let me first dispel that notion for there was no mystery in it and, as for confusing the enemy, the local people did just that with the many alternative names, many unofficial, that they used when they referred to an airfield. A good example is Bottesford which even to this day is still referred to as Normanton.

Before the Second World War the airfields were usually named after the nearest village to the site and, with there being few aerodromes, the confusion of similar names did not cause any serious problems. But with the coming of the Second World War and the mushroom growth of airfields more care was needed with the choice of airfield names.

The basic rule was still the same, that being to use the village nearest to the airfield. However, if this had a phonetic similarity to an existing airfield another village name would be used, still in the area but now some distance from the airfield that was named after it. When Swinderby airfield opened No 93 MU, sited by Swinderby station, had their field renamed Norton Disney so that the new airfield could take the name of Swinderby.

A very good example of similarly named airfields is Scopwick in Lincolnshire and Shotwick in Cheshire. As one would expect, problems occurred. One story is that Scopwick had ordered some aircraft parts. After several months these had still not been received at the Scopwick workshops and while they sent urgent requests the workshops officer at *Shotwick* was trying to work out why he had been sent a load of parts he had not requested. So, to avoid further problems, RAF Shotwick was renamed RAF Sealand as per Air Ministry Weekly Order 462/1924.

Not all airfields were named after villages, some were named after the farm or Lodge whose land they had engulfed, an example being Dunholme Lodge. Other names were also taken from the local geographical features, an example being Elsham Wolds.

The USAAF airfields were named *and* numbered, but the RAF normally used numbers only for Maintenance Units. The first American-built airfield, which became Station 485, was named Andrews Field in honour of General Andrews, the first Theatre Commander of the VIIIth Air Force.

During 1942/43, village names came alive with the wartime spirit as new airfields opened almost overnight. It was from these obscure locations with queer sounding names that the greatest air war in history was carried out. Therefore, it is sad that these names that once held the wartime glory of an aerodrome should pass into oblivion and, with the help of *Action Stations,* it is hoped that they will live on in aviation history.

Decoy airfields

The Second World War brought many techniques of deception and decoy airfields were just one of many, but it was not a new idea for it had been used during the First World War. Decoy fires, originally called 'Crashdecks', but renamed 'Starfish', were also developed but these are outside the scope of this volume which deals only with the decoy airfields.

In June 1939 it was decided to build both day and night dummies for the parent and satellite stations, and these were to be known as 'K' sites for day use and 'Q' sites for night. However, in August the Air Ministry postponed the decoy airfields and decided to go ahead with only dummy flare paths at the permanent stations. Many newly arrived Canadians were given the task of laying false flare paths, using Kerosene wick type cans with long spouts. The flare path patterns were laid in adjacent fields which were occupied by sheep and haystacks.

During the summer of 1940, Colonel John Turner was put in charge of the deception programme and by June 1940 the Q sites came into being. The Q sites, which needed only two men to operate them, were attached to a parent station and sited up to six miles away, the lights being controlled from an underground shelter that was in contact with the parent station by telephone.

The dummy flare paths were provided with lights and headlamps were used to represent aircraft landing lights. Ground personnel moved these about so that they represented an aircraft moving. These were later improved when the head-lamps were mounted on carriages attached to wires running alongside the dummy flarepaths and were propelled along by a cordite cartridge which burned out after 650 yards, the headlamp then coming to a slow stop after another 350 yards. This was a more realistic decoy and gave a good impression of an aircraft landing.

The Q sites were backed up by QFs, the code-name for small fires, the first of which came into operation in August 1940. By the end of 1941 there were 90 QFs and just over 100 Q sites and they had received over 350 attacks which proved they had served their purpose well. However, as the Luftwaffe became more skillful their effectiveness diminished and by early 1942 they were more or less abandoned and had closed down by the end of the following year. The QFs, meanwhile, were gradually reduced until by August 1944 only eight remained.

The K sites, which had dummy buildings and aeroplanes for day use, became operational during the early part of 1940. By November of that year there were 60 in use but the early ones were found to be too conspicuous so the ground was scored to imitate rutting by aircraft. Also, to add realism the Air Ministry ordered the production of dummy aircraft and by the end of 1940 nearly 400— Battles, Hurricanes, Blenheims, Whitleys and Wellingtons—were in production. The film industry played a major role and much of the construction for the decoys was done by Gaumont British and Sound City Films at Shepperton.

But these dummy aerodromes caused many problems, not only in finding the right site but also in the high cost of construction and the fact that each K site needed a complement of 24 to operate it. The final blow to the K sites came in December 1940 when captured German maps showed that nearly all the K sites had been spotted, which makes one believe that German agents had given away the decoys as this seems a much more likely explanation than aerial reconnaissance.

By the end of 1941 there were only three K sites left in operation and by May 1942 all had been abandoned and over 400 dummy aircraft became redundant. It is a pity that no-one thought about preserving some of these dummies and other items.

The decoy airfields saved many lives and aircraft, yet were never really accepted by the Royal Air Force, while many night decoys were given away by carelessness. Many station commanders were critical of them and feared that the dummies would lead the enemy to the genuine aerodromes. Thus, they were not operated properly and in many cases the lights were not switched on. Many station records that I looked at reported the generators out of action rendering the decoy non-operational, which was one way of putting it, an example being Woolfox Lodge. An entry in the Station Records for March 31 1944 states 'Two 'Q' sites are operated by this station, one at Pickworth and the other at Swinstead, but both of these had been unserviceable for some time due to trouble with the generators. Steps were immediately taken to put these into operation, but they are not yet serviceable.' And this is as late as March 1944 when the 'Q' sites should have closed down anyway.

None of the three Commands accepted dummy aircraft for their operational stations for they all thought they would be more trouble than they were worth. Bomber Command was the one most against them and in May 1943 all dummy aircraft were taken over by the Army. It was often very difficult to find suitable grass land in the right place for the decoy sites and the exact positions are obscure. During my research I did come across rations that were still being drawn up to the war's end for the staff at the decoy station, but these had long since gone. I have listed the sites of the decoy airfields and it still might be possible to find some piece of equipment around these areas for no-one has yet been able to come up with any and when they were abandoned the equipment was not always returned to the parent station.

A bomber station

This station has ten hangars which is more than the average station. However, the layout for the dispersed sites and runways are the average layout for all World War 2 airfields. Bottesford does have both kinds of hardstandings, the 'frying-pan' and the 'spectacle'. The shooting butts on the western side are shown: an aircraft would reverse near the perimeter track and then the rear-gunner would align his guns for practice at the butts.

Some of the buildings that remain today at Bottesford. **Below** *No 6 airfield site— operations block with station headquarters on the left.* **Bottom** *Site No 2 No 158— Gymnasium.*

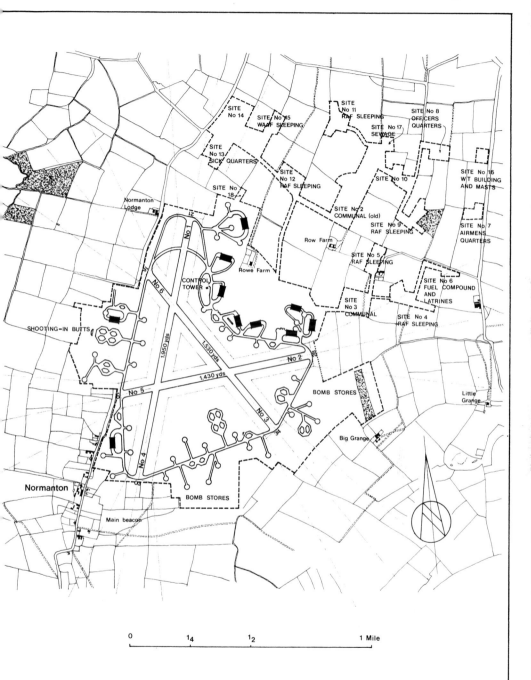

BOTTESFORD

Above *No 30 airfield site—Parachute Store.* **Below** *Site No 2 No 148—inside Airmens' Dining Room.* **Bottom** *Site No 2 No 159—Barbers', Tailors' and Shoemakers' Shop on the left. To the right the Gymnasium.*

Above *Site No 2—YMCA.* **Below** *Site No 3 No 180—Airmens' Dining Room.* **Bottom** *Site No 3 No 183—Sergeants' Mess and Shelter.*

1 Ashbourne	54 Kirmington		
2 Balderton	55 Kirton-in-Lindsey		
3 Bardney	56 Langar		
4 Barkston Heath	57 Langtoft		
5 Belton Park	58 Leadenham		SHEFFIELD
6 Binbrook	59 Leicester East		33
7 Bircotes	60 Loughborough		
8 Bitteswell	61 Ludford Magna		
9 Blidworth	62 Manby		67
10 Blyton	63 Market Harborough		
11 Bottesford	64 Market Stainton		
12 Bracebridge Heath	65 Melton Mowbray		
13 Bramcote	66 Metheringham		
14 Braunstone	67 Netherthorpe		
15 Bruntingthorpe	68 Newton		
16 Buckminster	69 North Coates		
17 Burnaston	70 North Killingholme		
18 Caistor	71 North Luffenham		
19 Castle Donington	72 North Witham		76
20 Coleby Grange	73 Nuneaton		
21 Coningsby	74 Orston	1	49
22 Cottesmore	75 Ossington		NOTTINGHAM
23 Cranwell	76 Papplewick Moor		
24 Desborough	77 Ratcliffe		DERBY
25 Desford	78 Rearsby	17	
26 Digby	79 Saltby		
27 Doncaster	80 Scampton		19
28 Donna Nook	81 Skegness		
29 Dunholme Lodge	82 Skellingthorpe		
30 East Kirkby	83 South Carlton		60
31 Elsham Wolds	84 Spanhoe		
32 Faldingworth	85 Spilsby		
33 Firbeck	86 Spitalgate		
34 Fiskerton	87 Strubby		
35 Folkingham	88 Sturgate		
36 Freiston	89 Sutton Bridge		
37 Fulbeck	90 Swinderby		
38 Gainsborough	91 Syerston		25 14
39 Gamston	92 Theddlethorpe		
40 Goxhill	93 Tollerton		
41 Grantham	94 Waddington	73	
42 Greenland Top	95 Wainfleet		
43 Grimsthorpe	96 Waltham		
44 Harlaxton	97 Wellingore		13
45 Harpswell	98 West Common		
46 Hemswell	99 Wickenby		8
47 Hibaldstow	100 Wigsley		
48 Holbeach	101 Winthorpe		
49 Hucknall	102 Woodhall Spa		
50 Immingham	103 Woolfox Lodge		
51 Ingham	104 Worksop		
52 Kelstern	105 Wymeswold		
53 King's Cliffe			

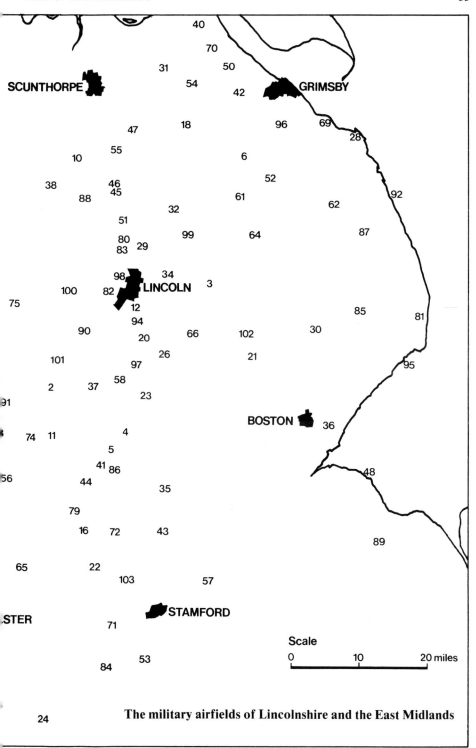

The military airfields of Lincolnshire and the East Midlands

The airfields

Apethorpe (King's Cliffe), Northamptonshire
See King's Cliffe

Ashbourne, Derbyshire
128/SK195455. SW of Sheffield off Derby road

Situated on the edge of the moors, this was one of the few airfields to be sited in Derbyshire. Construction work started in 1941 and in order to accommodate the airfield a farm and several private houses fringing Derby road were demolished. The airfield opened during the summer of 1942 as a training airfield in No 38 Group. Ashbourne was constructed as a standard bomber airfield with three 50-yard-wide runways, 1,700, 1,540 and 1,340 yards long and with the usual dispersed accommodation and hangarage. On July 10 1942 No 81 OTU formed here with an establishment of Wellington Ic and III aircraft. This unit moved out to Tilstock on September 1 1942.

On October 26 1942 No 42 OTU arrived and the training programme continued. The Operational Training Unit was divided into four separate flights, initial training being on Blenheims, followed by the Whitley V and finally the Albemarle. From June 6 1943 until February 1945, Darley Moor was used as a satellite airfield and this was used by the OTU's Ansons and Oxfords for the training of air-gunners and wireless-operators. On March 20 1945 the unit disbanded and the airfield then closed to flying. No 28 MU moved in and the runways were used for storage of bombs which were gradually moved on to the Derbyshire Moors and exploded. The station finally closed in 1954.

During the mid-1950s one hangar was dismantled and up to the mid-1970s many other buildings, including the flight offices and dispersal huts, were demolished, along with some stretches of the perimeter track. Today, several light industries are housed at the eastern end of the airfield, but the Commanding Officer's house and the southern part of the airfield are now privately owned. The control tower, which had been left to decay over the years, was renovated and put into use as offices by one of the companies.

Balderton, Nottinghamshire
120/SK815495. 2 miles S of Newark, W of the A1 road

Sited just south of Newark, this Nottinghamshire bomber airfield saw only limited operational life which came at the latter part of the war.

Balderton opened in June 1941 as a satellite for No 25 OTU, Finningley, in No 7 Group, and housed the Hampden bomber until November of that year. The following month the station transferred to No 5 Group as a satellite to Syerston and No 408 'Goose Squadron' (RCAF code letters 'EQ') moved from the parent station on December 8 1941 to take up residence.

The squadron's Hampden Mk I aircraft took part in many raids on both naval and industrial targets during the early war years, while bombing was still in its adolescence. Minelaying was also a major part of the early war missions and the squadron took part in the first 1,000-bomber raid on Cologne. An operational echelon was detached to North Luffenham from January to March 1942, while the runways were under repair. In September 1942 the squadron moved to

American officers inspect aircraft availability. One of the many C-47 Dakotas at Balderton, February 1944.

Leeming, Yorkshire. Work started the same month on runway construction in order to make the airfield capable of housing the four-engined bombers and in August 1943 the work was complete. During this period in 1942 the airfield had been used as a RLG by 14(P)AFU for day flying with their Oxfords.

From April 1943 to April 1944 the airfield was used by the Ministry of Aircraft Production, along with other airfields in the region, to store 32 Airspeed Horsa gliders which were serviced by a detachment of No 2 Heavy Glider Maintenance Unit until they were delivered to the Allied Airborne Forces. Also during this 12-month period the airfield was used by Whittle for the Meteor jet trials, and housed the Flight Trials Unit, but it became necessary to vacate the airfield because of growing activity in the 'Overlord' preparation.

The airfield re-opened and had the standard three runways which were 4,390, 6,000 and 4,620 ft long with an encircling perimeter track from which there were 15 pan-type and 20 spectacle-type dispersals. No 1668 HCU formed on August 15 1943 equipped with 16 Lancasters and 16 Halifaxes, but this unit moved out on November 17 1943 and after their departure the airfield was loaned to No 12 (P)AFU for circuits and bumps during December 1943. Then, on January 2 1944 the airfield came under control of the 9th TCC, USAAF, and several servicing wing units arrived that same day. Balderton now became Army Air Force Station 482.

Between January 22 and 30 1944 the C-47 and C-53 transport aircraft of the 437th Troop Carrier Group arrived but, by February 5, they had departed to a permanent base at Ramsbury. This unit was followed by the 439th TCG on February 21 who were also equipped with C-47 Skytrains and C-53 Skytroopers. The unit took part in only local flying before moving south on April 26.

During this period the airfield had been used as a transport base and as a store for American gliders. But, the wartime flame was only a flicker at Balderton and this looked like dying until on June 15 1944 it came back to life when the airfield was used by units of No 5 Group, the main one being the Lancasters of No 5 Lancaster Finishing School for circuits and bumps.

During the first week in September, ground units of the 439th TCG began arriving back at the station. Then, at the end of the second week, the air unit of the 439th TCG under Colonel Charles H. Young arrived. The task ahead of them was operation 'Market' and on the morning of September 17 1944, 50 C-47s, each towing a glider, filled with men and artillery, and 30 aircraft with American paratroopers, took off for Nijmegen, Holland. A few nasty moments arose when the 440th TCG aircraft from Fulbeck flew over the Balderton area and caused confusion as dozens of heavily laden aircraft struggled to gain height.

However, for the 439th the mission was successful and after dropping the paratroopers and releasing the gliders all aircraft returned to Balderton. On the 18th, the 439th again set out to the battle zone with gliders filled with supplies, but this

Balderton, March 1944: airmen of the 9th TCC make use of the fine day for a game of American baseball.

was their last mission from Balderton and by September 23 all American units had moved south.

The airfield then passed to No 5 Group, Bomber Command, and the flame was made to glow when, on October 21 1944, the station became operational with the arrival of No 227 Squadron, that had formed at Bardney from No 61 Squadron. Equipped with Lancaster Mks I and III, code letters '9J', the squadron brought at long last the bomber atmosphere to the station and it could now do the job it was built for. October also saw the arrival of the Aircrew Commando School from Scampton, which remained until March 23 1945.

On November 26 1944, Lancaster 9J-C roared down the runway at 23.45 hours and climbed into the dark night sky over Newark. The pilot was Flying Officer Britton and the airbomber was Warrant Officer Alan Cuthbertson, a Canadian on his first operational sortie. He recalls that first mission. 'My vivid recollection is that we crossed over the Alps which were ruggedly beautiful in the full moonlight. One or two of the large Swiss cities were also visible since they were not 'blacked out' indicating the status of a neutral country surrounded by nations at war. We approached Munich on track, on time at the approximate hour of 04.00 hours. Other aircraft became visible in the strong light of moonlight above, and fires below.'

The Munich sortie took nine hours five

minutes and Lancaster 'C' made it safely back to Balderton. Other missions followed and on January 1 1945 Warrant Officer Cuthbertson and crew were returning from an attack on Gravenhorst when they were hit while over 'friendly' territory. One engine was put out of action and to add to their predicament Balderton was fogged in and they had to be diverted to Marston Moor, where they landed safely.

Gravenhorst was again the target on February 21 but, for Lancaster PB666, 'J'-Jigg and crew, it was to be their last. The aircraft had just released its bomb load and was trying to clear the target area when a Lancaster a thousand feet above burst into flames; a few seconds later another Lancaster a little below them burst into flames, then, seconds later they were hit. It was a Bf 109 that raked PB666 with cannon fire which blew the front turret off and set fire to the outer starboard engine. The flash fire from the explosion was so close it burnt off all the hair, eyebrows and lashes from Warrant Officer James Cassidy, the bomb-aimer. Before the crew had time to assess the damage they were hit again, this time the shells setting fire to the two port engines and causing fire to break out in the centre of the fuselage. It is thought that Sergeant 'Jock' Edwards, the mid-upper gunner, was killed in this second attack.

Flying Officer Peter Green, the pilot of the stricken aircraft, yelled into the intercom, 'Bail out! Bail out!' as he fought to hold the doomed bomber on course and give his crew time to jump. Because the bomb-aimer was temporarily blinded he asked the navigator, A.F. Dales, to open the escape hatch but, it had jammed. He recalls, 'I stood up and stamped on it but nothing happened. I stamped on it again, this time out went the door and also my foot. The slipstream slammed it back against the back of the opening and broke both bones in my leg and bent it at a 90° angle along the bottom of the aircraft. I managed to pull it back inside of the aircraft.'

In terrible pain, Dales parachuted to safety from the doomed Lancaster. He was caught and taken to hospital in Bocholt, Germany, and after three moves was liberated and flown in an old Anson, made into an ambulance aircraft, to a Canadian hospital near Hamburg. Then back to England and after another three months in hospital was then returned to Canada on the hospital ship *Letitia*.

Three of the crew, the pilot, Flying Officer Pete Green; Sergeant Jock Edwards, mid-upper gunner; and Sergeant John Ling, the flight-engineer are buried near Winterswijk, in Holland.

During the first week in April 1945, No 227 Squadron moved out to Strubby, Lincolnshire, and on April 25 the station was put on C & M. On June 1 1945 it transferred to 40 Group, Maintenance Command (55 Wing) and No 1 Equipment Disposal Depot formed that same day. Later, on June 15 1945, it was redesignated No 254 MU and remained as such until 1954. During this period 4,000 lb bombs were stored on Balderton's runways. They were then removed and the airfield closed later in that year.

During the construction of the Newark A1 bypass in the mid-1960s the airfield was totally destroyed and only a few small sections of the perimeter track can be found in the surrounding fields. The machine-gun and cannon firing butts are still there, albeit in a very sorry state and now overgrown. In a copse on the north-west corner of the field are a couple of air raid shelters. From the air the runways can still be made out in the dark earth, a silent cenotaph to those who never returned home.

Bardney, Lincolnshire

121/TF140710. E of Lincoln and NE of the village of Bardney, E of B1202 road

Located some ten miles east of Lincoln in wooded country, this airfield was built between Scotgrove and Austacre woods during 1942-43. It was one of the numerous bomber bases in Lincolnshire and was designed to the standard plan with three concrete runways and with all the facilities widely dispersed. A tower of the standard wartime pattern was constructed on the south-eastern perimeter, not far from a minor road leading north from the village of Bardney, after which the airfield was named. Scotgrove drain runs at the south end of the airfield which was bordered on three sides by woods.

The airfield opened in April 1943 and was occupied on the 14th by No 9 Squadron which moved in from Waddington. Most of the squadron Lancasters took off from their former base the previous evening to raid Spezia in Italy and then landed back at Bardney the following morning. Such was the pace,

Lancaster EE136—'Spirit of Russia'—that was at Bardney with No 9 Squadron.

The ceremony in the village of Bardney on Sunday, October 19 1980, when a memorial to No 9 Squadron was unveiled. Over 250 people from around the world attended for the service and the chance to remember those who did not return.

with new bomber stations opening almost monthly, that the ground crew left Waddington at 21.00 hours, *after* the squadron aircraft had got airborne, and then dashed across to Bardney in time for their return.

No 9 Squadron remained at Bardney for the remainder of the war and only returned to Waddington on July 7 1945. During those hectic war years the squadron made attacks on targets throughout enemy-occupied Europe. In the fateful Nuremberg raid of March 30/31 1944 it put up 16 aircraft and lost one. In conjunction with No 617 Squadron, and using 12,000 lb Tallboy bombs, the squadron made three attacks on the German battleship *Tirpitz* and on the third attack put an end to it. The greatest honour came when Flight Sergeant George Thompson was posthumously awarded the Victoria Cross.

On January 1 1945, during the daylight raid on the Dortmund-Ems Canal, Thompson's Lancaster had just released its bomb load when it was hit by a heavy shell in front of the mid-upper turret. Fire broke out and dense smoke filled the fuselage. Next second the nose of the aircraft was hit and the Pespex screen was blown away. The sudden rush of air cleared the fuselage to reveal complete devastation of the aircraft and one engine on fire. Flight Sergeant George Thompson, the wireless operator, saw the mid-upper gunner was unconscious and immediately plunged into the flames and exploding ammunition and pulled the gunner from his turret. He sustained serious burns on his hands, face and legs but despite this he returned into the flames and worked his way painfully to the rear gunner whose clothing was alight and who had been overcome by the fumes. He carried him clear and used his bare hands to beat out the flames. The flow of cold air gave him great pain and frostbite developed. When he reported to the pilot he was in such a state that he was not recognised. The Lancaster made a crash landing 40 minutes later and just three weeks afterwards Flight Sergeant Thompson died of his terrible injuries. For his very brave action he was awarded the Victoria Cross.

On October 7 1944 No 227 Squadron reformed and 'A' Flight was attached to No 9 Squadron, but in under two weeks they moved out to Balderton. As they prepared for this No 189 Squadron was formed as a heavy bomber squadron in No 5 Group (October 15), equipped with Lancaster Is and IIIs. The squadron flew its first operational mission on November 1 1944 when five Lancasters were despatched to bomb Homberg. It was a poor first effort for two bombed the primary target, one the alternative and the other two aborted. On the following day the squadron moved to Fulbeck, Lincolnshire, taking with it 'Spirit of Russia', Lancaster EE136, which had originally been with No 9 Squadron and which went on to top the 100 mark.

After the war Bardney was one of many redundant airfields in eastern England and closed to flying in late 1945. The site enjoyed a brief period of military activity again when it was selected to become part of the Hemswell complex of Thor ICBMs. In 1959, No 106 Squadron moved in with the missiles but in 1963 the unit disbanded and the station closed, being finally vacated by the RAF in the same year. It was used from time to time by light aircraft after that and in 1979 the tower was still standing in good condition, apparently used as a house; while a 'B1' and 'T2' hangar, both in the south-eastern part of the site, were in use as warehouses.

Barkston Heath, Lincolnshire

130/SK970415. NE of Grantham on B6403 road, 2 miles S of Ancaster

This airfield was sited on the western side of Ermine Street, the old Roman road now known on this section as the B6403. It was built on Barkston Heath, from which it gained its name. The airfield was first brought into use in April 1941 as a Relief Landing Ground for nearby Cranwell since the college FTS was then operating a fleet of over 150 Oxfords and the circuit was very congested. Because of the frequent air raids during 1940 Barkston Heath had a decoy airfield at Willoughby Walks, which also 'doubled' for Cranwell, although there is no trace of it ever being used. Barkston continued in its opening role and, when Cranwell closed for several months during 1943, all flying sections operated from Caistor and it. During April 1943, Cranwell vacated the airfield for it had been earmarked for

Bomber Command, and it closed later that month.

Over the next few months Barkston Heath was converted from a grass satellite airfield to a full class 'A' bomber station, it being intended that the airfield should house a Heavy Conversion Unit parented by Swinderby. However, like many other airfields in the area, Barkston was allocated to the American IXth AFTCC and when it re-opened on January 11 1944 it was under American control.

The airfield was built to the standard pattern of the period with three concrete runways with an encircling perimeter track. The main runway was 6,000 ft and the two intersecting ones were 4,290 and 4,020 ft long, all being 150 ft wide. The main site with one 'T2' hangar and the tower were on the southern boundary with a 'B1' and a further 'T2' on the eastern side. A row of four 'T2' hangars was also erected on the east side of the B6403 road. During the reconstruction of the airfield the accommodation was used by an aircrew commando school.

On February 18 1944 the Air Echelon of the 61st TCG with its component four squadrons, Nos 14, 15, 53 and 59, equipped with 51 C-47 aircraft, arrived at Barkston Heath—now USAAF Station 483. This group, under the command of Colonel Willis W. Mitchell, had just arrived in England from its last theatre of operations in North Africa and Sicily and it was to find over the next few months that the natives here were friendly and

Paratroopers of the 9th TCC tumble from Douglas C-47s. The aircraft, coded 5X, are the 59th Squadron of the 61st TCG from Barkston Heath, photographed on a training exercise during May 1944 over Lincolnshire. Note: the first and second sticks have come out perfectly from the first aircraft, but not so from the second one.

Above *Joe Louis and Billy Conn entertain personnel on the base at Barkston Heath.*
Below *Varsity T1 WF392 at Barkston Heath in 1961.* **Bottom** *Barkston Heath in June 1980. The post-war addition is the concrete-based dome-shaped building which is a radar installation. To the left of it is a 'B1' hangar and in the background are 'T2's.*

'Yank' was welcome with the Lincolnshire people.

For the first few weeks training was limited because the airfield was not fully completed. However, new aircraft began to arrive and training missions increased. On May 29 a demonstration was held by the 52nd TCW which gave the locals a chance to see the Americans at work.

On June 1 and 2 1944 a large number of paratroopers arrived at the airfield and, on the 3rd, ground personnel began to paint broad black and white bands on the aircraft. These strange goings-on were clear to everyone when, on June 5 at 23.52 hours, the C-47s began taking off from Barkston Heath. Within six minutes 72 were airborne and heading with their cargo of 1,167 men of the 507th Parachute Infantry Regiment for drop zone 'T' near Ste-Mère-Église in Normandy. One aircraft was shot down over France and six others received minor damage, including that of Colonel Mitchell, who was hit on the right hand with a piece of shrapnel. At 04.15 on June 6 the aircraft began to return to Barkston Heath, having helped start what was to be the greatest invasion ever.

The next day at 03.25 hours, 52 aircraft took part in a re-supply mission but, this time, the battle raged and 20 aircraft were damaged, three ditching in the Channel on their return. On June 8 Joe Louis arrived at Barkston Heath and entertained the American forces, while on the 24th many high ranking officers visited the station. An air display was put on and Colonel Mitchell received an Oak Leaf Cluster to his DFC while two others received DFCs for their action during the D-Day operations.

Over the next few weeks the training continued and on July 28 two C-47s collided just west of Sleaford, nine crew being killed. The group now prepared for its part in 'Market Garden' and, at 11.21 on Sunday September 17, 72 aircraft began taking off with their 1,268 paratroopers on board. The 61st also carried 432 parapacks and their target was drop zone X near Heelsum. The next day, D + 1, 40 aircraft, each towing a Waco CG4A glider, took to the heavens with their load of troops, guns, Jeeps, equipment and ammunition and headed again for Arnhem. Four C-47s failed to return to Barkston.

Having played a major role in the D-Day and Arnhem operations, the group returned to routine duties and flew many supply missions to airfields in France. It had now received a few C-109 fuel tankers and with these the group flew this badly needed commodity to the advancing Allied armies. Many of the group's aircraft would, on their return journeys, bring the wounded back to airfields in southern England before returning to Barkston Heath.

By early 1945 it was necessary for the group to move in support of the rapidly advancing Allied Forces and, on March 13, the 61st TCG said goodbye to their Lincolnshire home and moved to France. They were replaced by another American Group, the 349th TCG, whose four squadrons, Nos 23, 312, 313 and 314, were equipped with C-46 Curtiss Commando aircraft, which were rarely seen in Europe. Having been assigned to the European Theatre the 349th TCG arrived from the US via the southern route, the first aircraft touching down at Barkston Heath on March 30. The group was commanded by Colonel Leonard J. Barrow, Jr, who was the youngest (28 years) Group Commander in the IXth Air Force Troop Carrier Command.

In early April the 349th received two C-109 fuel tankers and some gliders. On the 18th it moved with its 64 C-46s to a new base in France. In early May the 349th returned to Barkston Heath with eight aircraft and the airfield was used as a base from which to transport British Airborne troops to Scandinavia. By May 15 they had gone for the last time and the airfield was returned to the Royal Air Force on June 1 1945. On September 1 the station was transferred to No 22 Group, Technical Training Command, and became Sub-Depot No 2, RAF Regiment, under the parent unit at nearby Belton Park. The function of the 1,000-strong unit was to train RAF Regiment personnel, but with rapid demobilisation it remained only a few months and by the end of 1946 Barkston Heath was one of the many airfields in eastern England for which there was no further need. From that date it does not appear to have been used for flying, although the hangars were used for storage. Then, in 1954, it re-opened as a satellite for Cranwell and to date is still used as a RLG for the Royal Air Force College. By 1979 most of the accommodation had been demolished when additional radar was installed. The hangars remain although most are hired to civilian warehousing firms. No longer the cry of 'Any gum chum', only shadows.

Belton Park, Lincolnshire

130/SK930390. N of Grantham

Although not an airfield, Belton does warrant a mention by virtue of the fact that in both wars it had strong military connections. In the First World War it was a training camp and in October 1914 received a visit from Lord Kitchener. In the Second World War Belton Park became a depot for the RAF Regiment from December 1941 until it was closed in August 1946. The RAF Regiment was formed with the specific role of defending the airfields and other RAF stations. Belton also played a part in the training for the Arnhem raid by men of the Royal Parachute Regiment.

Binbrook, Lincolnshire

113/TA190960. NE of Market Rasen, N of the B1203 road NW of Binbrook

A high and windy site perched on top of the Lincolnshire Wolds overlooking the village of Binbrook, this bleak location was one of many in the Wolds selected for construction of a bomber airfield in the late 1930s.

It was a typical airfield of the period with five hangars on the eastern edge of the grass-surfaced landing area. Behind these hangars to the east were the workshops, barracks, messes and other buildings, all grouped closely together. However, work had been slow and by the time war was declared the airfield was far from ready. All the hangars were built as 'C' types, the austerity version of the more familiar 'C1' types found on so many of the bomber stations. A decoy airfield was set up at Wyham a few miles to the east but there is no trace of it today.

Binbrook opened in June 1940 in No 1 Group, Bomber Command, but it was far from complete and building work was still in progress. However, the following month, Nos 12 and 142 Squadrons arrived. Both units were equipped with Fairey Battles and up to a few weeks previously had been based in France.

No 12 Squadron (code letters 'PH' and, on some 'C' Flight Lancasters, 'GZ') had returned to Finningley in June and then moved into Binbrook. The squadron was already famous for Flying Officer D.E. Garland, a pilot, and Sergeant T. Gray, his observer, had been posthumously awarded the Victoria Cross—the first Royal Air Force VCs of the Second World War. In Battle P2204 'K', Garland led five aircraft on a low level attack on the bridge over the Albert Canal at Vroenhoeven which had been captured by German paratroops. As expected, the bridge was heavily protected by enemy fighters and over the target they encountered heavy machine-gun and anti-aircraft fire but despite all this the formation successfully bombed the bridge. But the price was high and Flying Officer Garland and Sergeant Gray, along with three other aircraft and crews, did not return.

No 142 Squadron had returned first to Waddington and then on to Binbrook. On

No 12 Squadron Wellington at Binbrook during July 1941. Note the Firebird nose insignia and the few strands of barbed-wire which were the airfield's defence.

'A' Flight Dispersal before take-off: Q 'Queenie' of 460 (RAAF) Squadron stands in readiness on dispersal, Binbrook, July 1944.

August 13 1940 both 12 and 142 Squadrons moved to Eastchurch in Kent so that building work could be completed, but in September they returned to Binbrook which was now functional as an operational bomber station. However, the defences left much to be desired (although this was the same at all airfields): at Binbrook they consisted of a few wooden poles stuck in the ground with figures stuffed with hay alongside them, these being sited at various points to simulate light ack-ack posts! They were supplemented by a few machine-guns.

In November, both resident units began to re-equip with Wellingtons and trained on them during the winter months. No 12 Squadron used them operationally for the first time on April 10/11 1941 during a raid against Emden. During September the Lysanders of No 1 Group Target Towing Flight arrived, which in November was re-named 1481 TTF. Meantime, No 142 Squadron had been destined for other theatres of war and during November moved to Waltham before being sent to North Africa.

No 12 Squadron made sure they lived up to their motto, 'Leads the field', in November 1941 when the squadron was top in No 1 Group with 31 sorties and 55 tons of bombs. During June and July 1942 'A' and 'B' Flights were detached to Thruxton and in September 1942 the squadron moved to Wickenby.

The station now became inactive and closed in order that three concrete runways, one main and two intersecting with an encircling perimeter track, could be laid. The airfield was brought up to the standards necessary to operate four-engined heavy bombers.

In early 1943 the station received a small force of No 460 Squadron and on February 10 1943 Group Captain H.I. Edwards, VC, DSO, DFC, arrived to take over as station commander. One of his first jobs was to attend the Court Martial of 'Bluey' Freeman on Wednesday, April 21 1943. The Grimsby police had brought charges after 'Bluey' had got a little high, but given the pressure the aircrews were under it was only understandable. As the President of the Court Martial, Group Captain Edwards knew this only too well and 'Bluey' got off on every charge.

The airfield officially re-opened on May 14 1943 with the arrival of No 460 Squadron, Royal Australian Air Force (code letters 'AR'), the only Australian unit in No 1 Group. The squadron arrived from Breighton with the aircrew and maintenance party in Lancasters and the main body being flown in a train of Horsa gliders. Binbrook was to remain its base for the remainder of the war and the crews soon became accustomed to the valley at the end of the main runway. The heavily loaded Lancasters would roll down the runway, disappear, then climb slowly into view of the crew behind awaiting their turn.

After only a few weeks of operations, disaster hit the station on the evening of July 3 1943 when an electrical short circuit on Lancaster DV172 caused the entire bomb load to drop to the ground. Within minutes the 'cookie' and two 500-pounders exploded. The Lancaster disintegrated and incendiaries were scattered over a wide area, setting on fire R5745 with blast damage to ED774 and W4783. The Aussies quickly had control over what could have been a very serious disaster, however, and later that same evening 17 aircraft took off for Cologne.

During its operational career, No 460 Squadron attacked many major targets, and took part in the air campaign to crush Berlin which began at the end of 1943. From November 18 to 27, No 460 Squadron made four trips to Berlin and despatched 28, 25, 16 and 24 Lancasters with an overall loss of four aircraft. The next month proved to be a different story and on December 2/3, 25 aircraft were despatched by 460 Squadron; from the 40 aircraft missing the total force of 458, the Binbrook squadron lost five. Then, on December 16/17 a total of 25 aircraft were missing on a raid, a further 29 crashing in the UK because their airfields were shrouded in fog, and four of these were aircraft from 460 Squadron. One crashed on an emergency airfield, a second crashed short of the runway at Binbrook, a third struck a tree and then crashed into the bomb dump of a nearby airfield while the fourth bomber just ran out of petrol and crashed.

LAC John Burrows was one of the groundcrew working with 460 Squadron and he was fascinated by their unorthodox approach to life. To him they were the bravest of men and he remembers clearly the times he prayed alongside them with the camp Padre just before take-off. He recalls: 'We used to clean out the rear gun turret areas of sick and blood after many a raid, a voluntary task, and we were paid an extra two shillings and six pence for this unpleasant job.'

On the fateful Nuremberg raid of March 30/31 1944 the station put up 24 aircraft of which three failed to return. This was the last of the raids into southern Germany at this time and Bomber Command now switched to pre-invasion targets. On one of these targets, railway yards in France on April 9 1944, a replacement Lancaster, ME727, on its first operation, took off as normal but instead of climbing it dipped its port wing and went round and round in a circle, obviously out of control, and at such a low height it was doomed. After half-a-dozen circuits it crashed in Scallow Wood and blew up. There were no survivors but in memory of that gallant crew, the landowner erected a marble cross with their names on.

The squadron then played its part in the battle for Normandy and, on one of the Caen raids, Group Captain Edwards piloted one of the Lancasters which bombed from heights between 3,000 and 6,000 ft. Pilot Officer G.M. Lindenburg did not return to Binbrook: his Lancaster was hit by several batteries at once and three of his engines were set on fire. On only one engine he managed to crash-land behind the Allied lines.

After the battle of Normandy, Bomber Command once more resumed the strategic bombing offensive and the Binbrook Lancasters were again making the long haul into the heart of Germany. The pace had now increased and, on August 12 1944, Lancaster AR-'K' King rolled down the runway and climbed into the night sky to join 378 other Lancasters and Halifaxes headed for Brunswick. For the crew of 'K' King it was their 13th sortie. Half-way to target they were hit by flak which cut through the hydraulic pipes to the rear-turret. Sergeant Andy Andrew, the flight-engineer, was kept very busy from then on. To add to their problems they had oxygen trouble and dropped from 18,000 to 8,000 feet; only with the help of the flight-engineer did the pilot, Flying Officer Jarratt, manage to 'rock it' and pull out of the dive. They bombed from 7,000 feet but as cloud was so thick no attempt was made to mark the target with flares, and crews bombed on timed runs from their last navigational 'fix' or with the help of H2S. Consequently the bombing was spread over a wide area. Coming out of the target area the Lancaster was attacked by night fighters and, seeing a burning light coming towards him, Jarratt managed to climb out of its path. This turned out to be an early type of air-to-air missile magnet warhead. An Me 110 followed up the attack and as compensation for a disappointing raid and a shot-up Lancaster the mid-upper gunner, Bob Compton, destroyed the fighter. Flying Officer Jarratt, from Sydney, brought the crippled, but victorious, bomber back to Binbrook.

Above *Canberra T11 WH904 of No 85 Squadron at Binbrook on September 27 1964. Note Lightning aircraft in the background.* **Below** *No 5 Squadron Lightning at Binbrook.* **Bottom** *The King's Head. In the neighbouring village of Tealby, 'mine host' served many a pint to Australian aircrew of 460 Squadron.*

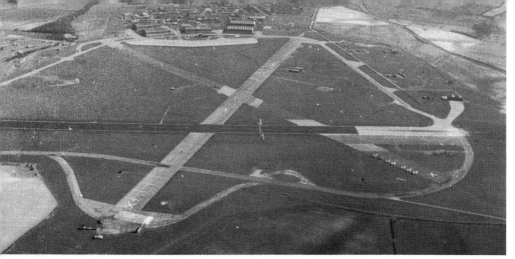

Aerial view of Binbrook taken in March 1980. Note the two subsidiary runways are displaying 'unfit for use' white crosses. Looking east one can see the five 'C' type hangars and, further to the right, Binbrook village. The Quick Reaction Alert hangar is to the right at the end of the main runway. The seven Lightnings on the subsidiary runway are left over from Christmas.

Towards the end of the war the squadron took part in the campaign against enemy communications and the station conducted 14 operations on 13 nights during February 1945. On the second of these raids one Lancaster was shot down while another was involved in a mid-air collision and crashed near Abbeville, the only survivor being Group Captain (later Air Commodore) K.R.J. Parsons, the new commanding officer of Binbrook.

The last mission of the war was on April 25 1945 when 20 Lancasters set out to bomb Berchtesgaden. 'Post Mortem' exercises were carried out during May and June and on July 28 the squadron was transferred to East Kirkby. One of its Lancaster Mark Is, W4783, 'G' George, completed 90 sorties between December 6/7 1942 and April 20/21 1944 and is today in the Australian War Museum at Canberra.

September 1945 saw the return of No 12 Squadron which, since its first visit in 1940, had flown a total of 1,370 successful sorties. The following month No 101 arrived from Ludford Magna, and it too had achieved an outstanding war record. April 1946 saw No 9 Squadron arrive only to depart again in July and then re-appear in September, equipped this time with Lincolns. In May 1946 the famous 617 Squadron arrived and began to re-equip with Lincolns. In July No 12 Squadron moved to Waddington then, in September 1946, equipped with Lincolns, it arrived back for the fourth time. The winter of 1946/1947 was very bad on the Wolds and flying was at a standstill. Binbrook was cut off and the situation got so bad that supplies were dropped by parachute from Dakotas of Transport Command.

The Binbrook squadrons made many goodwill trips to all parts of the world and in 1947, No 617 Squadron made a tour of the United States. That same year the Lincolns of 50 Squadron were detached to Binbrook from August to December. The unit returned again in August 1952 having re-equipped with Canberra B2s. It remained until January 1956 when it then moved to Upwood and was replaced that same month by Nos 109 and 139 Squadrons, both being equipped with Canberras.

Meanwhile, on December 15 1955, No 617 Squadron disbanded, having re-equipped in 1952 with Canberras. No 101 Squadron had also re-equipped with Canberras in 1955 but, on February 1 1957, both 101 and 109 Squadrons disbanded.

The three remaining Canberra squadrons continued to take part in exercises involving long distance flights. During 1956 No 9 Squadron was detached to the Middle East to take part in the Suez operation. June 1959 saw the unit moved to Coningsby where, the following month, it was joined by No 12 Squadron. This left only 139 Squadron, which had also taken part in the Suez operation and was detached at various times to Malta and Cyprus, but on December 31 1959 this squadron also disbanded.

From January 1 1960 Binbrook was

reduced to C & M. Then, the following April, the station was transferred to Fighter Command and a programme of reconstruction and expansion was carried out. The two auxiliary runways were retained and the main runway was extended to 2,500 yards, becoming the only one that is still used. The old bomber base was transformed into an airfield capable of operating supersonic jet fighters.

Binbrook re-opened on June 1 1962 with the arrival of No 64 Squadron flying the Javelin delta wing all-weather fighter, which was the standard aircraft at that period for all-weather squadrons. The station then saw the arrival of the Central Fighter Establishment in October, equipped with Hunters, Javelins and Lightnings, the role of this unit being to work out up-to-date fighter tactics.

May 1963 saw the return of the Canberras when No 85 Squadron arrived, but in a much different role: target towing for air-to-air firing and radar interceptions. The unit was also equipped with a few Meteors. It worked in conjunction with the other two units in this role for almost two years, until No 64 Squadron left for Singapore in April 1965.

It was now the era of the ear-splitting Lightning and, on October 8, No 5 Squadron re-formed, equipped with the Royal Air Force's first truly supersonic jet fighter.

On February 1 1966 the Central Flying Establishment disbanded but one section, the Air Fighting Development Squadron, was renamed the Fighter Command Trials Unit and continued to operate from Binbrook until it too disbanded on June 30 1967. The following April, Fighter Command became No 11 (Fighter) Group, Strike Command, and Binbrook remained a main fighter station. In January 1972 No 85 Squadron moved into Norfolk and in March of that year No 11 Squadron, equipped with Lightnings, moved in from Leuchars to make Binbrook an all-Lightning station. The role of the squadrons was interception with two Lightnings on Quick Reaction Alert which scrambled when there were any unidentified radar plots.

In 1974 the Phantom, having a longer endurance, took over the Lightning's role in air defence. In September 1974 the Lightning Conversion Unit was formed. The role of this unit was to provide training for the Lightning squadrons. It was later re-named the Lightning Training Flight and operates with Lightning T5s. Today Binbrook houses the surviving Lightning squadrons which are expected to remain operational until the mid-1980s.

Bircotes, Nottinghamshire
111/SK639938. W of Bawtry

Sited near the village of Bircotes after which it was named, this airfield is known to many as Bawtry, because No 1 Group made its HQ at Bawtry Hall from July 20 1941. The airfield opened in November of that year but never operated fully and it seems to have been used merely as a landing field for No 1 Group officers. The airfield did accommodate a few aircraft, all from OTUs, the first to arrive being No 25 OTU which operated with a variety of aircraft during its stay. These included Ansons, Hampdens, Lysanders, Martinets, Wellingtons and even Manchesters. During 1942 the airfield was upgraded as a satellite for the Finningley OTUs and further construction work was carried out. The buildings added included two Link Trainers, two Ground Instructional buildings, two extra blast shelters, a machine-gun and cannon range, and a crew procedure centre. Nothing was done to the runway which remained grass surfaced.

Throughout 1942 No 25 OTU continued to use the airfield and, during that year, the unit had three major accidents. The first was on February 10 when Manchester L7478 crashed in forced landing 1½ miles north of Bawtry. Then, on June 12, Wellington N1375 undershot and ripped its undercarriage off on a pile of stones. The third accident was on September 18 when Wellington DJ976 overshot the runway and crashed about a mile to the west of the airfield. The unit survived the year with a few other minor accidents and on January 7 1943 vacated the airfield.

August 1943 saw No 82 OTU arrive with Wellingtons, Hurricanes and Martinets, but this unit did not stay very long, moving out on October 8 1943. A week later No 18 OTU moved in with Wellingtons. From June to July 27 1944 the Wellingtons of 28 OTU paid a brief visit but in August 1944 No 18 OTU left and Bircotes closed to flying.

Today the airfield has virtually disappeared. However, there is a converted hangar near the main entrance on the

Tickhill road and in the far corner at the edge of a wood is a large dark green hangar in very good condition. Both are used as storage warehouses while part of the technical site is in use as a transport depot.

Bitteswell, Leicestershire

140/SP510845. Approximately 2 miles W of Lutterworth on the A427 and the junction of the A5

Construction of the airfield started during 1941 and it opened in February 1942 as a satellite for Bramcote. It was used by the parent unit, No 18 OTU, which covered all aspects of crew training, chiefly with Wellington aircraft and Polish aircrews.

In June 1943 the airfield became the satellite of Bruntingthorpe which was the home of No 29 OTU, 92 Group. Bitteswell still had the role of training aircrews, but this time British. The aircraft used were Wellingtons and Ansons.

During November 1944 the station reverted to a satellite for Bramcote and housed No 105 OTU. The heavy demand for bombers was now on the decrease and this was the reason for the change, since Bramcote was now part of Transport Command and the home of No 105 OTU with an establishment of Dakota aircraft.

Aircrew training continued until July 1945 when 105 OTU moved out and Bitteswell was placed on care and maintenance under Bramcote. An MT Section then moved into the first hangar and this, with a strength of approximately 20 personnel, had the task of salvaging anything possible from the station. It is interesting to note that in June 1946 two of the salvage unit witnessed the test flight of the AW52. Having heard a Whitley land, then take off from the airfield, and knowing there should be no flying, they went to investigate and saw what looked like a double sycamore leaf fluttering to the ground. It was a tailless glider and they noticed it was all covered in little pieces of wool about three inches in length. They had time to speak to the test pilot before personnel from Armstrong Whitworth arrived.

This company had used the airfield since late 1943 to assemble and test-fly Lancasters which were produced at their Coventry factory. After the RAF cut all ties with the airfield in July 1946 the aircraft manufacturers moved in to keep the hangars in use by overhauling military aircraft. During the 1950s the company used it as a base to produce and test fly their Argosy aircraft. Other aircraft, Hunters, Seahawks, Meteors and Javelins, were also built and test-flown during this period.

The next decade saw a change of ownership when the Hawker Siddeley Group took over Armstrong Whitworth and for a time they continued to turn out a large number of Argosies and Hunters for the overseas market.

Today, Bitteswell is part of the Kingston Brough Division of British Aerospace and used as a repair and modification centre. The Coventry factory closed in 1965 and there is no production line at Bitteswell. The airfield is still used by Vulcans and Shackletons but with these being phased out one can only wonder for how long.

Blidworth, Nottinghamshire

120/SK590540. SE of Mansfield between the A614(T) and A60 roads

Sited to the east of Blidworth Lodge, this tiny airfield was established as 35 Satellite Landing Ground and was parented by No 51 MU, Lichfield. Blidworth opened in 1941 and was only a grass strip of approximately 1,000 yards, used mainly for the storage of fighter aircraft. No records are available but according to local inhabitants, Westland Whirlwinds were flown in and out during 1942/43. Also, up to June 6 1944, Lockheed Lightnings were stored here.

Immediately after the war, Blidworth had no further use and it was abandoned by the Royal Air Force in 1945. The Guardroom at the one-time Main Gate has been renovated into a bungalow and it is now difficult to recognise its original function. However, the store room at the back of the bungalow still retains its original service character. The only other surviving structure, at the time of writing, is a brick-built shaft at the western end of the landing strip, which appears to be ventilation for an underground structure of some kind.

Blyton, Lincolnshire

112/SK870955. 5 miles NE of Gainsborough, at the junction of the A159 and B1205 roads

Situated just north-east of the village of Blyton, from which it derives its name, the airfield was a perfect site for a heavy bomber station, but for some reason it had a sad atmosphere and was only used for under three months in that capacity.

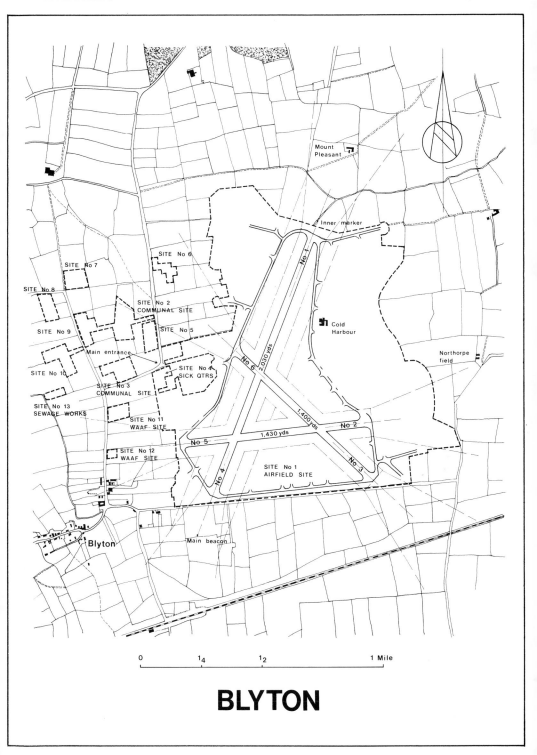

SITE No 7

SITE No 8

SITE No 9

SITE No 6

SITE No 2
COMMUNAL SITE

SITE No 5

Main entrance

SITE No 10

SITE No 3
COMMUNAL SITE

SITE No 4
SICK QTRS

SITE No 13
SEWAGE WORKS

SITE No 11
WAAF SITE

SITE No 12
WAAF SITE

Blyton

Main beacon

Mount
Pleasant

Inner marker

Cold
Harbour

Northorpe
field

No 1

2,030 yds

No 6

1,400 yds

No 2

1,430 yds

No 5

No 4

No 3

SITE No 1
AIRFIELD SITE

0   1⁄4   1⁄2   1 Mile

BLYTON

Construction started during the early part of 1942 and Blyton opened in November of that year as a standard pattern three-runway heavy bomber station in No 1 Group, Bomber Command. The first occupants were No 199 Squadron which re-formed there on November 7 equipped with Wellington bombers. This unit had originally formed in World War 1 and had disbanded in June 1919 at Harpswell, only a short distance from Blyton.

Just a month after being re-formed the squadron made its first operational mission when, on December 6/7 1942, five Wellingtons from the six despatched bombed Mannheim. The squadron took part in many bombing missions, but it was soon on the move and on February 1 1943 left Blyton to be immediately replaced by No 1662 HCU, with an establishment of 32 aircraft which included Lancaster Mk Is and Halifax Mk Is and IIs.

The role of the station now changed and it became part of the No 1 Group training organisation that had been set up to provide the Group with its urgently needed crews. This was to remain the role of Blyton for the duration of the war and No 1662 HCU remained here until it was disbanded on April 6 1945, along with all the other HCUs immediately after the war. Lindholme was No 11 Base HQ which housed No 1656 HCU and Blyton was a sub-station with 1662 HCU, 1667 HCU being at Faldingworth. In October 1943 the unit's Lancasters went to No 1 LFS at the parent station and were replaced by Halifaxes which it operated until November 1944, when the supply of Lancasters made it possible to change over completely to them. During this period the unit worked hard and, from September 1943 onwards, there were many crashes. In August 1944 there were two, a Halifax at West Butterick and a Stirling at Laughton Marsh. The next month there were also two crashes, both Halifaxes, and so it went on, a tragic existence for those gallant aircrews and people around the stations.

On November 3 1944 there was a command structure change and Blyton was transferred to 7 Group, with No 71 Base, Lindholme, and Sandtoft now being the other sub-station with No 1667 HCU. To help relieve the congestion in the circuit, Sturgate was used as an RLG after it opened in 1944. After No 1662 had disbanded just before the end of the European war, the station ceased flying activities and closed towards the end of

1945. The site was then put on a C & M basis and in the mid-1950s it was one of the six Lincolnshire airfields designated as reserve USAF bases, but it never saw any active presence and by 1978 most of the facilities had been dismantled and the land returned to farming. Today, it has an even sadder atmosphere with the runways in the process of demolition and the control tower standing in a derelict condition on the western side of the site. There are also some slit air-raid trenches, Nissen huts and a few other buildings on the technical and administration sites to the north of the airfield.

Bottesford, Leicestershire

130/SK820415. Approximately 10 miles NW of Grantham between the A52 and A1(T) roads

The airfield was sited between the villages of Bottesford and Long Bennington in the beautiful Vale of Belvoir and blended in very well into the countryside. Construction work started on this airfield for Bomber Command in late 1940 and it was to have a decoy airfield at Tithby, some 12 miles to the west.

It was a standard three-runway design with the main runway on a north-east, south-west axis running parallel to the joining village road. At the north end was Folly Hill and at the southern Beacon Hill, behind which lay the village of Bottesford; because the church was in a direct line with the main runway a red light was fixed on top of the spire.

Immediately to the north of the airfield is a thicket, Normanton Thorns, where the county boundaries of Lincolnshire, Leicestershire and Nottinghamshire meet, and the airfield is neatly bisected by the boundary between the first two of those counties, the technical site and much of the living accommodation being in Lincolnshire and the western part in Leicestershire. In addition to 'T2' hangars on the technical site there was another of this type in the south-west corner of the airfield adjoining the minor road linking the villages of Bottesford and Long Bennington, and there was a 'B1' hangar on the opposite side of this road about half a mile further north.

Bottesford, known as Normanton to everyone in the area, opened on September 10 1941 in No 5 Group, Bomber Command, but the station did not have a resident unit until No 207 Squadron arrived from Waddington in November

No 467 Squadron at Bottesford in 1943. The Aussies get a helping hand with their cumbersome gear. Jock the Scottie gets a final pat from the crews.

1941. The squadron was equipped with Manchester Mk I aircraft, and it was with these aircraft that the squadron attacked the German warships *Scharnhorst* and *Gneisenau* on February 12 1942. However, like all of their breed, the Manchester continually gave trouble and their Vulture engines were unreliable when needed most at take-off. During the summer months the unit re-equipped with Lancaster Mk I aircraft and during September 1942 moved to Langar, Nottinghamshire.

On November 7 1942 No 90 Squadron re-formed as a heavy bomber unit equipped with Short Stirling Mk I aircraft (code letters 'WP'). That same day No 467 Squadron, RAAF, was formed at Scampton, Lincolnshire, and it moved to Bottesford on November 24. The station housed the two squadrons for a few weeks only, since on December 29 1942 No 90 squadron moved to Ridgewell, in Essex.

No 467 made their first operational mission on January 2/3 1943 when five Lancasters laid mines in the St Jean de Luz and Bayonne areas. The first bombing mission was on January 7/8 1943 when three Lancasters took part in a raid on Essen. The pace increased as our Australian cousins settled in for the task ahead, but they also had to fight the elements of nature. During the last week in February, No 467 was to despatch nine aircraft for an attack on Milan but, after three had managed to get airborne, the

fourth got bogged down and blocked the main runway so only three took part.

As the supply of Australian crews increased so did competition between units. Wing Commander Gomm was Station Commander and the Squadron Commander was Squadron Leader Green, and they concentrated on achieving the highest total of operational flying. This is shown by the fact that, during April, there was a suspected epidemic of diphtheria at Bottesford and everyone was confined to camp for ten days. Yet, during this period, No 467 Squadron made six major raids and a few 'gardening' sorties.

On the night of April 20 1943, Lancaster ED545 took off from here along with 13 others from 467 Squadron on a raid against Stettin. They were part of a Main Force of 339 Lancasters and Halifaxes of which 22 were lost, but all 13 returned safely to Bottesford. Sergeant Harry White, bomb-aimer in Lancaster ED545, piloted by Sergeant (Ginger) Ball recalls: 'I remember it most vividly for it was the only occasion that I had to fire my front turret guns in defence'. The route for the bomber force was via the North Sea, low level, crossing the Danish coast into the Baltic, still low level, crossing the German coast west of Stettin then gaining altitude to 10,000/12,000 ft for target.

During the first week in October the squadron operated on four nights in succession. While returning from one of these missions on the 3rd of the month,

The old wartime control tower at Bottesford photographed in June 1980.

Pilot Officer K.A. McIver, DFC, was killed when he crashed into the Channel. His was one of two aircraft that failed to return to Bottesford that night. What with night flying tests and then the actual mission it must have been a continuous roar of engines for the locals. But they made the Aussies welcome and much of their free time was spent at the 'Reindeer' pub in Long Bennington.

On November 13 1943 the unit moved back into Lincolnshire, to Waddington, and Bottesford ceased to be a front line operational bomber station for it was then transferred to the US IXth AF to house their troop carrier aircraft, many paratroop units being concentrated in the Grantham area. On November 18 1943 the 50th TCW moved in from Cottesmore. Then in January the 436th TCG, made up of No 79, 80, 81 and 82 Squadrons, arrived with Douglas C-47 aircraft. The 436th TCG was under Colonel Adriel N. Williams and moved out on March 3 1944 to Memburg. The build-up continued, the 440th TCG, equipped with C-47 Dakotas, being one of the last remaining groups to come to England, its No 95, 96, 97 and 98 Squadrons arriving at Bottesford during March under Lieutenant Colonel Frank Krebs but moving out to Exeter on April 18. Both Groups had been engaged in paratroop training, frequently dropping men and supplies by parachute in the surrounding districts.

After the American phase in the airfield's history it returned, in July 1944, to No 5 Group, Royal Air Force, and became the home of No 1668 HCU, flying Lancaster Mk Is and IIIs as well as Hurricane IIcs. No longer was it to be an operational bomber airfield and, on September 1 1944, No 1321 Bomber Defence Training Flight was formed with an establishment of eight Hurricanes.

However, this unit disbanded on November 1 because a change of policy decreed that these aircraft should be attached to the HCUs for fighter affiliation. No 1668 HCU took on charge Beaufighters, Hurricanes and Mosquitoes for this purpose.

From November 1944 the airfield came under control of No 7 Group, Bomber Command, but that was the only change for the resident HCU remained until September 17 1945 when it then moved to Cottesmore. Flying ceased at the airfield and Bottesford closed before the end of the year.

During the 1950s the domestic and workshop sites were demolished and the airfield itself was purchased by Mr John Rose of Kilvington, Nottinghamshire, who founded the Newark Storage Company which now uses the remaining hangars and buildings for storage purposes. All the concrete hardstands have been demolished and the runways are in a deteriorating condition. There are still many buildings, both Maycrete and Nissen, on the site, and the ten hangars are all in good condition. The owner is in the process of recladding them one at a time and should be congratulated on his policy of preservation with regard to many of the wartime buildings. The control tower stands derelict and silent. Now all that remains are memories, all have gone, except the two aircrews who lost their lives in aircraft accidents while at Bottesford and are interred in the local churchyard. While on night flying test on August 19 1942, Lancaster R5863, piloted by Sergeant W.D. Fordwych, crashed on the road at Normanton. The other fatal crash was Lancaster R5694, piloted by Flight Lieutenant R.J. Hannan, DFC, which crashed on the aerodrome on November 25 1942.

Bracebridge Heath, Lincolnshire

121/SK985673. S of Lincoln, E of the A15 road

During the First World War Lincoln became a major centre of aeroplane production, one of the engineering firms engaged in this work being the old-established Robey & Co Ltd, whose factories were in Canwick Road. In May 1916 they received a contract to build 30 Maurice Farman Longhorn aeroplanes and they established a small aerodrome at Bracebridge Heath from which these could be test flown.

The site was on high ground near an asylum and, indeed, the original wooden aeroplane shed was constructed at the side of the wall of the asylum cemetery. Robey's Aerodrome, as it was known at the time, was also used for testing the Sopwith Camels and Triplanes constructed by Clayton & Shuttleworth Ltd, another local firm.

Only part of the order for Longhorns had been completed when the contract was cancelled and Robey went on to produce Short 184 seaplanes. However, in late 1917 work started to develop the aerodrome to accommodate No 4 Aeroplane Acceptance Park which was operating under unsatisfactory conditions from a temporary aerodrome on the West Common, Lincoln.

Hangars of the 1917 RFC pattern were erected together with ten canvas Bessonneau hangars, the latter adjacent to St John's Farm in the south-eastern corner of the site, and the aerodrome was extended to make it capable of accepting

Robey-Peters aircraft at Bracebridge Heath in 1916.

the largest aeroplanes of the day. No 4 AAP duly moved in but by this time the war was over and Bracebridge Heath saw little use before the unit disbanded in 1920. It was also briefly the home of No 120 Squadron after the unit's return from France in 1919 but, as part of the post-war reduction in the size of the armed forces, the unit was disbanded in the same year and in 1920 the aerodrome closed.

The original aeroplane shed constructed for Robey was dismantled, as were the temporary hangars, but most of the remainder of the buildings were retained, several of the brick-built hangars surviving in 1979 in fair condition as warehouses and garages. Part of the site of the former aerodrome was occupied by A.V. Roe & Co Ltd during the Second World War as a maintenance base especially concerned with the salvage and rebuilding of Lancaster bombers.

Bramcote, Warwickshire

140/SP406883. NE of Coventry, S of the B4114 road

Bramcote was one of the bomber training airfields planned for the Midlands during the pre-war Royal Air Force Expansion period. Sited just south of the Shelford to White Stone road and with the River Anker as its north-eastern boundary, construction work started in the early part of 1939. The airfield was earmarked as a possible dispersal site for bombers should the operational airfields in eastern England be attacked.

During September 1939 some Wellington bombers of No 215 Squadron scattered to the airfield, which was still far from complete. However, they remained only two weeks and had moved to Bassingbourn before the end of the month. The

construction work continued and Bramcote opened on June 4 1940 in No 6 Group, Bomber Command. A decoy airfield at Wibtoft was also set up for Bramcote.

The airfield was first used to form four Polish bomber squadrons. No 300 (Masovian) formed on July 1 1940 with the code letters 'BH' and equipped with Fairey Battles, while No 301 (Pomeranian) formed on July 22, code letters 'GR', also with Battles. No 300 Squadron was the first Polish-manned bomber squadron to form in the Royal Air Force. However, British advisers and technical specialists were attached to the squadrons. Both squadrons moved to Swinderby in August 1940 and were soon in action in the offensive by Bomber Command—vengeance would be theirs.

The next Polish squadron to form was No 304 (Silesian), code letters 'NZ', on August 22 1940. This unit formed from No 6 (Training) Group and was the first 'French-Polish' squadron to be formed from those who had fled to England in order to carry on the fight. This unit also had British personnel attached to it. The squadron was first equipped with Battles but converted on to Vickers Wellingtons.

The fourth and last of the Polish squadrons to form was No 305 (Ziemia Wielkopolska), code letters 'SM', on August 29 1940, again initially equipped with Battles but converted to Wellingtons, the aircraft in which both squadrons were to make their operational debut after they had moved from Bramcote in December 1940 to Syerston.

On June 15 1940, No 18 (Polish) OTU, which had previously formed at Hucknall, arrived with their Wellington Mk 1cs and IIIs. This unit specialised in the training of Polish aircrews, which became the main role of the airfield, although during the OTU's stay other units paid brief visits. During November 1940 No 151 Squadron arrived with Hurricanes but departed the following month to Wittering after they had re-equipped with Defiants. In May 1941 the station received a detachment of No 605 Squadron, also with Hurricanes, which departed the following September. Also during 1941, No 1513 BAT Flight took up residence with their Oxford aircraft and remained at Bramcote for the duration of the war.

February 1942 saw the station take on Bitteswell as a satellite which remained under Bramcote's control until June 1943. Meanwhile, No 18 OTU had continued with its training programme and had also participated in the 1,000-bomber raid on Cologne, Essen and Bremen in May and June 1942. During 1943 many changes took place. A new satellite opened at Nuneaton in February for No 18 OTU, but on March 7 this unit moved to Finningley, Yorkshire, and in April the airfield was transferred to No 44 Group, Transport Command. That same month No 105 (Transport) OTU took up residence, with an establishment of 35 Wellingtons, and this became the main resident unit. The status of the station on June 6 1944 was No 105 (T) OTU with Wellington 1cs and Xs and 1513 BAT flight with Oxfords, both units in No 44 Group. During 1944 the Oxfords of No 1514 BAT Flight put in a brief visit and on November 1 the station again took on Bitteswell as a satellite until July 1945. During May 1945 No 105 OTU re-equipped with Dakota IIIs and IVs. The following August the unit was re-designated 1381 (T) CU and towards the end of October it moved to Desborough.

In May 1946 the long-reigning 1513 BAT Flight departed to be replaced on July 16 by the Oxfords of 1510 BAT Flight. This unit left the following November and on December 3 1946 the station was transferred to the Royal Navy and became HMS *Gamecock*. For the next decade it was to serve as a Royal Navy airfield and was mainly used by 1833 (RNVR) Squadron flying Seafires. However, soon after the disbandment of the RNVR squadrons Bramcote was closed to flying and in 1959 the site was transferred to the Army. Today, it is known as Bramcote Camp and contains very few traces of the former bomber airfield. However, it looks as if the main runway 03-21 will be reborn for the route of the planned M69 motorway follows the full length at the point it crosses the old wartime airfield.

Braunstone (Leicester), Leicestershire

140/SK540040. Between the A50 and A47(T) roads W of Leicester

This airfield orginally opened as Leicester Airport on July 13 1935 and was thought to have a great future, but today it is no more than an overspill of Leicester. Sited to the west of Leicester, the airport had 534 acres reserved for development, construction work starting in April 1933. The aerodrome licence was issued on March 27

Braunstone Clubhouse and Airport Office photographed just after they were completed.

1935. 72½ acres had been laid out and constructed as a grass landing area and this gave a maximum runway of 783 yards. The club house, hangar and other buildings were sited on the western side of the airfield and were leased to the Leicestershire Aero Club, which at that time was flying Moths and Puss Moths.

Suggested future development of airfield buildings was planned on the eastern side near the proposed town planning ring road that would give access. However, these plans were not carried through and at the outbreak of war the airfield was taken over by the Royal Air Force and was used as a satellite of No 7 EFTS at Desford. It played an insignificant part and immediately after the war it closed. The site was restricted for modern day aircraft and with so many surplus airfields available just after the war the site was never developed and today houses an industrial site with many new buildings although two wartime hangars still remain, the only structures to survive.

Bruntingthorpe, Leicestershire

140/SP595885. S of Leicester between Bruntingthorpe and Gilmorton

Bruntingthorpe was one of a number of airfields in the East Midlands that was used by operational training units of Bomber Command. It was sited a few miles south of Leicester between the villages of Bruntingthorpe and Gilmorton, taking its somewhat unwieldy name from the former.

The airfield opened in November 1942 in No 92 Group as a satellite for North Luffenham, and housed part of No 29 OTU which had formed at the parent station on April 25 1942. This unit flew mainly Wellingtons and in June 1943 it moved in completely so that runways could be built at North Luffenham. That same month Bitteswell was taken over as a satellite and No 1683 Bomber Defence Training Flight with an establishment of Tomahawk IIa aircraft took up residence. The role of this unit was to provide fighter affiliation practice for the crews under

Aerial view of Bruntingthorpe as at August 10 1945 (DOE). Bruntingthorpe village lies top right of the photograph and the V-shaped road junction, top left, is Peatling Parva.

Top *Lancaster being used for testing with test engine ASX fitted in the bomb-bay. For a short period just after the war, Armstrong Siddeley used the airfield at Bruntingthorpe, but the stay was brief and no records are available.* **Above** *RB-66B Destroyer of the 19th Tactical Reconnaissance Squadron coming in to land at Bruntingthorpe.*

training for front-line bomber squadrons.

No 1683 BDTF moved out during May 1944 and, on November 1 1944, Bitteswell was relinquished and control transferred to Bramcote, although 29 OTU (which, during October 1944, had no fewer than 204 Australians under training) remained until June 19 1945. The airfield was used for a short time in 1945 by Power Jets Ltd for flight testing of the Meteor jet fighter but the stay was brief and by the end of the year the airfield was reduced to care and maintenance.

For a few years it was just another redundant airfield. Then, on November 13 1953 it was allocated to the USAF. Although it was not used at that time and returned to Air Ministry control by the end of the year, Bruntingthorpe had been earmarked for possible future USAF use and on February 15 1957 it was re-allocated

for that purpose. The airfield was re-activated and a single runway, 3,400 yards long, was constructed in order to accept high performance jet bombers.

Bruntingthorpe became a satellite for the USAF at Alconbury, the first unit to arrive being the 3912th Air Base Squadron. This unit was replaced in January 1959 by the 3912th Combat Support Group. That same month the 100th Bomb Wing (part of SAC) arrived with B-47s and remained until April. The following August the 19th Tactical Reconnaissance Squadron (10 TRW) with RB-66B aircraft arrived and stayed until the autumn of 1962. The USAF abandoned the base in September 1962. Between their arrival until departure no fewer than ten different detachments had been at Bruntingthorpe, although the only two types of aircraft had been the B-47 and RB-66B.

After the departure of the Americans in 1962 the airfield closed once again. The site has been used by the Talbot car manufacturer and up to 1979 several hangars were still standing, including a 'B1' type on the eastern boundary of the airfield. It is a pity that an airfield with such an excellent runway (that could, in fact, take Concorde), is not used for the purpose of flying. The airfield's close proximity to the M1 and M6 motorways, the main A5(T) and the A50 roads make it an ideal airfield and it is sad in a way that it should now only be used as a Vehicle Testing Station.

Buckminster, Leicestershire

130/TF893235. 1 mile E of Buckminster

A small field used in the First World War by the Home Defence squadrons, the airfield was in fact just over the county boundary and in Lincolnshire. It was opened in September 1916 and housed 'C' Flight of No 38 Squadron whose HQ was at Melton Mowbray. This unit was equipped with FE2b biplanes, acting in an anti-Zeppelin role, but by the time they moved from Buckminster they had not made a single interception.

May 1918 saw this unit move out to be replaced in August by No 90 Squadron which had re-formed as a Home Defence unit equipped with Sopwith Camels and Avro 504s, which were used as night fighters. HQ was at Buckminster and 'A' Flight at Leadenham. With the war over the unit became a post-war casualty and disbanded in June 1919. The airfield, which had also been used as an Aircraft Acceptance Park since 1918, closed before the end of 1919 and the site was taken back for agriculture. It was never reactivated during the Second World War, possibly because of the one at Saltby instead, and today there is no trace at all of Buckminster airfield.

Burnaston, Derbyshire

128/SK290305. SW of Derby just S of the village of Burnaston, W of the A38

Burnaston officially opened on Saturday, June 17 1939, as Derby's Municipal Airport. The airfield was already established and housed the RAF Volunteer Reserve Training Centre which had been formed in September 1938. In his opening speech, Sir Kingsley Wood, the Air Minister, gave mention of the RAFVR and stressed the necessity for strong defences of this country. How right he was.

On September 29 1938 No 30 Elementary and Reserve Training School for the Royal Air Force formed, although it had in fact been operating for some months and was run by Air Schools Ltd under the control of Captain N. Roy Harben, DFC, who had also formed the Derby Aero Club. After the outbreak of war No 27 E & RFTS arrived from Tollerton and amalgamated to form No 30 Elementary Flying Training School. The unit was equipped with Tiger Moths, Miles Magisters, Hawker Harts and Fairey Battles. It is interesting to note that during the 1940 invasion scare bomb racks were fitted to the training aircraft.

The little yellow training aircraft soon became a familiar sight and sound over the Derbyshire countryside. During 1940 the aerodrome was attacked by the Luftwaffe and on one occasion a stick of incendiaries fell on the airfield but no aircraft were damaged.

Under war conditions and heavy demands the airfield rapidly expanded and had four grass-surfaced runways, the maximum being 1,000 yards long. However, the airfield could not cope with the increased aircraft activity and the heavily congested circuit. To ease the congestion Burnaston took on two satellite airfields, one at Battlestead Hill and the other at Abbots Bromley, near Uttoxeter.

In 1942 the station had a new role—the pilot training of the first Glider Pilot Regiment, which was part of the Airborne Division. It must have been very strange to see soldiers, the majority being Army Corporals, in full flying kit and learning to fly RAF trainers. The men wore ordinary battledress but were distinguished by the word 'Airborne' on their shoulders and the famous 'Pegasus' badge of a winged horse. Many of these gallant young men went on to fly the gliders used on D-Day and at Arnhem.

Throughout the Second World War training was the main role of the station. The original development of visual training on the Link Trainer was carried out here, this method being adopted as a standard part of a pilot's training. Some 300 civilians were employed at the airfield.

After the war the station reverted to its pre-war status as a civil airport. Derby Aviation Ltd began to operate charter services from Burnaston in 1949 and the post-war story is closely linked with that company. On July 21 1953 the RAF officially closed down No 3 Basic Flying

Top *Canadair DC-4M Argonaut, G-ALHS, and* **(above)** *Douglas DC-3, G-AOFZ, both of Derby Airways at Burnaston on May 19 1962.* **Below** *Squadron offices on the main site at Caistor, 1979.*

Training School and all RAF personnel were posted away. Derby Aviation continued to expand and passengers were flown on schedule and charter flights from Derby airport which, in 1960, handled 35,000 passengers. These included flights to the Channel Islands, Dublin and Glasgow. However, it was the increased traffic that led to its closure for it was only a grass airfield and however well maintained could never hope to be as safe or efficient as one with runways. There were now hundreds of redundant airfields with concrete runways and in the early 1960s Burnaston lost out to Castle Donington, which was the obvious choice for development as the regional airport. Today, the only remains are two hangars and the control tower, the other building on the site appearing to be a recent addition.

Caistor, Lincolnshire

112/TA085020. Approximately 10 miles N of Market Rasen, W of Caistor

This airfield is immediately adjacent to the minor road that joins the villages of Caistor and North Kelsey. This road was part of the old Roman road and formed the southern boundary of the airfield.

Caistor was only a small grass-surfaced airfield with very primitive amenities but it did have a concrete perimeter track. It opened in 1941 as a Relief Landing Ground for Kirton-in-Lindsey and was used by their fighter squadrons until May 1942. From June 1941 the airfield was also used by Cranwell as an RLG. From May until November 1942 the airfield served as an RLG for Leconfield and was frequented by the Oxfords of 15 (P) AFU.

At the end of 1942 the station was transferred to the control of Manby and brought into use as an RLG for the parent station. From 1943 until May 1945 it was again brought into use as an RLG for Kirton-in-Lindsey, but closed to flying soon after the end of the Second World War. The site was re-occupied in 1960 as part of the Hemswell Thor complex and housed 269 Squadron equipped with Thor ICBMs. However, this unit disbanded in 1963 and the site was abandoned.

Today there is very little trace of the airfield. Only a piece of perimeter track, a Blister hangar and a few huts that have weathered the passage of time are evidence of its wartime connection. The concrete walls of the Thor site are still there to mark its post-war role.

Cammeringham (Ingham), Lincolnshire

See Ingham

Castle Donington, Leicestershire

129/SK450260. SE of Nottingham between the village of Castle Donington and Diseworth

To augment the bomber expansion during the Second World War a number of airfields were planned for the Midlands to house bomber operational training units, Castle Donington being one. The site was surveyed in 1941 and work started early the following year. The airfield opened on January 1 1943 in 92 Group, Bomber Command, as a satellite for Wymeswold. It was a standard OTU airfield with three paved runways and was situated immediately to the south of the small town of Castle Donington.

The airfield was used by part of 28 OTU equipped with Wellington 1cs, IIIs and, later, Xs. Martinets and Masters were used for target towing, but these were later replaced by Hurricanes. July 11 1944 saw the start of a training programme for crews of the Pathfinder Force, but the scheme was shortlived.

With the growing importance of Transport Command the unit converted to transport aircraft and on October 15 1944 the bomber OTU disbanded and was replaced by 108 OTU, a transport unit equipped with 40 Dakota III aircraft. Castle Donington was transferred to Transport Command but remained a satellite for Wymeswold.

On August 10 1945, 108 OTU was renamed 1382 TCU, still with Dakotas although a few were now the Mark IV aircraft. The station came under No 4 Group, Transport Command, which was opening many trunk routes through the liberated countries of Europe and to the Middle and Far East. The unit's aircraft were used to ferry troops and supplies along these routes.

Castle Donington closed to flying in September 1946 and was abandoned as an RAF airfield that same year. However, there was still a hope for the airfield and when it became apparent that Derby's regional civil airport at Burnaston was not capable of being developed to meet the growing traffic needs, a number of former wartime airfields in the area were inspected. Castle Donington was finally selected because of its site and close

proximity to the M1 motorway that runs past the eastern end of the airfield.

Work started in 1964 and, at a cost of over £1.4 million, a new airfield was constructed on the old wartime site in just over 12 months. Little use was made of the wartime facilities for the airfield had deteriorated badly. The original Civil Engineering contract for the runway, taxiway, terminal, apron and other buildings was carried out by Richard Costains Ltd. The new 5,850-ft runway was laid on the original 10/28 runways, east to west, and in 1970 this was extended by A. Monk and Company to its current length of 7,480 ft. The runway extension caused the closure of the B5401 Diseworth–Castle Donington road and the re-routing of the B5400 Diseworth–Kegworth road to form part of A5129.

Gone, the many kinds of aircraft that used the airfield, Wellingtons, Master IIIs, Oxfords, Hurricanes, Dakotas, Stirlings and Yorks. Gone too the familiar wartime triangular pattern with only now the main 10/28 runway with a parallel taxiway, and an auxiliary grass runway, 01/19, which is 2,900 feet long and 330 feet wide. A new airport for a new breed of aircraft, still transporting passengers like the old Dakota did, but for a more peaceful purpose.

The new airfield, now known as the East Midlands Airport, re-opened as a civil aerodrome on April 1 1965 as a joint venture by Leicestershire/Derbyshire and Nottinghamshire County Councils together with the cities of Derby and Nottingham and, in the first year of operation, handled 103,966 passengers. Traffic expanded rapidly under the careful direction of Mr E.C. Dyer, the Airport Director, and by 1979 the total passenger through-put at the airport was 732,661.

There are now many operators out of East Midlands Airport which include British Midland Airways, ex-Derby Airways who moved here with the closure of Burnaston; KLM, Pan-Am, Air-Bridge, Alidair, Field Aircraft Services Ltd and the Rolls-Royce Executive Flight. There are also Donair Flying School and the East Midlands School of Flying. Also, Castle Donington handles aircraft of about 30 different commercial airlines.

For the 1980s the expansion plans at the East Midlands Airport include an application to further extend the runway to 9,500 ft, together with expansion of all relevant areas, and the development programme should roll from 1981 through to 1985. The future is bright for the airport which will play a major role in the medium and long haul traffic to many places far afield.

Below *Castle Donington—an oblique photograph looking across the main runway towards the vast concrete apron of the new East Midlands Airport.* **Above left** *Winter time at East Midlands; an old veteran looks on with approval. From left to right a Dakota, Boeing 707, HS 125, behind the lorry an ex-RAF Andover, and another Boeing 707.* **Left** *A Boeing 747 (Jumbo) at East Midlands Airport—a far cry from the early wartime days. The maximum fuel load of the '747 is 44,260 imperial gallons which would keep a family car a lifetime.* **Below left** *Air France Concorde prepares for take-off from East Midlands Airport.*

Above *Refuelling a Hurricane of 402 Squadron at Coleby Grange. Note the mud and working conditions.*

Left *Bob Corbett's 402 (RCAF) Squadron Hurricane nosed over after landing in bad weather.*

Below *F/O Morrow's Hurricane Mark II of No 402 (RCAF) Squadron in June 1941.*

Below right *Waiting to Scramble at Coleby Grange in September 1943; 410 (RCAF) Squadron. F/O Walter Dinsdale (with Mae-West) who today is a prominent MP in the House of Commons, Ottawa, and F/Lt Vern Williams.*

Coleby Grange, Lincolnshire

*121/TF005605. S of Lincoln, between the
A15 and A607 roads, alongside the B1202*

One of a number of airfields situated on
the relatively high ground south of the city
of Lincoln, Coleby Grange opened in the
spring of 1940 as a Relief Landing Ground
for RAF Cranwell. The B1202 road was
closed and part of the southern perimeter
track laid on the site of the road. A control tower of the standard wartime pattern
was constructed on the eastern boundary
of the field, almost alongside the A15
road which paralleled the perimeter track
at that point. A 'T1' hangar was erected
in the shelter of the small thicket near
Heath House on the opposite side of the
A15.

Although the facilities in early 1940
were minimal, by May the airfield housed
a detachment of Hurricanes from 253
Squadron, Kirton-in-Lindsey, and these
were followed at the beginning of August
by the Defiants of 'B' Flight of 264
Squadron, also based at Kirton-in-
Lindsey. This unit moved out three weeks
later and Coleby Grange reverted to being
a RLG for Cranwell and also received
occasional use by Waddington, two or
three miles to the north.

In May 1941 the airfield became a
satellite of Digby, the nearby No 12
Group fighter station, the other satellite
being Wellingore. The two airfields were
coded WCI and WCII from the Sector
name, Coleby Grange being the latter.
The first to occupy the airfield with
Hurricane Is was a unit of the Royal
Canadian Air Force, No 402 Squadron,
on May 16 1941. The pilots were housed
at Coleby Lodge, a fine old country house
near the airfield. The Canadians quickly
settled into their Lincolnshire home and

one pilot, Bob Corbett, somehow
managed to keep, and ride, a horse while
at Coleby.

The Canadians were a likeable bunch of
young men, eager to fight, and during
their stay many romances blossomed in
the wartime Lincolnshire countryside.
While at Coleby the pilots taught the
station dental officer to fly and one day he
arrived at the airfield in a Tiger Moth. He
told one of the pilots, Flying Officer
Robert Morrow, that Group Captain
Murlis-Green, the Digby Commanding
Officer, had given him the aircraft in
exchange for a new set of dentures. The
teeth stayed in place but the Tiger Moth
went back.

After 402 Squadron had moved out on
June 23 1941 they were replaced on July
25 by No 409 Squadron, another unit of
the Royal Canadian Air Force that had
formed at Digby the previous month.
Initially 409 Squadron was equipped with
Defiant Mark I night fighters and it
operated with these, and the subsequent
Beaufighters Marks IIF and VIF, from
Coleby until February 27 1943 when the
unit then moved to Acklington, North-
umberland. No 410, another RCAF
squadron, equipped with Mosquito NF
Mark IIs, the best night fighters of all,
had arrived from Acklington six days
previously to replace the outgoing 402
unit. With the closure of Hibaldstow,
Coleby Grange became the major base for
night fighters in Lincolnshire in 1943
although the role of 410 Squadron was
not solely the night air defence of Britain,
for the unit also took part in 'Ranger'
operations. These involved individual
aircraft strafing road and rail targets in
occupied Europe. This unit remained until
October 19 1943 when it then moved to
West Malling. It was replaced on

November 7 by No 264 Squadron, also with Mosquito II aircraft, but they remained only a few weeks and departed on December 18 1943. A few weeks earlier, on November 25, No 288 with their Blenheim IVs and Defiant IIIs had vacated Coleby Grange.

During February 1944 No 68 Squadron arrived with Beaufighters but the following month they departed and were replaced by No 307 (Polish) Squadron equipped with Mosquito XIIs. This was to be the last operational squadron to be housed at Coleby and gave Lincolnshire the final night cover of the war. Coleby's operational role came to an end when the unit moved out on May 6 1945.

Thereafter the station was merely used as a landing ground and housed only non-operational units, one being No 1515 BAT Flight with Oxford I aircraft from February 28 1945 to June 2 1945. After this unit departed the airfield closed to flying, a closure hastened by the fact that it had remained a grass airfield with very limited facilities despite being used by such advanced aircraft as the Mosquito.

In 1959 Coleby Grange re-opened to house No 142 Squadron, a unit equipped with three Thor missiles—part of the American Thor ICBM complex under the control of Hemswell—but these sites soon became too vulnerable and No 142 Squadron was disbanded in 1963.

The airfield closed that same year after having played a vital part in the air war and quickly reverted back to agriculture, a 'T1' hangar to the east of the A15 being taken over by a local farmer. The tower was still standing in 1979, albeit in a somewhat derelict condition.

Coningsby, Lincolnshire

122/TF225565. Just S of the village of Coningsby and W of the B1192 road with the main entrance to the station from the village

The south-east of Lincolnshire is flat and lightly populated and would therefore seem to be a perfect location for bomber airfields. But it is fenland and therefore not suitable because of the drainage problems inherent in this type of soil. However, Coningsby was surveyed during the Expansion period and preliminary work started towards the end of 1937. Construction proceeded very slowly and it was not until November 4 1940 that Coningsby opened as a bomber airfield in No 5 Group, Bomber Command. It was a grass airfield with two 'J' type hangars in the north-west corner, and it was provided with substantial barracks and other permanent accommodation. A decoy airfield was sited at Hagnagy some eight miles east of Coningsby.

Having opened, the station then had to wait until the New Year before it received its first flying unit. In February 1941, No 106 Squadron arrived from Finningley and began mining operations with their Hampdens. The first bombing raid was on March 1/2 when four Hampdens attacked Cologne. That same month No 97 Squadron arrived with Avro Manchesters and both squadrons participated in many raids against Fortress Europe.

However, problems were being encountered in operating the heavier bombers from the grass surfaces so, in March 1942, No 97 Squadron moved to Woodhall Spa. No 106 remained and after

Below *Boeing B-29 Washington B1s at Coningsby. Tattershall Castle is in the distance on the right.* **Above right** *Anson at Coningsby in July 1961.*

a brief spell with Manchesters began to convert to Lancasters during the summer months. Having thus re-equipped, the squadron moved to Syerston and Coningsby closed for the construction of concrete runways.

The airfield re-opened in August 1943, now equipped with three concrete runways and additional hangars which included a 'B1' and a row of three 'T2's. That same month the new runways welcomed the famous 617 'Dam Busters' Squadron under the command of Wing Commander Guy Gibson. 617 were soon putting their special skills in action and on September 15/16 1943 they attacked the Dortmund-Ems Canal, using for the first time the 12,000 lb high capacity bomb. But, like the famous dams-raid, the squadron paid a very high price, only three Lancasters returning from the total force of eight despatched. In January 1944 the squadron moved to Woodhall Spa, possibly in order to give them greater security, and No 619 Squadron, which was based there, moved to Coningsby to replace 617.

The following month the Lancasters of No 61 Squadron moved in from Skellingthorpe to join No 619 and both units took part in many major raids on enemy targets before they both departed in April 1944, No 61 back to Skellingthorpe and No 619 to Dunholme Lodge.

That same month No 83 Squadron was transferred from No 8 Group and Wyton to No 5 Group and Coningsby. April also saw the return of No 97 Squadron from 8 Group and with these two units the station's role changed to precision marking of targets. These squadrons formed the No 5 Group Special Marker Force, the Pathfinders, and attacks were made on railway targets in France and Belgium. The units also played a part in

'Operation Overlord' and on the eve of the invasion, the night of June 5/6 1944, the squadrons bombed gun emplacements at La Pernelle on the Normandy coast.

On Saturday, August 18 1944, Sergeant R.F. Powell was on stand-down and looking forward to the weekly dance at Boston. Aircrew in wartime snatched what pleasure they could and the Saturday dance was a treat not to be missed. For Sergeant Powell, midday brought the bad news. Group had laid on a sudden and unexpected daylight raid to a target somewhere in France—six crews were needed, and 97 Squadron was to supply them. His luck did not hold for his was one of the crews picked for the mission.

There target was the oil refinery plant at Bordeaux and, as the opposition would be light, no fighter cover would be necessary. It was a beautiful sunny day and the flight to the target was uneventful. By late afternoon the bombers neared Bordeaux and the oil refinery tanks, uncamouflaged, gleamed in the brilliant sunlight. As they started their bombing run they were met with extremely accurate ack-ack fire and Sergeant Powell, who was the mid-upper gunner, felt helpless:

'Great tension and fear gripped me, when suddenly we were hit, the aircraft rocked violently and a shell exploded near my mid-upper turret, shattering the Perspex. I was blinded as pieces of Perspex and shrapnel hit my face and entered by unprotected eyes. My helmet and oxygen mask had undoubtedly taken a lot of the impact but I was still in a bad way. With the unending stream of blood from my face and eyes, panic gripped me at the thought that I had been blinded—perhaps for life.'

Meanwhile, the skipper had continued on target course and held the Lancaster steady until bombs were away. This had

Above *Phantom of 29 Squadron takes off at Coningsby. Note re-heat.* **Right** *Four 29 Squadron Phantoms from Coningsby join a Victor tanker of No 55 Squadron from Marham. Note the underwing refuelling pods on the tanker.*

been difficult for the fuselage was full of holes and damage had been done to many of the flying instruments. The aircraft had only three engines for one port engine had been put out of action.

The mid-upper gunner was no use in his condition so he left his shattered turret, a very difficult task for it was only a small restricted space, and crawled in a sea of blood and darkness, up front until he touched Flight Sergeant Nicholson, the wireless operator. He was placed on the rest bed and a first aid dressing was put over his face.

The pilot brought the crippled Lancaster back and crash landed at Manston, Kent. In the fuselage alone it had over a hundred holes. The comradeship shown during the mission was typical of aircrew in such a situation and because Sergeant Powell was in a semi-conscious state one crew member remained with him during the return flight home. Sergeant Powell was awarded the Distinguished Flying Medal and after a short spell in hospital he went on to complete a second tour of operations. Such was the spirit that made victory possible.

On their last operational missions in World War 2 both squadrons took part in an attack on an oil refinery at Tonsberg in Norway on April 25/26 1945. No 83 Squadron had flown a total of 5,117 sorties during World War 2 and had won 429 decorations and honours—one VC, one OBE, one MBE, 29 DSOs, 209 DFCs, 36 bars to DFCs, one CGM, 147 DFMs, three bars to DFMs and one DCM. No 97

(Straits Settlement) Squadron also had a fine war record and had flown 4,091 sorties while its members had won 21 DSOs, 222 DFCs, two bars to DFCs, 157 DFMs, two bars to DFMs, one OBE and one BEM.

After the war both No 83 and 97 Squadrons remained at Coningsby and in December 1945, after No 5 Group had disbanded, the station came under No 1 Group at Mildenhall. Both squadrons re-equipped with Lincolns during July/August 1946 and in November they moved to Hemswell. The station still had a role to play in the post-war RAF as a heavy bomber station but, during the late 1940s and early 1950s, it was only with four Mosquito units. These were No 16 OTU and No 231 OCU with T3s and B16s and Nos 109 and 139 Squadrons with B16s and B35s. Both of the squadrons arrived in November 1946, No 109 from Wickenby and No 139 from Hemswell, for Pathfinder duties. During their stay at Coningsby both units sent out several detachments, No 109 to Thorny Island, Coltishall and Shallufa, Egypt; No 139 to East Kirkby and Shallufa. In March 1950 both squadrons moved to Hemswell to prepare to receive Canberras.

The piston-engined Lincoln was now obsolete and in order to boost Bomber Command, American aircraft were ordered to build up the heavy bomber squadrons. Coningsby received its first B-29 Washingtons (Boeing Superfortress) when No 149 Squadron, having worked up at Marham, arrived in October 1950.

Next to arrive was No XV Squadron in February 1951, followed by No 44 (Rhodesian) Squadron in May and finally No 57 from Waddington, in April 1952, to make a total of four squadrons all equipped with B-29s. But, by this time the B-29 was outdated and in 1953 Nos XV, 44, 57 and 149 Squadrons re-armed with Canberras.

In October 1953 in swept an old broom, No 40 Squadron, also equipped with Canberras. The squadron badge was a broom and their motto was 'Hostem Acoelo Expellere' ('To drive the enemy from the sky'). This had now been done and the squadron had returned home to its first UK base since 1942, having spent its time in Egypt, Libya, Tunisia and Italy. In February 1954 the squadron moved to Wittering and the following May the four resident squadrons moved to Cottesmore, Rutland. The station then closed for reconstruction and runway extension.

When it re-opened in late 1956 it had only a main runway 9,000 ft long and 200 ft wide with a subsidiary which was now the normal layout for the jet age requirements. Over the next few years Coningsby housed several squadrons of Canberras as a back-up to the RAF's nuclear strike force, the first being No 57 Squadron which had arrived from Honington in November 1956, but this disbanded at the end of the following year. No 9 Squadron arrived from Binbrook in June 1959 and was joined the following month by No 12 Squadron. In July 1961 both units disbanded and in 1962 re-formed here along with No 35 Squadron as V-force units equipped with Vulcan B.2 medium bombers.

In November 1964 the three resident squadrons moved to Cottesmore and Coningsby closed, its long period of service in Bomber Command finished. But it had closed for an important reason since it had been selected as the main base for the TSR2, and work started to make the airfield suitable for this advanced aircraft. However, when the TSR2 was cancelled, largely for reasons which were witheld from public scrutiny, Coningsby reverted to care and maintenance until 1966. It was then chosen as the first base for the Phantom fighter-bomber and the station received No 5 School of Technical Training to train the ground crew. In February 1968, under 38 Group, ASC, No 228 OCU formed to train the Phantom aircrews. The unit's aircraft wear the markings of No 64 Squadron, their shadow number for front line employment in an emergency. The following years saw several Phantom squadrons come and go, Nos 6, 54, 41, 111 and 29 which, today, is the resident squadron in support of our front line air defence. Coningsby also witnessed the training by No 228 OCU of all Phantom aircrew in the Royal Air Force, and the specialist training of all Phantom groundcrews. The station looks as if it will continue in this role, being updated with aircraft and by mid-1984 it will house a Tornado Operational Conversion Unit.

As a bonus, RAF Coningsby is the home for the Battle of Britain Memorial Flight which the station received in March 1976 to renew its link with the spirited past. The Battle of Britain Memorial Flight was formed in 1957 at Biggin Hill. It has an establishment of Spitfire II P7350, Spitfire V AB910, Spitfire XIXs

PM631 and PS853, Hurricane IIs LF363 and PZ865, plus Lancaster 1 PA474. This is now in the markings of Guy Gibson's aircraft of 617 Squadron but, having a mid-upper turret and a normal bomb bay, it does not look right in these markings. A reminder of the past also exists in three of the four main hangars on the station for two are 'J' type from 1939 and one the 'B1' type from 1942, the fourth being a Gaydon type built in 1960. The three 'T2's are also still in use.

Cottesmore, Leicestershire (Rutland)

130/SK905155. Approximately 10 miles NW of Stamford, W of the A1 and N of the B668 roads

Sited west of Ermine Street and north of the village of Cottesmore from which it was named, this was another of the sites selected close to the old Roman road on which work started in 1935 during the planned Expansion period. The technical and domestic buildings were immediately to the north of Cottesmore village.

The airfield officially opened on March 11 1938 but the station was not fully ready and work continued during the next few months. Cottesmore opened as a bomber station in No 2 Group, designed to accommodate two squadrons. In April two squadrons from Worthy Down arrived, No 35 with Wellesleys (code letters 'WT') and No 207 with Battles

(code letters 'WJ'). The latter moved to Cranfield in April 1939 and No 35 Squadron re-equipped with Battles and followed in August.

The Battles were replaced that same month by the Hampdens of No 185 Squadron which arrived from Thornaby. At the outbreak of war the unit had on strength 15 Hampdens, one Hereford (code letters 'GL') and four Ansons. The station had now been transferred to No 5 Group, Bomber Command, and the defence of the aerodrome was placed under the control of detachments from local Army units. Eventually a rifle squadron of 250 airmen was formed, complete with two armoured vehicles— converted lorries that looked like the fore- runners of Heath Robinsons! On the airfield itself, air raid shelters, pillboxes and gun positions were constructed, but many of the latter never housed any guns and the overall defence position was pathetic.

By the middle of September, No 106 Squadron had arrived from Thornaby and Evanton. This was also a Hampden squadron (code letters XS' and 'ZN') but, for some reason, it was decided not to retain Cottesmore as a bomber station and in October No 106 Squadron moved to Finningley.

By this time No 185 Squadron had become a Group Pool Squadron and the station transferred to No 6 (Training) Group. The unit continued as a reserve

9th TCC at Cottesmore on D-Day. Engines are started as these fully equipped airborne troops march in formation to board their aircraft. They are part of the greatest airborne troop armada ever assembled.

squadron, engaged in the training of bomber crews, but could not keep pace with the rapid growth of Bomber Command. Thus, the operational training units were organised on a station basis and, on April 5 1940, No 185 lost its squadron status and merged with SHQ Cottesmore to form No 14 OTU with an establishment of 32 Hampdens, 16 Herefords and 24 Ansons (code letters 'GL' and 'AM'). Even though the role of the station was now firmly sealed, that same month No 185 (B) squadron was re-formed as a Hampden bomber squadron. After a false start it disbanded, however, on May 17.

On June 26 1940 the airfield was bombed on what was to be the first of several such raids, but damage was slight and it did not affect the training programme or stop the unit taking part in operational missions. The aircraft were dispersed on hardstandings around the perimeter and at the outbreak of war the families had been evacuated from the married quarters which were then used to billet the increased Service personnel. As a further precaution Cottesmore had a decoy airfield at Swayfield some six miles to the north-east but records do not show if this was ever used.

On July 25 three Hampdens from No 14 OTU took part in the first 'Nickel' over Northern France. The normal training continued but the unit continued to fly 'Nickels' until December 23 1940, at which time Cottesmore ceased these duties. By then a total of 35 sorties had been flown, with no loss of aircraft but equally with little gain except flying experience.

Throughout 1941 the training of crews increased and the airfield was attacked in April, May and June, but very little damage was done. A break from routine came on May 30/31 when Cottesmore despatched 29 Hampdens against Cologne in the first of the 1,000-bomber raids. Three aircraft failed to return but on the second raid against Essen on June 1/2, all 24 aircraft returned to base safely. Cottesmore also took part in the third and last 1,000-bomber raid on June 25/26 1942 against Bremen when 22 of the stations's Hampdens took part, one failing to return.

The unit continued in the training role and also to provide aircraft for some bombing raids. The last operational raid for the station's aircraft was on September 16 1942 when 12 Hampdens

A well-earned decoration: First Lieutenant Woodrow V. Timo of 316th Troop Carrier Group, 9th Troop Carrier Command, is presented with the Distinguished Flying Cross by Lieutenant General Lewis H. Brereton during a ceremony at Cottesmore, April 25 1945.

joined the main force in a raid against Essen. A total of 151 sorties were flown from Cottesmore during this period with a loss of nine aircraft and 23 crew members.

On August 1 1943, No 14 OTU was transferred to Market Harborough and with their departure the wartime training duty was to end. Cottesmore had played a useful role and, during its peak period of 1942, 1,047 pilots, navigators, wireless operators and air-gunners successfully passed to the squadrons. A total of 63 aircrew were killed during training.

The airfield was now placed on a C & M basis and work began with the laying of concrete runways which were essential for the heavier aircraft now coming into service. It was also obvious that Cottesmore had been marked as a probable base for the Americans and one to be used in the preparation for the invasion of Europe. During April 1943 Horsa gliders were flown in by Whitley and Albemarle tugs and held in dispersed storage. These were maintained by a detachment of No 2 HGMU from Snailwell.

Argosy of No 115 Squadron coming into land at Cottesmore.

The airfield re-opened in August 1943 and was now complete with three standard 50-yard-wide concrete runways, the main being 2,000 yards and the two intersecting runways 1,600 and 1,500 yards long each, with an encircling perimeter track which was rather bitty in order to accommodate 35 concrete and 17 tarmac hardstandings. It was normal practice for the American airfields in the UK to have this number. The airfield now had four 'C' type hangars and one 'T2'.

Cottesmore was now transferred to American control with a small muster of Royal Air Force personnel which included the glider detachment. It was now USAAF Station 489 and, on September 24 1943 the Headquarters Troop Carrier Command arrived and took over the whole station. The HQ unit was then re-named 9th TCC and on December 1 1943 moved back to St Vincents, Grantham. The next to arrive was the 50th Troop Carrier Wing HQ but their stay was also brief and on November 18 1943 they moved to Bottesford.

Throughout the winter of 1943/44 the build-up of USAAF personnel continued and Cottesmore was used as a transit base for many American ground units. Then, on February 16 1944, the first 26 aircraft arrived. These were of the 316th TCG under Lieutenant Colonel Burton R. Fleet, comprising Nos 36, 37, 44 and 45 Squadrons equipped with C-47 Skytrains, C-53 Skytroopers and Hadrian gliders. The following day the 52nd Troop Carrier

Wing HQ arrived and took up station at Cottesmore under the command of Brigadier General Harold L. Clark. This Wing had seen action in North Africa and Sicily and had nine months of combat experience behind it. With the 52nd TCW were four groups, the 61st TCG at Barkston Heath, 313th TCG at Folkingham, the 314th TCG at Saltby and the 316th TCG here at Cottesmore. By February 20 there were 50 aircraft on the airfield and the number of personnel had risen to nearly 3,700. To house this sudden influx, tented accommodation mushroomed overnight and local properties were requisitioned including Exton Hall, the home of the Earl of Gainsborough.

February also saw the arrival of the Pathfinder School of the IXth AFTCC. This unit had seven C-47s, two being equipped with 'GEE' and the others with SCR-717 radar. The unit was immediately involved in extensive training, but this interferred with the resident unit so on March 22 the Pathfinder School moved to North Witham.

These units trained with one objective in mind—the invasion of Europe—and many paratrooper drops were carried out around Cottesmore. The 316th trained hard and, on May 9 1944 when the station was honoured by a visit from Prince Bernhardt of the Netherlands, they put on a demonstration of a new glider pick-up which was to play an important part in the D-Day operations.

On May 11/12 operation 'Eagle' was staged, this including all the troop carrier groups belonging to the 50th, 52nd and

53rd Wings. Heavy clouds covered most
of England that night and, as the 52nd
TCW assembled over March, Cambridgeshire, on the return, two aircraft of the
316th TCG collided, killing the pilots,
Lieutenant Colonel Burton R. Fleet and
Lieutenant Shorber. Those killed were
buried a few days later at Madingley.
Lieutenant Colonel Harvey Berger was
appointed the new CO.

72 aircraft of the 316th TCG took part
in 'Operation Overlord' and, on June 6
1944, paratroopers were dropped and
gliders released at drop zone '0' near
Ste-Mère-Église. The 316th began to
arrive back at Cottesmore by 04.00 hours
after a successful mission. These initial
drops were followed up later the same day
by further reinforcement drops.

After the assault on Normandy the
316th TCG continued with training and
supply missions into Europe. The Group
subsequently took part in the Arnhem
airborne operations when, on the morning
of Sunday, September 17, 90 transport
aircraft took off from Cottesmore
between 10.35 and 10.50 hours loaded
with 1,362 American paratroopers which
included General Jim Gavin, the 82nd
Airborne Division CO, and the war
correspondent Ed Morrow.

The following day, D+1, 82 aircraft
towed 82 Waco CG4 gliders carrying 384
American troops, 28 Jeeps, five 75 mm
howitzers and nearly 44,000 lb of supplies
into the Arnhem area. By the third day the
weather had closed in, but Arnhem was
now lost. Because of bad weather conditions it was not possible to fly the next
mission until D+6 and the last Arnhem
run was flown on D+9.

After Arnhem the 316th again settled
down to training and supply missions.
Cottesmore provided many facilities for
those on base and most evenings there
were film shows or live entertainment with
the 316th Dance Band. At 01.00 hours on
March 4 1945 they had some extra live
entertainment when a German aircraft
attacked the base and dropped 17 anti-
personnel bombs. Two aircraft and a
Waco glider were damaged. However, on
March 21 all aircraft moved to
Wethersfield, Essex, in preparation for
the assault crossing over the Rhine on
March 24 1945.

Immediately the war in Europe was
over, the Americans began to depart. A
final parade was held on the station,
which was attended by Lieutenant
General Lewis H. Brereton, Commander

*HP Victor B1, XA929, at Cottesmore in
July 1961.*

of the First Allied Airborne Army. During
the parade a cheque was handed over to
the Oakham hospital and a bronze plaque
mounted near the main entrance: 'May
the memory of the comradeship sown in
the skies of Europe forever be as green as
the fields of Cottesmore.' By June 11 all
Americans had gone.

The station was then handed back to
the Royal Air Force and, on September 17
1945, No 1668 HCU moved in from
Bottesford, while by the end of the month
there were over 2,000 Service personnel,
including a large number of WAAFs.
However, many of these were just
awaiting demobilisation and by January
1946 the station's complement had fallen
by half.

The airfield was now back in the
training role and, up to the time it
disbanded in March 1946, No 1668 HCU
had successfully trained 57 crews and had
flown 4,285 hours. This unit was replaced
by No 16 OTU which arrived from Upper
Heyford equipped with 15 Mosquito
Mark T3 and Mark FB6 aircraft and four
Oxfords whose identity letters were
'FMO'.

The flying training programme was very
much reduced for there was now an acute
shortage of servicing personnel and many
aircraft had to be put into storage. The
programme was brought to a complete
halt during the severe winter of 1946/47
and in February not one aircraft managed
to leave the airfield. It was so bad that on
March 6 a Lancaster from Lindholme had

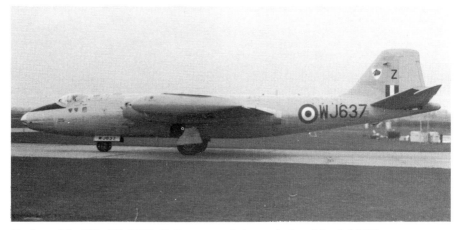

Canberra B2 of No 231 OCU, Cottesmore, photographed on March 8 1972.

to drop food and medical supplies. To help in the task of snow-clearing the German PoWs who were already housed at Cottesmore were put to work daily. Also, an extra 100 were brought in from the PoW camp at Woolfox Lodge.

By the end of March 1947 all bombing training ceased and the role of the unit changed from operational to crew training. Peacetime training meant a more leisurely programme and an intermediate stage was introduced. No 16 OTU now became No 204 Advanced Flying School and re-equipped with Mosquito Mark 6s. The station was transferred to No 21 Group, Flying Training Command.

On March 10 1948, No 204 AFS moved to Driffield, being replaced by No 7 SFTS, and the station became part of No 23 Group. The first task of the unit was to revert to its old title of No 7 FTS. Its role was to train pilots for the Royal Navy which did not have separate Flying Training Schools. The school, equipped with Tiger Moths and Harvard Mark 2B aircraft, also ran pilot refresher and instrument rating courses. In June 1950 the faithful old Tiger Moth was replaced by the Prentice. By the summer months the school had reached over 2,500 sorties a month and, like all Flying Training Schools, it had its share of accidents, the most common being either landing with wheels up or landing too heavily with resultant collapse of the undercarriage.

The passing-out parade is the highlight of any Forces training establishments and the 'Wings' parade for the school was no exception. For No 9 Pilots' course, the

presentation of 'Wings' to graduating students on June 2 1950 was made by The Earl of Ancaster, who was then Lord Lieutenant of the County of Rutland.

The training increased and in order to ease the congested circuit, Spitalgate was used as a relief landing ground for the Prentice aircraft and Woolfox Lodge for the Harvards. By March 1953 the Harvards had been replaced by Balliols and in March 1954 No 7 FTS disbanded. The Women's Royal Air Force also departed and Cottesmore prepared for another change of role.

The station had not long to wait for in May it was transferred to No 3 Group, Bomber Command, and four front line squadrons arrived from Coningsby, Nos XV, 44, 57 and 149, flying Canberra B2 aircraft. But further changes were in the wind for Cottesmore had been earmarked for development as a V-bomber base. The first to leave was No 149 squadron on August 24 1954 to Ahlhorn in Germany. The other three squadrons moved to Honington in the early part of February 1955 and on the 15th the station was placed on C & M.

Over the next three years a vast airfield complex was built, extending the main runway to 3,000 yards and laying down new taxiways and hardstandings suitable for V-bombers. New buildings were also needed on the technical site to house the special equipment for the new air traffic control facilities. The domestic site was also enlarged and modernised.

The station re-opened in March 1958 as an operational base and on April 15 No 10

Squadron re-formed as a V-force squadron with Handley Page Victor B1 aircraft. On September 1 1958 the second Victor squadron, No XV, re-formed here.

The Government had pinned its faith on the V-force and with the modern day technology in airwar it was estimated the UK would have about four minutes' warning of an imminent air attack. In order to achieve fighter-type scrambles with a V-force bomber, a modification was made to the engine starting cycle whereby all four engines started simultaneously. It was now commonplace for four Victors to be airborne in under four minutes and over the years it became an attraction to see a V-bomber scramble.

In November 1961, No 232 OCU ('C' Flight) moved in from Gaydon for Cottesmore had been chosen to carry out the intensive flying trials of the Victor B2. The following March the unit was renamed Victor Training Flight and in February 1964 it moved to Wittering. The Victor V-bomber role at Cottesmore was changing and, at the end of March, No 10 Squadron disbanded. On October 31 1964, No XV Squadron also disbanded and on November 2 Nos 9, 12 and 35 Squadrons arrived from Coningsby, flying Vulcan B2s which were to form the Cottesmore Wing. The station was now transferred to No 1 Group. The role of the Cottesmore Wing was to maintain both their nuclear and conventional roles and carry out training to this effect. Apart from normal training the Vulcan squadron crews carried out many missions abroad, including to the Far East.

Then, with a change in Government defence policy and the transference of the nuclear deterrent to the Royal Navy the V-force was reduced and No 12 Squadron disbanded on December 31 1967. The following year saw further changes that affected not only Cottesmore but the whole of the Royal Air Force for, on April 30 1968, Bomber Command amalgamated with Fighter Command to become Strike Command, the bomber section being No 1 (Bomber) Group. In January 1969, Nos 9 and 35 Squadrons left Cottesmore for the warmer climate of Akrotiri, Cyprus.

The role of the station now changed again and April 1969 saw the arrival of Nos 98, 115 and 360 Squadrons from Watton. No 98 Squadron, flying Canberra E15s, and No 115 Squadron, flying Argosy E Mark 1s, had the task of flight checking all Royal Air Force Navigational, airfield and runway approach aids on a world-wide basis. No 360 Squadron, made up of 75 per cent Royal Air Force and 25 per cent Royal Navy personnel, was the joint RAF/RN electronic warfare training squadron flying Canberra T17 aircraft.

In May 1969 No 231 OCU arrived from Bassingbourn and this unit, equipped with Camberra B2s and T4s, completed the change. But there were still further changes and in 1971, after it was decided to reallocate all of No 90 (Signals) Group's aircraft, the station was transferred to No 1 Group, Strike Command.

In the Defence Review of 1975 which

Tornado BT002, ZA320, on take-off at Cottesmore, June 6 1980. This was the first aircraft to arrive but stayed only a few hours. It arrived officially on July 1 1980.

resulted in the closure of 12 stations, there were many changes at Cottesmore. The first sign came in August 1975 when No 360 Squadron moved to Wyton. During the summer months the Canberra airframe had many Category 3 problems and not only No 71 MU but a contractor's working party had to move in to iron out the problems. These proved so difficult that many airframes were still being worked on in hangars after the station had been placed on care and maintenance.

In early February 1976, No 231 OCU moved out to Marham, followed at the end of the month by No 115 Squadron with their Argosies to Brize Norton. The saddest moment came when, on February 27 1976, No 98 Squadron disbanded and its aircraft handed over to 100 Squadron at Marham. No 98 Squadron, RFC, had first formed at Harlaxton, Lincolnshire, on August 30 1917 as a day bombing unit equipped with DH9s. It had been based in France, Belgium, Germany as well as many UK bases and had a varied history.

On March 31 1976 Cottesmore was placed on a C & M basis, until March 31 1978 when it was reactivated. Extensive works services began in preparation for Cottesmore's new and vital role of the 1980s. These preparations ranged from the most detailed office work to major construction on the airfield. This included runway resurfacing, new hardstandings and converting one hangar into an engine test centre. In addition there are many new buildings, including accommodation blocks, a far cry from the wartime tented housing. The station is the home of Tri-National Tornado Training Establishment (TTTE) and one of the most important military bases in Western Europe. Cottesmore will train all the crews, pilots and navigators who will fly the British, Italian and German Tornadoes. A total of 809, which includes four present service aircraft, will be produced. These will be 671 operational and 138 trainers with operational capabilities. A further break-down is 385 for the RAF, 324 for Germany (of which 112 are for the German Navy) and 100 for Italy. The latter will be last in line for the Tornado and will make do with their F-104s until they come into service. Cottesmore will have 50 Tornados based here, the first two of which arrived on July 1 1980 and were welcomed by Air Vice-Marshal Michael Knight, AOC No 1 Group. The Tornado is being jointly produced in Britain, Italy and West Germany. It has a crew of two and will eventually replace five types of aircraft now in Royal Air Force service.

On October 22 1979 the Tornado Ground Servicing School (TGSS) started training its first students. It has the role of training men who will maintain and service the Tornado in the Royal Air Force. TGSS is under the control of RAF Support Command while the rest of the station is in No 1 Group Strike Command.

The Germans will again be at Cottesmore but this time with their families and not as PoWs. Rutland (now part of Leicestershire), will house the air force personnel and their families from the three nations. It is a small price to pay for security and the Tornado will make an essential contribution—in all conditions. It is a welcome Tornado that is now at Cottesmore. As at June 1980, English-Electric Canberra PR 7 WH791/8187M is Gate Guardian and I trust it will be retained for the future.

Cranwell, Lincolnshire

130/TF015490. NW of Sleaford, between A17(T) and B1429 roads

Bordered on three sides by roads, the airfield is sited just west of the village of Cranwell and goes back as far as 1915. During November of that year some 3,000 acres of farmland were commandeered, mainly from the estate of the Earl of Bristol. On December 28 1915 work started on the construction of the wooden huts that were to become HMS *Daedalus*. The first buildings erected were for the unit personnel and their airships and balloons. The aerodrome, with wooden hangars and two flight sheds, was sited just south of the B1429 road. To the north of this road was a separate aerodrome which also had several balloon sheds sited on the northern edge of the airfield, and this was Cranwell North. The first three free balloons arrived from Wormwood Scrubs in May 1916. A single track branch railway line was also laid just west of Sleaford from the main Grantham–Boston line and this was used by two locomotives from 1917 until after the Second World War. What used to be the railway station is now the main guardroom.

The station opened on April 1 1916 as the RNAS Training Establishment, HMS *Daedalus,* and the role of the unit was to train officers and ratings of the Royal Navy on aeroplanes, kite balloons and dirigibles. In July 1916 Their Majesties

Above *Airship at Cranwell. This one was scrapped here in 1920.* **Below** *Bristol Bulldog (IM) K3923 and Siskin IIIA J9305 at Cranwell in 1932.*

King George V and Queen Mary paid their first official visit.

When the Royal Air Force was formed in April 1918 it took over Cranwell and there were many changes. After the heavy losses in France in April 1917 when the RFC lost 131 aircraft there was a reorganisation in the training structure and from April 1918 to 1919 the station housed 201, 202 and 213 TDS, later renamed 56, 57 and 58 TDS respectively. Cranwell was a very large station even in the early years, and during the summer of 1918 comprised the Airship Training Wing, Boys' Training Wing, Wing Aeroplane Repair Section, PT School and Wireless Operators' School. There had even been an American unit the previous year, but in the early part of 1918 it was gone. The Electrical and Wireless School also operated during this period from May 1916 to June 1918.

However, at the end of the war its future was in the balance. A Bill was put before Parliament in 1919 by Winston Churchill, then Secretary of State for Air, which included proposals to establish a cadet college for the Royal Air Force, and it was suggested this could be at Cranwell.

The Churchill-Trenchard Memorandum, as it became known, was accepted and the first course for officer cadets was officially opened at the Royal Air Force Cadet College, Cranwell, on February 5 1920. It was later renamed the Royal Air Force College from 1929 until September 1939. Lack of finance meant that the old wooden huts had to be retained for many years and more permanent buildings, including the new college structure, were not completed until 1933, being formally opened on October 11 1934 by HRH the Prince of Wales. The old wooden hangars

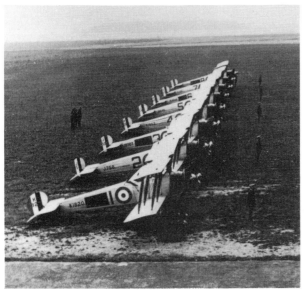

Above *Avro Tutor K3215 just takes off at Cranwell. This aircraft now flies in the Shuttleworth Collection, sadly all painted yellow, not its true colours.*

Left *Avro 504 Ns and Ks of 'A' Flight, Cranwell 1932.*

Below *K1991—the Fairey Long-range Monoplane which flew non-stop from Cranwell to South Africa—at Cranwell in 1933.*

Above right *Valetta T2 WG260 at Cranwell in September 1964.*

were replaced by two 'C' type hangars. Because Cranwell was within 50 miles of the sea a flashing beacon was added at the insistence of the first Commandant, Air Commodore Longcroft, and this also acted as an aid to aircraft navigation. The revolving light installed in the 130-ft high tower flashed white every three seconds and was visible for 20 miles on a clear night.

Training at Cranwell continued unabated between the wars, but the airfield was congested and large fields in the area were used as forced landing grounds, one being at Temple Bruer and one at Wellingore. During this period only pilots were trained here and a wide variety of aircraft flew from the two airfields, including Avro 504Ks with different coloured wheels to denote the Flight, later replaced in 1927 by 504Ns, the DH9A and the Bristol Fighter from 1920 to May 1930. The Armstrong Siddeley Atlas entered service for the prospective bomber pilots and the Sopwith Snipe came to Cranwell in July 1921, remaining until September 1927. The Siskin then arrived for those cadets who would go on to fighter aircraft but was later replaced by the Avro Tutor which, like the Hawker Hart, remained at Cranwell until the outbreak of World War 2. Many well-known personalities graduated from the College, including Group Captain Douglas Bader in 1930.

Cranwell was also associated with epoch-making long-distance flights. In May 1927, a modified Hawker Horsley set up an unofficial record when Flight Lieutenant C.R. Carr was forced to land in the Persian Gulf after flying 3,420 miles in 34½ hours. Two years later, in a Fairey Long Range Monoplane, Squadron Leader A.G. Jones-Williams and Flight Lieutenant N.H. Jenkins succeeded where Carr had failed by flying 4,130 miles from Cranwell to Karachi in 50 hours 37 minutes. These came under the RAF Long Range Development Flight that existed from 1927 until mid-1938, but information on this unit is regrettably sparse.

On August 6 1929 the Electrical and Wireless School was established, renamed No 1 E & WS then No 1 Radio School, training both air and ground wireless operators. There was also No 8 Radio School from March 10 1941 until June 26 1946. Aircraft used by the Wireless Schools were varied, including Wallace IIs from 1939 to November 1940, Valentias from 1936 to October 1941, Tiger Moths from 1937 to October 1952, and the Mentor and Harvard, but the main ones were the Proctor and Dominie being used from November 1940 until November 1947, and the Oxford from May 1943 to October 1952. Others used were the DH89A (Dragon-Rapide) from 1941 to 1943, Oxfords up to 1952, Halifaxes from September 1945 to August 1949 and Ansons from June 1949 to October 1952. Also, in the 1920s Cranwell housed the No 4 (Apprentices) Wing from 1920 until 1926 when Halton was then ready. Frank Whittle, the jet engine pioneer, was one of the first apprentices trained at Cranwell.

The Royal Air Force Hospital was also here to serve the airfields in the area from 1922 until 1940, when it moved to a more peaceful environment at Rauceby mental hospital. Many new units were created during the expansion of the Royal Air Force in the 1930s and some were at Cranwell: for example the School of Store Accounting and Storekeeping in July 1934, which in December 1936 became the Equipment Training School which remained until June 1941; a Supplies Depot from October 1936 until November 1949; and the School of Clerks Accountancy from May 1939 to January 28 1941. Cranwell was also HQ No 21

Group, Training Command, from December 1938 until July 1944.

At the outbreak of the Second World War the college was closed, only to be re-opened immediately as the Royal Air Force College Flying Training School, one of six new schools to be established. In May 1941 Whittle's Gloster E28/39 jet aircraft made its maiden flight of 17 minutes from the South Airfield. That same month Twentieth Century Fox filmed *A Yank in the Royal Air Force* which was used as a morale booster.

Throughout 1940 the airfield received many enemy attacks, but the bombs were dropped on the surrounding countryside and the decoy airfield at Willoughby Walks proved effective. During October of that year the enemy raids became more frequent and flying accidents increased. In August 1941 an incendiary bomb hit the college, the only damage being a cracked tile, and this was the sole bomb to hit Cranwell. The only major damage done to the college during the war was on March 18 1942 when, in fog, Whitley P5052 of No 3 OTU hit the roof and fell on the lecture room—then being used as a dormitory. The crew of three were killed and a large fire ensued which caused a lot of damage.

During the war years the college broadened its scope but training was still its main role and by early 1941 the Royal Air Force College SFTS had approximately 150 Oxfords. In order to ease the congested circuit, relief airfields were used at Fulbeck, Wellingore, Coleby Grange, Barkston Heath, Caistor and Spitalgate. The situation eased a little when the Oxfords of No 2 CFS, which had formed in July 1940 as 2 FIS with Tutors and Oxfords, becoming 2 CFS in November, moved out in June 1941 to Church Lawford. This unit was then replaced by 3 (Coastal) OTU which arrived on August 6 1941 equipped with Whitleys. These were replaced in May 1943 by Wellingtons, some of which had Leigh Lights, and Martinets. The role of 3 OTU was to train Coastal Command crews in operational techniques and the syllabus included long cross-country and overseas training flights from Cranwell. The unit remained here in that capacity until June 23 1943 when it moved to Haverford West.

During 1943 the Royal Air Force College FTS was operating Oxfords, Masters, Tiger Moths, Blenheims and Spitfires. In March it was retitled 17 SFTS and in May 1945 was transferred to Spitalgate. The Flying Training School at Cranwell had done an outstanding job of training aircrew for the operational squadrons. The college was always over-crowded and most of the time food was short, but wartime life was exciting. The majority of aircrew trained here were from Commonwealth and Allied countries including Free France, Belgium, Ceylon, Czechoslovakia and Turkey. Some idea of the wartime population can be judged from the fact that in September 1943 a parade to commemorate the Battle of

Close up of a Jet Provost T5 outside the hangar at Cranwell, May 1979 (MOD).

Aerial view of the College Hall with its Italianate domed tower, and three Jet Provost Mark 5As flying past (MOD).

Britain was held in which an estimated 7,000 Service personnel plus 3,000 civilians participated at Cranwell.

On July 21 1945, No 1 Officers' Advanced Training School moved out of College Hall to Digby, having been at Cranwell since March 1944. On June 13 His Majesty King George VI revisited the college. During the war years 326 Cranwell graduates lost their lives out of the 931 who served, and over 600 won decorations. These included one VC which was awarded posthumously to Wing Commander H.G. Malcolm for his attacks on Bizerta and Chonigni airfields in North Africa during 1942; three GCs, one of which was the Empire Gallantry Medal won by Flight Cadet W.N. McKechnie on October 18 1929 and converted to a George Cross on July 28 1942; 82 DSOs and 269 DFCs.

The post-war years saw No 19 FTS, which had replaced No 17 SFTS, using the airfield with their Tiger Moths until they moved to Feltwell, Norfolk, in April 1947. That same month the Royal Air Force College was officially re-opened. During 1947 there were more changes

when the Secretarial Branch Training Establishment and Equipment Officers' School moved in, but it was short-lived and they moved out in 1948. That same year saw the replacement of the de Havilland Tiger Moth by the Percival Prentice as the *ab initio* trainer.

In October 1950, No 1 Radio School moved to Locking and the apprentice element which remained at Cranwell was renamed No 6 Radio School but, on December 1 1952, this also moved to Locking and Cranwell became responsible for officer training only. From January 1951 to March 1953 the Chipmunks of No 3 Initial Training Wing (later No 3 ITS), buzzed around the airfield.

To permit the introduction of the Meteor and Vampire in 1954, two concrete runways were constructed on the south airfield and Barkston Heath once again became a satellite, remaining in use even today as an RLG.

In 1960 the old wartime huts were cleared away as a vast building programme got underway. This cost over £2 million and included a new Sergeants' Mess (opened 1963), Airmen's Social Club (opened

1964), a further Officers' Mess, a large instructional block, an aerothermodynamics and engineering complex, plus married quarters. In 1966 the RAF Technical College moved to Cranwell from Henlow.

1970 saw the college 50 years old and in June Her Majesty The Queen and His Royal Highness The Duke of Edinburgh visited it. The following year His Royal Highness the Prince of Wales trained at Cranwell for five months and received his Wings from the Chief of the Air Staff. In November 1971, on the disbandment of No 22 Group, Cranwell assumed direct control of all the University Air Squadrons. January 1974 saw the College of Air Warfare move in from Manby, a unit which remained with their Dominie aircraft until 1978.

On May 30 1975 the Commandant-in-Chief of the College, Her Majesty the Queen, again visited the college to present a new Colour. In April 1976 the Central Flying School moved to Cranwell when their former home at Little Rissington had closed. However, its stay was short and, on November 21 1977 the CFS HQ moved to Leeming. Also in the move was the Spitfire that had been on display, leaving only a Vampire in front of Flying Wing.

The evolution of the training programme had continued over the years and the aircraft were numerous, from the post-war Tiger Moths and North American Harvards, then the Percival Prentice which, in turn, was replaced by the de Havilland Chipmunks and, for a short period, the Boulton & Paul Balliol T2. The combination of the Piston Provost and Meteor 7 or de Havilland Vampire T11 made way for the Jet Provost and for the college to embark on all-through jet training. Cranwell is constantly changing to keep its place as the RAF's No 1 college.

Derby (Burnaston), Derbyshire

See Burnaston

Desborough, Northamptonshire

141/SP815860. Approximately 4 miles W of Corby between Wilbarston on the A427 and Desborough on the A6(T)

Designed to Class 'A' standards as a heavy bomber airfield, but like so many others in the Midlands, Desborough opened as a bomber OTU in No 92 Group, Bomber Command.

The airfield was sited between the villages of Wilbarston and Desborough, after which it was named, and lies east of the B669 road that joins the two villages. Work started here in late 1942 to transform the ironstone uplands into a bomber station and when it opened on September 1 1943 it was to the standard specification with the standard 50 yard-wide concrete runways, the main being 2,000 yards long and lying on an east-west axis. There were two intersecting runways, each 1,400 yards long, with an encircling perimeter track, off which there were 29 hardstandings of the 'frying pan' type. There were four 'T2' hangars and one 'B1' which were sited two in the northern section of the airfield near Walter Wood, two in the southern part and one to the east near Pipewell Wood.

The domestic accommodation for permanent staff and pupils was located on seven sites dispersed about a mile to the south-west of the airfield, some being in Brampton Wood just west of the B669 road. The Communal Site and sick quarters were on the B669 road and many sites were adjacent to it, including the SHQ, operations and briefing rooms.

The station opened on September 1 1943 to receive No 84 OTU which was equipped with Wellington IIIs and Xs plus five Hurricane IIs for fighter affiliation and two Master IIs. The station also received a surprise visit from a Wellington of No 22 OTU, Wellesbourne Mountford, that crashed on the airfield at 09.50 hours on the opening day, fortunately without injury to any of the crew. However, over the next 18 months many others were not to be so lucky for there were many crashes.

During 1944 the flying programme was intense and the unit average was about 2,000 flying hours per month. The year started badly when, on January 21 1944, Wellington LN238 crashed into Geddington Chase Wood, just four miles north of Kettering, killing three and injuring four others. Then, just six days later, there were two more fatal crashes, Wellington X3392 crashing at 20.14 hours near Molesworth followed by Wellington HZ484, 2½ hours later, at nearby Arthingworth.

The role of the OTU was to bond together aircrew members as a team and give them further training on an operational basis. Every two weeks 11 each of pilots, navigators, wireless operators, bomb aimers and rear gunners were posted in to crew up and start a ten-week course, which was about 80 flying hours.

Throughout the war years Desborough stayed the home of No 84 OTU and remained a training station. On April 1 1944 the satellite at Harrington was handed over to the American VIIIth Air Force for their B-24 Liberators. Desborough continued with a reduced establishment of 40 Wellington Xs and, on April 17 1945, Course No 38 started what was to be the last for, on June 14, No 84 OTU disbanded before the course was finished and the crews were posted away. The aircraft were dispersed, 16 going to 8 MU, Little Rissington, 13 to 48 MU, Hardwarden and six to 12 MU Kirkbridge.

During July 1945 the runways were tested by staff from 44 Group Transport Command and some repairs were carried out. After they were completed in August the airfield was used for landing practice by Dakotas from 107 (T) OTU at Leicester East. However, by the end of the month the station closed to flying and was put on a care and maintenance basis. Then, on October 4 1945, it was transferred to No 4 Group and, on October 31, No 1381 (T) CU moved in from Bramcote with Dakota aircraft but, with the rapid rundown of the Royal Air Force, they did not remain long and before the end of the following year the station had closed down and was put on C & M until it was de-requisitioned.

Today the airfield is almost derelict and most of the land has reverted to agricultural use. The control tower and most of the buildings have long since gone, but a few still survive on the Administration Site and the perimeter track remains intact to serve as a road. One of the two remaining hangars was burned down in January 1979 while Amey Roadstone Ltd have just moved in and will speed up Mother Nature.

Desford (Leicester), Leicestershire

140/SK480020. S of Desford between the A47(T) and B582 roads

This was a small grass airfield that opened in 1935 as a civilian-manned Elementary and Reserve Flying Training School. Sited to the south of the village after which it was named, Desford was also known as Leicester because of its close proximity to the city.

At the outbreak of the Second World War Desford became the home of No 7 EFTS, in No 51 Group, Flying Training Command, equipped with Tiger Moths. This small site, wedged between a triangle of roads, operated with three grass strips with the airfield buildings at the north and south ends of the site alongside the minor roads. To help ease these cramped conditions, Kirkby Mallory, just over a mile to the west, was used as a satellite landing ground. Desford also took on

Desford today—far removed from the small grass airfield of 1935.

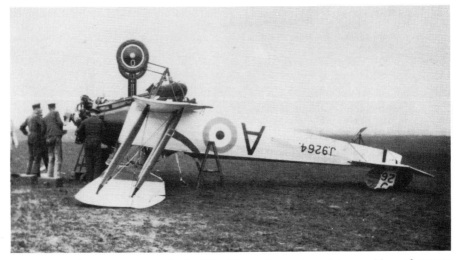

Avro 504N of No 2 FTS at Digby in 1928, illustrating early training problems that were just the same during the Second World War.

Braunstone as a satellite from just after the beginning of the war until the end.

No 7 EFTS remained until the end of the war and the station then became No 7 Reserve Flying School. In 1953 the airfield closed and the few buildings that remain today are used by industry.

Digby, Lincolnshire

121/TF045570.   W   of   B1191   from Scopwick village

In 1917, near the hamlet of Scopwick, workmen began transforming the lush pasture land of Lincolnshire into a station equipped with aircraft sheds and domestic accommodation to take the overflow of aircraft and cadets from HMS *Daedalus,* the Royal Naval Air Service training school at Cranwell.

Construction, which consisted of three pairs of 1917-pattern brick-built hangars and a single of the same pattern to serve as an aircraft repair hangar, plus numerous single storey barracks, messes and other buildings, was not completed until October 1918. However, work was far enough advanced to allow the airfield to operate as a separate station and during March 1918 a group of officers and men left Portholm Meadows aerodrome, Huntingdonshire, and moved to Scopwick.

On March 28 1918, just three days before the Royal Air Force came into being, Scopwick Aerodrome was officially opened with the arrival of Handley Page

bombers. The field was administered by 12 Group and the first officer Commanding was Major D'Albiac, DSO, RFC, who assumed the rank of Squadron Leader from April 1 1918—he was later to be Air Marshal Sir John D'Albiac, KCVO, KBE, CB, DSO.

In November 1918, No 59 Training Depot Station was formed but, with the war over, the unit did not become fully established. As far as can be ascertained, early in 1919 it was renamed No 59 Training Squadron to train both fighter and bomber pilots. By May that year it consisted of four flights, Nos 209, 210 and 213 (formerly Nos 9, 10 and 13 RNAS, brought in with their Sopwith Camels from France); plus No 273.

In April 1920 No 3 Flying Training School was formed and Scopwick was transferred to 23 Group. The new officer commanding from April 21 1920 was Squadron Leader A.T. Harris, AFC— later Marshal of the RAF Sir Arthur 'Butcher' Harris, GCB, OBE, AFC. Then, in July 1920, to end the confusion between the similarly named Shotwick Aerodrome in Flintshire, Scopwick was renamed Digby and Shotwick became Sealand. No 3 FTS flew various types of fighter trainer aircraft, but with the run down of the post World War 1 Royal Air Force, it was disbanded in 1922 and Digby was placed on care and maintenance.

It was not until June 1924, when No 2 Flying Training School moved in from

Digby during the winter of 1940/41. This is a very good example of the 'Fort' type control tower with centrally-placed side door and internal spiral staircase. It was usually built in red brick and left unclad.

Duxford, Cambridgeshire, with its Avro 504s, Bristol Fighters and Sopwith Snipes, that the roar of aircraft engines was again heard at Digby. From September 17 that year the unit commander was Wing Commander A.W. Tedder, later to be Marshal of the RAF the Lord Tedder, GCB, DCL, LLD.

There was considerable development of the aerodrome and, as it expanded, married quarters were, built on the station. During 1926 Vickers Vimys were added to the unit's other aircraft, and these lasted until 1931-32 when they went away with the Bristols and, in March, the Avros. In December 1933, after a period of running down, No 2 FTS disbanded and Digby was handed over to Cranwell. Ten months later No 2 Flying Training School was reformed, flying Avro Tutors, Hawker Harts and Furies before moving to Brize Norton on September 7 1937. During 1935/36 the seven original hangars were demolished and replaced with barrack blocks for the airmen. It was intended to construct three new hangars of the 'C' Type but only two were built for, with the close proximity of war, the building programme was shelved.

Digby was now transferred back to No 12 Group of Fighter Command and two months later, in November 1937, two squadrons of biplanes arrives—No 46 with Gloster Gauntlets and No 73 with Gloster Gladiators. During 1938 the

squadrons were re-equipped with Hurricanes and, in August 1939, they were joined by the Hurricanes of No 504 (County of Nottingham) Squadron. They were all engaged on fighter defence and convoy patrols.

On September 10 1939 No 611 (County of Lancaster) Squadron arrived with Supermarine Spitfires and remained until July 1940. On October 6 No 229 Squadron arrived, flying Blenheim 1fs operationally from December on 'Kipper' patrols over the fishing fleet and, from January 1940, on night training and RDF co-operation duties, remaining at Digby until June 1940.

During 1940 there was a great deal of movement of squadrons, several being posted in for re-forming after taking part in the Battle of Britain. January 1940 saw the arrival of No 46 Squadron with Hurricanes, and this unit remained until May. That same month 111 Squadron with Hurricanes, 222 Squadron with Spitfires and 56 and 79 Squadrons, both flying Hurricanes, arrived. During June No 29 Squadron arrived, shortly to be equipped with the famous Beaufighter. This squadron remained until April 1941. From September to November Digby housed 151 Squadron and in December the Hurricanes of No 46 Squadron returned. With so much fighter movement and build-up it was decided to give Digby a decoy airfield, the site chosen being at Ruskington, a few miles to the south of the station. Records do not show if it served any purpose and there is no trace of it today.

On December 11 1940 the arrival of a group of Canadian officers marked the beginning of Digby's association with the RCAF when No 112 (City of Winnipeg) Squadron, later to become No 2 Squadron, RCAF arrived. With the arrival of No 1 (Canadian) Squadron these units were allocated new numbers in the 400 series and were re-numbered 401 and 402.

The Canadians soon had things well organised and, as the first crop of pilots from the Joint Air Training Plan in Canada arrived, Flight Lieutenant Ed Reyno set up a small OTU at the station to train the pilots on Hurricanes, and later Spitfires. The crash rate was high for all Hurricanes and Spitfires were nose heavy on the ground and would go nose over if the throttle was opened too quickly, especially the later Spitfire IXA. However, the crash rate was low once the squadron was trained, about five per cent of the pilots causing 75 per cent of the accidents. Second class pilots were not kept in first class squadrons and were ruthlessly weeded out, sometimes with the help of the Germans, for the poor pilot was often a straggler and easy pickings.

To give a brief look into fighter life, the following is an extract from the Flying Log Book of Flying Officer Robert E. Morrow, who bravely fought to defend our shores and lived to tell the tale. Today he is a prominent QC in Montreal, Canada.

1941 Early months—402 in training—various activities such as gunnery at Sutton Bridge—chase a few recce Ju 88s.

March 23 Morrow intercept Ju 88 40 miles off Yarmouth—17,000 ft. Killed rear gunner—Navy confirmed—confirmation never became official.* This was first 402 engagement.

April 14 Ju 88 daylight—cloud cover bombing of Digby. One bomb hit a small truck. Killed LAC Owen of 402 Squadron. First casualty.

April 13 V.B. Corbett became CO. G.R. McGregor—Digby Wing Leader.

April 15 First offensive patrol—To France with Wittering Wing†—three

---

Spitfires lost. *Note* This was crazy—flying from Wittering to France. Everybody fell into southern England out of fuel. Adolph Galland claims two Spitfires with his 'wheels down'—two of those Spits were shot down by a 109 with 'Wheels down'.

April 27 Re-equips Hurricane Mk II.

May 1 Attack Ju 88 at night over North Sea. Inconclusive.

No 402 Squadron at Digby to June 23 1941: there were 28 pilots, of whom ten were killed and five became prisoners of war. Two were ex-service medical and two dropped out. From this small number, the senior ranks obtained were one Group Captain and five Wing Commanders. A proud record of leadership.

On May 17 1941 a tragic loss occurred when Flight Lieutenant C. Hyde was killed over Metheringham, Lincolnshire, while doing aerobatics for a war-drive. He was the first 402 pilot killed and was buried in Scopwick churchyard, where a plot was set up for Canadians. Flight Lieutenant Morrow took over Hyde's flight command.

With a build up of men and aircraft more RCAF squadrons followed, Nos 409, 411 and 412 in June 1941. No 409 exchanged their Boulton Paul Defiant night fighters for Beaufighters and operated from the satellite airfield of Coleby Grange. During its role as an operational fighter station Digby made use of the two satellites, Wellingore and Coleby Grange. On September 16 1942 the station became officially Canadian and was re-named RCAF Digby with Group Captain A.E. McNab DFC (RCAF) the Commanding Officer.

Over the next two years, numerous fighter squadrons were to pass through Digby and, although it was RCAF, some RAF squadrons used it, as did the Belgians with No 609 Squadron and again in 1943 with the two Spitfire squadrons Nos 349 and 350 from August to October. But, as the tide of the air war turned, so did the pressure on the home defence fighters and Digby changed from operational activity to training. During the latter part of 1943 and early part of 1944 the squadrons, which included many Canadians, were No 438 from November 20 to December 18 1943, No 416 from October 2 1943 to February 11 1944, No 402 from September 19 1943 to February 11 1944 and a complete Canadian Spitfire Wing of three squadrons, Nos 441, 442

---

*   To this date there is no confirmation of this, and any Navy report has disappeared.
†   Not strictly the 'Wittering Wing'—Nos 65, 266 and 402 Squadrons.

and 443, that formed on February 8 and departed on March 17 1944. They all moved to southern bases, nearer to the invasion beaches in time to take part in the pre-D-Day operations. This left at Digby No 116 Squadron with Airspeed Oxfords and Nos 527/528 with Bristol Blenheims engaged on air-sea rescue and radar calibration duties. No 310 (Czech) Squadron flew in with their Spitfires in July in order to rest from the heat of battle, and after they left in August 1944, Digby's role changed to non-operational.

In May 1945 the station reverted to RAF Digby and the remaining Canadians were posted out. Finally, on July 22 1945 Digby was transferred from Fighter Command to Technical Training Command. No 1 Officers' Advanced Training School moved in from Cranwell that same month and remained until April 1947 when it then moved out to Hornchurch. Flying resumed in January 1946 when the de Havilland Tiger Moths of No 19 Flying Training School were kept at and flown from Digby until February 1948. For several years a number of training units were housed at Digby, including No 1 Initial Training School from 1948 to 1950 and No 2 Initial Training School from 1950 to September 1951.

In 1951 the firm of Airwork Ltd set up No 2 Air Grading School to give flying training to would-be pilots, but not on the hard wartime lines. In February 1953 this unit moved and in September Digby went on to a care and maintenance basis until October 1 1954 when work started in order to receive No 399 Signals Unit, in No 90 Group, and more buildings both domestic and technical were erected. No 399 SU arrived in January 1955 followed in July by No 591 Signals Unit. In September 1959 the Aerial Erectors School arrived and, in February 1969, No 54 Signals Unit.

Today the two hangars are empty of aircraft and the roar of their engines have long ceased. Where they used to take-off and land, wireless aerials now sprout from the grass airfield—paved runways were never constructed. The glamour days of the fighter squadrons have long since passed but Digby has claim to many 'Personalities'. ACM Sir Kenneth Cross, CBE, DSO, DFC, who was CO of No 46 Squadron in 1939; Group Captain D.R.S. Bader, CBE, DSO and Bar, DFC and Bar, and

Dispersal hut at Digby in 1940/41. From left to right are Johnston, Rocky St Pierre, Cape Hyde and Jimmy Walker (later W/C DSO & bar—killed in an accident just before D-Day).

Wing Commander Guy Gibson, VC, DFC, from 29 Squadron; Wing Commander Yeo-Thomas, the 'White Rabbit', of Intelligence; Air Marshall Sir George Beamish, KCB, CBE; Air Commodore Sir Frank Whittle, KBE, CB, FRS, LLD and Wing Commander The Honourable C. Cochrane were all Flying Instructors here. Flight Lieutenant J.A. Rae, DFC, RCAF, of television fame was another who passed through Digby. However, Digby still has a key role to play and is one of the oldest stations still in use by the Royal Air Force.

Doncaster, Yorkshire
111/SE595020. SW of racecourse on A638 road

Even before the First World War Doncaster racecourse was used to hold the first British aviation meeting in October 1909 with such early aircraft as the Bleriot XI and Colonel Cody in a British Army Aeroplane No 1. Colonel Cody became a naturalised British subject during one of the non-flying days. So naturally, like many other racecourses, Doncaster was used as a landing ground during the First World War. The hangars and accommodation were sited to the north-west of the racecourse. Early Home Defence squadrons, No 15 RAS and No 15 RS, had used the racecourse since January 1916 and in June of that year a detachment of No 47 Squadron equipped with BE2e aircraft moved in, but departed before the end of the month. No 46 Reserve Squadron formed here on October 23 1916 and on December 12 1916 moved to Bramham Moor. No 80 Training Squadron formed here as a Canadian unit on January 1 1917 and moved at the end of the following month to Camp Borden in Canada. No 90 TS then formed on March 15 and moved to Beverley a month later.

On February 7 1917 No 82 Squadron RFC was formed here, equipped with Armstrong Whitworth FK8 aircraft, and remained until November 20 1917 when the squadron then moved to France. On September 15 1917, No 49 Reserve Squadron moved in and remained until July 15 1918 when it then disbanded. The site then became the home of No 47 Training Depot Station, formed from 41 and 49 Training Squadrons and equipped with 24 SE5A and 24 Avro 504 aircraft. The Depot remained at the site until it was closed in 1919.

Between the wars Crilly Airways with Dragon aircraft started a service in 1935 to Croydon and on November 1 1938, No 616 (South Yorkshire) Squadron, AAF, was formed as a bomber unit but its role was quickly changed to that of a fighter squadron and a flight of Gauntlets moved in June 1939 to Finningley, Yorkshire, as part of No 12 (Fighter) Group. The rest of the unit moved to Leconfield after equipping with Spitfires.

During the 1930s it was decided that Doncaster should have an airport, but space at the north-west site was very restricted and a new site had to be found. This turned out to be just across the A638 road, south-west of the racecourse. It was a very poor choice for it was a small site bounded on all sides by roads and railway lines, but it still opened as Doncaster Airport in 1939.

Doncaster was nominated one of the 'Scatter' airfields to which RAF aircraft could be dispersed in the event of war, and it was taken over by the RAF later in 1939. It was also considered important enough to need a decoy airfield, and this was sited at Armthorpe a few miles north-east of the racecourse. No 7 Aircrew Operational Training Unit was formed here under No 5 Group and this unit flew Hampdens and Ansons. The unit had the task of training crews for the operational squadrons, but facilities at Doncaster proved to be very inadequate and unsuitable for night flying. So, on September 15 No 7 (Aircrew) OTU moved to Finningley. The next to take up residence during September was the Civil Aircraft Flight of the National Air Communications unit flying Ensign, HP42, and Fokker aircraft, becoming 271 Squadron Royal Air Force on May 1 1940 flying a strange variety of transport aircraft which included a Ford Tri-Motor, HP42s and Bombays, but mainly the Harrow. Most of the time the Harrows were used to move squadron personnel around the country.

On December 6 1940 a fierce gale damaged many of the aircraft and completely destroyed two: Handley Page Harrow K6974 and Handley Page HP42, ex-G-AAUE of Imperial Airways, which ended up on the London North Eastern railway line.

In March 1941, No 613 (City of Manchester) Squadron arrived with Curtiss Tomahawk aircraft and was based here until August 1941. The squadron returned for a short stay in January 1942. That same year No 1680 Flight was

Colonel Cody taking off in his British Army Aeroplane No 1 at Doncaster racecourse, October 1909. The racecourse stands are in the background.

detached to Doncaster and this unit had Albatross aircraft.

In June 1943, Wellingtons of No 18 OTU from Finningley were using the airfield as a satellite. Doncaster was then a modification centre for the C-47 Dakota aircraft of No 46 Group and during this period it was a very busy airfield. From January 7 to 21 1944 No 658 Squadron visited the airfield with their Auster (AOP) Mk III aircraft. The following month, 271 Squadron moved to Down Ampney, Gloucestershire, with their Dakotas and the Sparrow aircraft left behind were formed into an Ambulance Flight.

There was no place in the post-war RAF's plans for a small, grass-surfaced airfield incapable of any development so it was vacated by the RAF soon after hostilities ceased and re-opened as an airfield for light aircraft. However, the Royal Air Force did return in October 1947 when No 9 Reserve Flying School formed with de Havilland Tiger Moths, then Percival Prentices, Ansons and Chipmunks. The school closed in May 1954.

Today the aerodrome remains in existence and the facilities include two grass runways, hangarage, flying club and restaurant, but there have been many closure rumours.

Donna Nook, Lincolnshire

113/TF430985. Approximately 8 miles E of Louth off the A1031 road

This airfield was sited on low-lying land right on the Lincolnshire coast beside the North Sea. It is just a few miles south of the pre-war airfield of North Coates and it is believed that originally it was to have been laid out as a decoy for this airfield.

However, it opened in late 1940 as a very primitive RLG for North Coates, and even had a decoy site of its own at Marsh Chapel. The main aircraft to use the relief airfield—which was laid out in the shape of a 'T' with the leg being just over half a mile in length—were Lysanders, Beauforts and Beaufighters. Donna Nook never had any flying units officially based on it and closed to flying in 1945.

The Donna Nook Gunnery and Bombing Range had opened in 1926 and was used by North Coates. In the early 1930s there had been three bombing targets, one of which was illuminated for night bombing, and ten gunnery targets. Donna Nook range closed in 1946 but when Theddlethorpe bombing range closed in December 1973 due to complaints from local people, it was re-opened. Only practice weapons are used, flying is kept to the seaward side of the seabank and the beaches at Donna Nook are cleared of debris each Friday. Spectators are permitted to watch from the Stonebridge car park and, as most attacks are made below 500 ft, one can spend an interesting hour or so watching the Royal Air Force at work.

Dunholme Lodge, Lincolnshire

121/SK995785. 4 miles N of Lincoln between the main A15 and A46 roads at Dunholme Lodge

For a few brief moments the crew of Lancaster LM446, 'H' Harry, took in the beauty as they crossed the Alps towards Italy in the hope of drawing the German night fighters down that way. Then Pilot Officer Olsen of 619 Squadron turned and re-crossed the Alps and headed for Munich. His aircraft was one of the 260 that took part in this raid of April 24/25 1944. An experienced pilot on his 26th operational mission, he made a dummy run over the target in order to give the PFF cover whilst they made a low level pass to mark the target. The raid was a success and, after nine hours and fifty minutes, 'H' Harry touched down back at Dunholme Lodge.

The airfield had opened in May 1943 during the mushrooming of heavy bomber airfields that sprouted almost overnight in order to meet the demand of Bomber Command. Work had started on this site at the end of 1942 and it conformed to the standard design of the period with three paved runways linked at their ends by a perimeter track around which were concrete hardstandings for the aircraft. A tower was built on the eastern boundary, not far from the Lodge after which the airfield was named, and the hutted accommodation was dispersed around the surrounding countryside, some of it on the outskirts of the village of Welton to the north-east.

The first squadron to arrive was No 44 (Rhodesia) which moved in from Waddington while concrete runways were laid. During their stay the squadron equipped with Lancaster Marks I and III and made attacks on enemy targets in all weathers. In April 1944 the airfield became a two-squadron station with the arrival of No 619, which was also flying Lancaster Is and IIIs.

During the latter part of 1943 and early 1944 it was a very busy airfield. However, with such a demand on the air space it had become apparent that Dunholme Lodge was sited too close to other airfields: Scampton was only a couple of miles to the north-west whilst several others (including Fiskerton, Ingham, Faldingworth and Wickenby) were not much further away and this caused great operational problems through the overlapping of circuits.

So, despite having runways, it was decided to close Dunholme and on September 28 1944 No 619 Squadron moved out, followed two days later by No 44 Squadron. However, even with the overlapping of circuits which was made more serious when Scampton re-opened, Dunholme Lodge was brought back into operational use for a few weeks. On October 22 1944 No 170 Squadron (code letters 'TC') moved in with Lancaster Is and IIIs from Kelstern, Lincolnshire, where they had re-formed as a heavy bomber squadron a few days earlier. The squadron took part in many raids on enemy targets during their brief stay, but the airfield caused great operational problems and No 170 Squadron, whose motto was 'Videre non videri' (To see and not be seen) moved out on November 30 1944 to Hemswell, Lincolnshire.

The airfield now closed for operations and in the same month General Aircraft Ltd moved in and used the station as a modification base for their large Hamilcar gliders. Some of these were later used in the Rhine crossing airborne operation. In 1945 they moved out and the airfield closed to flying the same year.

Post-war the site was occasionally used for motor-cycle racing but it was brought back into use in 1959 to house 141 Squadron equipped with Bloodhound surface-to-air missiles. These were to defend the V-bomber airfields. However, this role only lasted until 1964 after which Dunholme Lodge was vacated and the airfield closed down again.

The former main entrance is still evident in the south-eastern corner of the site at a point where the A46 road has a sharp corner, but most of the facilities have been dismantled. The runways have been narrowed into access roads for farmers and the few old huts that remain are used to store fertilisers. Today, there are few traces of the former busy operational bomber base.

East Kirkby, Lincolnshire

122/TF345615. Situated just SE of the village of East Kirkby between the A155 and the main A16 roads

East Kirkby was one of the most southerly of the Lincolnshire airfields, being located on the edge of the fenlands. Two minor roads had to be closed to allow the airfield to be constructed just to the south-east of the village, and work started in 1942. The product was a heavy bomber station of standard mid-war pattern, widely dispersed accommodation and the usual trio of paved runways with the main one running east to west. The station had a decoy airfield at Sibsey, about seven miles to the south, but it could not have served any great purpose at that period of the war.

By mid-1943 one of the main bomber stations in Lincolnshire, Scampton, was still operating Lancasters from a grass airfield so it was a great relief when, in August 1943, East Kirkby opened and was able to accept one of the Scampton squadrons—the other, No 617, moved to Coningsby which had just been provided with runways—and Scampton was able to close for runway construction. The unit that moved to East Kirkby was No 57 Squadron which operated its Lancasters from the airfield for the duration of the war in Europe.

On November 15 1943 No 630 Squadron, whose motto was 'Nocturna Mors' (Death by Night) was formed from 'B' Flight of No 57 Squadron, equipped with Lancasters (code letters 'LE'), and also remained here for the duration of the war, being disbanded on July 18 1945. No 630 Squadron took part in many of the major raids, including the 'Battle of Berlin', and dropped 10,347 tons of bombs. On the fateful Nuremberg raid of March 30/31 1944 the squadron put up 16 aircraft and lost three. Its last bombing mission was on April 25 1945 when five of the squadron Lancasters took part in the raid on Berchtesgaden. The awards gained by the squadron were one DSO, one bar to DSO, one BEM, 42 DFCs, four bars to DFCs, 11 DFMs and one AFM.

No 57 Squadron also took part in the many raids on V-1 storage sites and oil targets. On April 8 1945 Squadron Leader Hodgkinson took off for one of these targets at Lutzkendorf in Lancaster DX 'J' and returned to find the airfield covered in fog. He had to be diverted to Wellesbourne, making a round trip of nine hours twenty minutes. On April 17 1945 an accident occurred when the aircraft were being bombed up. Two 1,000 lb medium-capacity bombs exploded while being fitted into Lancaster PB360 and this caused a chain reaction of bomb explosions. Three airmen were killed and 14 injured, two civilians also being casualties. Needless to say, operations were cancelled for the airfield appeared completely wrecked. Next morning it was found that five Lancasters were written off and 14 damaged.

No 460 Squadron arrived at the station from Binbrook on July 20 1945 as an element of Tiger Force. However, on August 17 all training here for Tiger Force ceased and for everyone, the war was over. The unit continued with local flying and the Australians did 'Cook's Tours' to Berlin, also helping to bring home troops

No 57 Squadron at East Kirkby in April 1945. Outside the 'A' and 'B' Flight Sections W/O Broadhead (second from left) relaxes with his other three crew members. Note the targets attacked, behind them and to the left.

East Kirkby memorial—see title page.

from Bari before being withdrawn from the line on September 22. On October 4 the Australians held their farewell parade, whcih was attended by Air Vice-Marshal Wrigley. On October 10 the squadron officially disbanded and by the 25th of the month all squadron personnel had been posted to Gamston for repatriation.

Post-war East Kirkby remained a bomber airfield until November 1945, acting as a preparation base for Tiger Force, the proposed heavy bomber force that was going out to the Far East. During August No 57 Squadron was the first unit to be equipped with three Lincolns for Service trials but on November 25 1945 the squadron disbanded here and re-formed the next day at Elsham Wolds. After the departure of 57 Squadron the airfield closed to flying but the site was retained by the Air Ministry. In August 1947 the airfield was reactivated when a detachment from 139 Squadron, Conings-by, used the station until February 1948. The station again closed to flying and was put on a C & M basis.

When the international situation required an increase in the size of the USAF in Europe in the early 1950s East Kirkby was one of the airfields in the UK that were designated reserve airfields for the Americans. Considerable work was put into inproving the basic facilities and from August 14 1954 until 1958 the airfield was used by the USAF with a few Dakotas of the 3917th Air Base Squadron of the 7th Air Division, SAC. The airfield closed in 1958, after it had returned to the RAF, and was held as an inactive site until it was finally disposed of in April 1970.

Today the airfield is used for factory farming and the control tower has been converted into site offices for Eastwoods Ltd who operate broiler houses along the runways. Sun Sparkle, a potato company, is using the 'T2' hangar, but this has been converted over the years.

Elsham Wolds, Lincolnshire

112/TA042135. Approximately 7 miles NE of Brigg, E of A15 road near Elsham village

Air raids by German Zeppelins and long-range bombers like Gothas and Zeppelin-Stakens in the early part of the First World War had such an effect on public morale that the RFC formed several Home Defence squadrons. Some of these were based in Eastern England for the area between the Humber and the Wash was an easily defined entry point for the Zeppelins and Lincolnshire received its fair share of bombs, although few did any damage. At first the squadrons were mainly equipped with obsolete aeroplanes such as the Avro 504 and the BE2, and consisted of three flights each at a separate aerodrome plus a headquarters and workshop which was usually at a convenient small town.

One of the fields used by a Home Defence squadron in defence of North Lincolnshire and the Humber was situated in north-east Lincolnshire on the bleak Wolds near the village of Elsham after which it was named. Facilities there were primitive for the base unit, 'C' Flight of 33 Squadron. It is impossible to imagine the courage of those early wartime pilots, having to make do with very primitive flying instruments. There was no airborne radio or radar in those days, and they were exposed to the cold. The head-quarters was several miles away at Gains-borough and 'A' and 'B' Flights were at

Brattleby and Kirton-in-Lindsey respectively, both of which were to become the sites of military airfields again a generation later. Elsham housed the FE2b fighters of 'C' Flight from December 1916 until after the end of the war in June 1919 when it was closed and reverted to agriculture.

With such a demand for bomber stations, Lincolnshire was again in the front line during the Second World War and Elsham was one of numerous former aerodromes to be surveyed to see if they were suitable sites for the construction of new airfields for the growing Royal Air Force in the early part of 1940. It was pronounced capable of development and work started in the same year.

The new airfield, named Elsham Wolds for it was actually built *on* Elsham Wolds, immediately north-east of the village of Elsham, was built to the early wartime pattern with a 'J' type hangar on the eastern side of the field and much of the accommodation grouped behind it. Eventually the airfield had three concrete runways, the main one on a north-west/south-east axis which led its flight path almost directly over the neighbouring airfield of Kirmington a few miles to the south-east. The decoy airfield for Elsham Wolds was at Great Limber a few miles south-east of the Kirmington airfield but records do not show clearly what purpose it served.

Elsham Wolds opened in July 1941 as a heavy bomber station in No 1 Group and for over four years was the home of No 103 Squadron which operated with Wellington 1cs, then Halifax IIs and finally with Lancaster IIIs, against a wide variety of long and short range targets.

The station had only been open three months when, on the night of October 22 1941, Pilot Officer Ken Wallis, RAFVR, was captain of Wellington 1459, PM-X of 103 Squadron, on a raid against Mannheim. That night there were intense thunderstorms, and trouble began almost immediately after leaving the coast. The oil coolers, presumably due to water in the system, froze, and the second pilot was unable to pump any fresh oil to the engines, the pump handle and piston assembly breaking from the pump. Wallis continued, however, and after bombing the target from 16,000 ft the aircraft started its return, suffering intense flak over Liège.

On reaching the Belgian coast, the new second pilot was allowed to take over, but after a short while he reported that one engine had failed and he was having difficulty in maintaining control in the cu-nimbulus cloud. Captain Wallis took over:

'I came forward from the navigator's compartment, and got the feeling that he was flying the aircraft in a 90° bank, a cloud "horizon" in the night sky appearing to be vertical. It was actually the side of a giant thunder-cloud. I climbed into the pilot's seat and tried to coax the engine back to life with de-icing fluid, only to have the other engine ice-up also. The windscreen was now covered in ice and it was impossible to see. Then, both cylinder head temperature gauges dropped to zero, and we lost height, completely "blind", from 14,000 to 1,000 ft.'

The wireless operator was sending an SOS, although there was little hope of a successful 'ditching' in the stormy sea. Just when there seemed no hope, one

P/O Ken Wallis' Wellington 1459, PM-X, of 103 Squadron, comes to a halt in a potato field.

Above *On dispersal—crew of* Santa Azucar, *No 103 Squadron, Elsham Wolds.* **Right** *Halifax of No 21 HGCU at Elsham Wolds during 1946.*

engine screamed out in fine pitch, then stopped again. It fired once more and Pilot Officer Wallis was able to nurse both engines back to life, just above the sea, and beneath the icing level.

With engines running irregularly, they resumed a course for home, and eventually arrived over Lincolnshire. Suddenly there was a flash and a bang, about 18 inches out from the fuselage on the port side, followed by a strange noise, a smell of molten metal, and a very rapid deceleration to near stalling speed. Pilot Officer Wallis immediately realised they had hit a balloon cable, and pushed the nose down to maintain some control. The cable cut through the wing like an oxy-acetylene cutter, severing the fuel pipes, engine controls and hydraulics, but fortunately the cable broke just after cutting half-way through the main spar.

With bomb doors open, undercarriage hanging down, the port engine idling in fine pitch, and no hydraulics for flaps, they slowly lost height and, unable to see the airfield lights, they fired off what Very lights they could. Next moment the Wellington ploughed into a wet potato field, burying the second pilot up to his waist in mud. The aircraft was intact and the crew quickly scrambled out. Pilot Officer Wallis:

'With fuel still draining from the cut pipes, and the hot engine ticking as it cooled, I counted my crew, and noticed we had six, though we'd set out with five. I then noticed that one had a rifle; when I approached him in the dark he saluted me and said "Good morning, Sir". He was the guard from the main gate, very near which we'd ground to a stop!'

Pilot Officer Wallis and his crew survived, and he went on to become a Wing Commander having completed 36 operations over Germany and Italy. Today he is famous for the Wallis Autogyro, 'James Bond's' aircraft code-named 'Little Nellie'.

On the first raid on the Peenemünde V-weapons station No 103 Squadron put up 24 Lancasters. The squadron also had the most distinguished Lancaster of World War 2—Lancaster III ED888 M^2 ('Mike Squared') which, on its retirement in December 1944, had logged 140 sorties including 98 to Germany, 15 of these to Berlin. A total of 974 operational hours. No other Lancaster in the whole of Bomber Command equalled this performance, yet it was not even selected for preservation after the war.

From May to October 1942 the station housed 103 Squadron Conversion Flight with Halifax II aircraft. From the end of January 1943 to April 6 1945 the airfield was also used as a relief landing ground for the Blyton-based 1662 HCU, using Halifax Mks I and II and Lancaster Mk Is. It was a very busy station and on November 25 1943, No 576 Squadron was formed (code letters 'UL'). The squadron was equipped with Lancaster Mks I and III with Merlin engines, and this played a part in their badge design which was a merlin

bird, wings inverted and addorsed, preying on a serpent. The squadron remained at Elsham Wolds until October 1944 when it then moved to Fiskerton, having taken part in all stages of the bomber offensive.

As on so many bomber stations the crews were a mixed bunch of Canadians, Australians and New Zealanders and when the Commonwealth boys received their food parcels it was red letter day on the station with such treats as tins of peaches and chocolates. Nancy Shenker, a WAAF who worked in the parachute room, remembers them well for it was her job to hand out and take in the aircrews' gear. Many of the aircrew left their personal belongings with these girls and Nancy recalls her tragic introduction to the section: 'It was a girl crying and me hoping never to get like that and having to hand over belongings to be sent back to parents or wives.'

Just before the end of the war, the station received No 100 Squadron which arrived on April 1 1945 and took part in the final bombing raids of the war from Elsham Wolds. The last operational action was on April 25 when 15 Lancasters took part in the raid on the SS barracks at Berchtesgaden. In December 1945 the squadron moved to Scampton along with No 57 Squadron that had re-formed here the previous month from the disbanded 103 Squadron.

With the bomber squadrons now departed the station was to house No 21 HGCU for almost a year from December 1945 to November 1946 when it then moved to North Luffenham. This Transport Command unit was equipped with Halifax Mk VIIs, Albermarle tugs and Horsa gliders. A far cry from the heavy bombers that the Lincolnshire people had become accustomed to seeing.

In 1947 the airfield closed and today the roar of Merlin engines has changed to the roar of traffic for the new motorway to link up the new Humber Bridge cuts right through the middle of the wartime airfield. A 'J' hangar, the old parachute room of Nancy Shenker's section, and a few other buildings on the technical site survive, along with a few sections of runway and the old control tower, part of which is being used as a house.

Faldingworth, Lincolnshire

112/TF035855. Approximately 5 miles W of Market Rasen and 3 miles S of Toft Grange

The airfield is sited three miles west of the village of Faldingworth, between Faldingworth Grange in the south and Toft Grange in the north. It was at the latter that, in 1940, a decoy airfield, a KQ site, was laid out for Hemswell, but in 1942 these sites were abandoned. It was interesting to note that work started only in late 1942 at Faldingworth, the site being developed as a standard heavy bomber station for No 5 Group, Bomber Command.

Work continued throughout 1943 and Dogland Wood in the centre of the airfield was almost completely removed. In October the airfield opened in an incomplete state and housed No 1667 HCU, equipped with Halifaxes and

Lancasters until the middle of February 1944. Also, for a few weeks during the winter of 1943/1944, 'C' Flight of No 1 LFS was also here.

On March 1 1944, No 300 (Polish) Squadron moved in from their primitive grass airfield at Ingham and became equipped with Lancaster Mk Is and IIIs. Faldingworth then became almost completely manned by the Polish Air Force during its operational life. These were men who had fled Poland and chose to wage the war from British soil. One such man was Sergeant Drozdz who graduated with Flight Engineer Wings and was posted to 300 Squadron at Faldingworth. They waged their war from their Lincolnshire station and attacked many targets deep in the Fatherland, including Essen, Nuremberg, Munich, Ludwigshaven and Hanover, to name but a few. Then, on April 14 1945 came the one that Sergeant Drozdz had been waiting for—Berlin. At 18.15 hours precisely their Lancaster, PB730 'R' Roger, with its bomb load of 11,000 lb, thundered down the runway and pulled away into the night sky. They passed over Beachy Head at 18,000 ft with the four Merlin engines beating out their rhythmic purr. They were part of the main force of 426 bombers which, like a drone of deadly wasps, winged their way to target. On their last leg and with Magdeburg to starboard they climbed to their bombing height of 19,000 ft. At 22.50 hours they released their bomb load and the Lancaster was soon making its way home, At 02.45 hours, skipper Jan Kozicki saw

the illuminated letters 'FH' on the runway beneath—Faldingworth was clear to land. 'R' Roger had been in the air 8½ hours and had journeyed 1,500 miles using 1,174 gallons of petrol and still had 440 gallons left.

Today Henryk Drozdz lives near Leicester with his English wife Doreen. 35 years after the end of hostilities, Henryk Drozdz looks back: 'It seemed a blow for freedom—fear was always with us because all sorties were dangerous. The cumbersome, though well-loved Lancaster was not exactly a lithe bird and with its full bomb load was a potentially laden arsenal and I saw many of my friends die in the sky around me . . . may we never see such a war again.'

The last operational mission of the war for No 300 Squadron came on April 25 1945 when 14 Lancasters bombed Berchtesgaden. The unit then took part in the peacetime operations 'Manna', 'Exodus' and 'Dodge'. On October 11 1946 the squadron disbanded having played a major part in the bombing offensive during which the squadron won 107 decorations.

From May 1944 to January 9 1945, No 1546 BAT Flight, flying Oxford Is, had also made Faldingworth their home. Then, after the Lancasters had departed, No 305 (Ziemia Wielkopolska) (Polish) Squadron (code letters 'SM') was transferred from Germany to the UK and Bomber Command and arrived with Mosquito VIs at Faldingworth during October 1946 only to disband on January 6 1947. Faldingworth was then without

Air and ground crew of 'R'-Roger, 300 Squadron, Faldingworth, after their first sortie on November 29 1944 on Dortmund. The captain is behind the Polish WAAF driver and Sgt Drozdz is first on the right in the flying kit.

any units but did not close until October 1948 when the station went on to C & M.

In 1957 the station opened in a non-flying capacity after a massive reconstruction programme had been carried out to make it a secure storage area for nuclear weapons. All of the south-west section now housed underground bunkers and special shelters. Around this special site sprang up watch towers and searchlights, barbed-wire fences and concrete walls between which was no-man's-land, a special sterile area. A 24-hour armed police guard made the security watertight.

No 92 MU moved in from Wickenby and the site continued as a main weapons store for the V-bombers until 1969 when the Polaris submarines took over and No 92 MU started to run down and the station closed in November 1972. No 92 MU was a sister unit of 94 MU, in which the author was responsible for security, and today the watch towers and barbed wire can still be seen from the Spridlington to Faldingworth road. Security was so high that, whereas most airfields are depicted in some detail on Ordnance Survey maps, Faldingworth is not even named. However, it is now beginning to appear on the 1980 ones. This special site is today used by the British Manufacture and Research Company (BMARC), belonging to Oerlikon, a Swiss-based armament firm who also use the Donna Nook range to demonstrate their shells to potential clients. BMARC, formed in 1938, made all the Hispano-Suiza aircraft cannon and ammunition for Britain during the Second World War. They also have a factory at Grantham but Faldingworth tests all the cannon and ammunition made there. Faldingworth also stores bulk explosives and, by 1985, £10 million will have been spent on the site.

Firbeck, South Yorkshire

120/SK555892. Approximately 7 miles N of Worksop, S of the A634 road

A very poor choice for an airfield, being bounded in the north by a river and a main road; to the east by heavy woods and, at the south-eastern end, by the village from which it takes its name; Firbeck was constructed as a grass-surfaced airfield with the minimum of installations and facilities dispersed around the airfield, in the grounds of Firbeck Hall and in the village itself.

Firbeck opened in September 1940 and was immediately occupied by No 613 (City of Manchester) Squadron, an Army Co-operation unit equipped with Lysanders, which remained here until April 1942 when it moved to Twinwood Farm, Bedfordshire. The next to arrive was another Army Co-operation unit, No 654 Squadron, on September 15 1942, flying Auster Mark I aircraft. This unit moved out on November 20 1942 and in February 1943 Firbeck was designated a relief landing ground for 25 EFTS at Hucknall. This unit used the airfield with their Tiger Moths until June 1945. During this period, on April 30 1943, No 659 (Army Co-operation) Squadron was formed here for air observation duties and moved out the following August. This unit eventually saw service in Normandy, engaged in the 21st Army Group's campaign in France and the Low Countries during the autumn of 1944. After No 25 EFTS ceased using the airfield it was then operated for a few weeks by 24 EGS but by the end of 1945 the airfield had closed to flying and was abandoned by the Royal Air Force.

Firbeck looks as bleak today as it must have done in 1940. At this moment in time two Blister hangars remain along with some of the airmen's quarters in the south-west corner. The admin-site in the south-east near Firbeck village and in a cottage on the opposite side of the road is the remains of the Station Armoury. A few of the officers' quarters in the grounds of Firbeck Hall, to the east of the airfield, still remain. At the side of Firbeck village the old HQ site can still be traced by means of a Nissen hut and a few foundations.

Fiskerton, Lincolnshire

121/TF045730. Situated 5 miles E of Lincoln, just S of the A158 between the villages of Reepham and Fiskerton

On April 25 1945 the 23 Lancaster bomber crews of No 576 Squadron filed in for their briefing at RAF Fiskerton on what was to be their last operational mission of World War 2. The Wing Commander stood up. 'The target, gentlemen, is Berchtesgaden'—the Fuhrer's notorious 'Eagle's Nest' and the SS barracks. 'That's the house where the gentleman lives. If he doesn't happen to be there, there will be plenty of SS men around.'

With an escort of American Mustangs the Lancasters arrived over the target area

Above *Fiskerton control tower (now demolished).* **Right** *'C'-Charlie landing at Fiskerton at the end of the war.*

and, with excellent visibility, gave the 'Eagle's Nest' and SS barracks a heavy 'pasting' with 1,000 lb, 4,000 lb and some 12,000 lb bombs. Flight Lieutenant Campbell and crew in 'C' Charlie were on that mission and one of the crew said it was the target he had been waiting for all the war.

During the afternoon as they touched down back at Fiskerton one of the skipper's pals was waiting at dispersal with brimming pints of beer. The navigator, Flight Sergeant Andrews remarked: 'Never found out how he carried them, and, by God, that beer was cold on an empty stomach after eight hours' flying.'

The small village of Fiskerton was introduced to aviation in World War 1 when it was hit by bombs dropped by a raiding German Zeppelin, but it was not until the Second World War that it began an association with the RAF. In the early years of that war a site immediately north of the village was surveyed and found suitable for development into an airfield for the RAF. The airfield opened in January 1943 in 5 Group, Bomber Command, as 52 Sub-Base Station controlled by Scampton, HQ 52 Base.

The airfield conformed to the standard heavy bomber base pattern with three concrete runways linked by a perimeter track around which were 36 hardstandings for the aircraft. The main runway, which runs east-west, points at the cathedral just like Skellingthorpe. The technical site was in the south-east corner of the site and was provided with two hangars, a 'B1' and a 'T2' with a further 'T2' on the opposite side. The living accommodation was dispersed on sites mainly to the south-east of the airfield, some of these being not far from the River Witham. As a result of the construction works the minor road linking the villages of Fiskerton and Reepham was closed as it was crossed by all three of the runways.

On January 19 1943 No 49 Squadron of No 5 Group, Bomber Command, was the first unit to occupy the new airfield. A veteran bomber squadron equipped with Lancasters, 49 remained at Fiskerton until October 17 1944. During its stay the squadron took part in the first 'shuttle-bombing' raid and on the Nuremberg Raid of March 30/31 1944, when 16 aircraft were sent and two failed to return. Other squadron targets were on Peenemünde, the coastal gun battery at La Pernelle and the V-1 storage sites.

After the departure of No 49 Squadron the station went on care and maintenance and was transferred from 5 Group to 1 Group. The station had a strength of only 33 officers and 116 airmen. But not for long for No 576 Squadron, of No 1 Group, equipped with Lancasters, moved in to replace No 49 Squadron on October 31 1944 and was joined on November 1 by another Lancaster squadron, No 150, which was re-formed after its return from Regina, Italy. The latter remained only ten days and moved out on 11th November 1944 to Hemswell.

From January 1944, No 1514 Beam Approach Flight with Oxfords was stationed at Fiskerton until disbanding in January 1945. During the runway resur-

facing, from September 10 to October 24 1944, the airfield was closed and operations were carried out from Dunholme Lodge. The airfield re-opened as a satellite for Scampton.

Fiskerton was one of the 15 airfields to be equipped with FIDO, the fog dispersing equipment, and continued to be an active bomber station until September 21 1945 when it finally closed to flying. No 576 Squadron, having disbanded on September 13 1945, brought to an end the hectic life and final roar of Merlins at Fiskerton. The squadron had flown 2,788 operational sorties with a loss of 67 aircraft. If had also taken part in operations Manna, Exodus, Post Mortem and Dodge. 576 Squadron also carried bombs from the dumps and dropped them into the sea.

The rundown process was then rapid and Fiskerton was reduced to care and maintenance on December 15 1945. In 1961, when the Royal Observer Corps changed its role to nuclear fall-out reporting and warning, a small part of the site was re-opened to become the headquarters of 15 Group Royal Observer Corps which moved from Waddington into the first purpose-built underground operations room. The majority of the rest of the airfield was handed back to the farmers.

By 1978 the tower still survived in a derelict state and one hangar, the 'B1' was still standing minus much of its cladding, but a few months later the tower was demolished. It was from this airfield that the bombers took off for Germany, but now all is silent—the heavy roar of engines as the bombers struggled to get airborne under their heavy loads are just a whisper in the night breeze.

Folkingham, Lincolnshire

130/TF050300. W of the A15 road between Aslackby and Folkingham

Situated in the flat south Lincolnshire countryside a few miles south-east of Grantham is the small village of Folkingham, and it was here that in 1940 a decoy airfield (KQ site) was laid out to attract enemy aircraft away from nearby airfields, particularly the one at Grantham.

This dummy airfield was abandoned in 1941 when daylight air raids had almost ceased and it was probably this site that was developed in 1943 as a standard pattern heavy bomber station for No 5 Group, Bomber Command.

However, the south Lincolnshire area was chosen as the base for large numbers of US Army paratroopers and several airfields were transferred to the USAAF to accommodate Troop Carrier Groups. Consequently, when Folkingham was ready for use it was handed to the US IXth AF as Air Station 484, opening on February 5 1944 as a permanent station under the 52nd Troop Carrier Wing. On February 24 1944, the 313th TC Group under Colonel James J. Roberts, Jr, arrived with the 29th, 47th, 48th and 49th Squadrons. The unit was equipped with 70 C-47 Dakotas divided between the four squadrons.

The unit took part in the D-Day landings and moved out just before midnight on June 5 to drop the 508th Parachute Infantry and the 82nd US Airborne in Normandy behind the assault coast. The 313th TCG had been allocated DZ 'N' which was about three miles south of Ste-Mère-Église. The 1,181 American paratroopers began dropping just after

Above *The last of several C-47 transport aircraft prepares to leave. Thought to be at Folkingham in February 1945, but records are not clear on this. Note: many men wearing winter greatcoats.* **Below** *C-47s parked nose to tail. Thought to be Folkingham but again records are not clear from this official USAF photograph.*

02.00 hours on June 6, but the German forces were alerted and many aircraft were hit by small-arms fire. One crashed near the dropping zone. Altogether the unit lost three aircraft and 21 others were damaged.

A back-up mission was needed and the following day, D + 1, operation 'Freeport' was the re-supply drop for the 82nd Airborne Division. At 03.10 hours 52 aircraft began taking off from Folkingham with the urgent supplies, but thick clouds hampered the formation and again many aircraft received damage and returned to Folkingham on one engine and a prayer.

Over the next months the 313th flew on supply and transport duties to the advanced air-strips in the liberated areas of France. The Group also continued with training and at 11.30 hours on Sunday, September 17 1944, 90 transport aircraft of the 313th TCG began to take off with paratroopers of the British 1st Parachute Brigade for Arnhem. The next day, D + 1, a glider mission was flown and 42 aircraft towed 42 gliders to LZ 'N'. Fog caused some take-off problems over Folkingham, but all became airborne and the gliders began releasing from their tug aircraft at 14.30 hours at a height of 800 ft and about a mile south-west of the landing zone.

After the Arnhem campaign, aircraft from Folkingham were flown to the continent almost every day with supplies and returned with wounded troops aboard.

With new airfields being opened on the continent the 313th TCG was ordered to move to France and all American units began to move out on February 23 1945. Folkingham closed to flying on March 20 after a brief but vital operational life. The station was finally vacated by the USAAF on April 15 1945 and was transferred to 40 Group, Maintenance Command, RAF, on June 4 with the intention of becoming a sub-site of 16 MU Stafford. But there were further changes for the airfield and on August 10 1945 it was handed over to 22 Group, Technical Training Command, to house No 3 RAF Regiment Sub-Depot. This unit trained and equipped members of the RAF Regiment for service overseas and remained here until mid-1946. After this unit had departed Folkingham closed down on June 27 and the site reverted to Maintenance Command in 1947. It appears to have been inactive until 1959 when work was undertaken to make it into part of the North Luffenham Thor ICBM complex, and by 1960 the missiles were in position.

From December 1959 the three Thor missiles of No 223 Squadron were housed at Folkingham. This unit disbanded in August 1963 and the airfield then closed. During the mid-1960s the airfield was used by the British Racing Motor Company under the management of Raymond Mays, for testing and development of racing cars. This was for only a short period and after Raymond Mays had moved out the Ministry of Defence disposed of the site which soon reverted to agriculture leaving very few traces of the former airfield and those hectic wartime days when Folkingham took part in two of the most momentous battles of the Second World War.

Freiston, Lincolnshire

131/TF385405. E of Boston on the Wash mud flats S of Freiston

A most isolated site, but perfect for live firing and bombing, were the mud flats and marshes around the Wash, and it was for this role that Freiston aerodrome opened in September 1917. It was a small RNAS station under the control of HMS *Daedalus,* the RNAS training station at Cranwell who ran their armament training school here until 1918.

With the amalgamation of the RFC and RNAS to form the Royal Air Force on April 1 1918, No 4 School of Aerial Fighting was formed with an establish-ment of DH5 and SE5 aircraft. July 1918 saw the school re-named No 4 Fighting School and the role of the unit was training scout pilots in gunnery. In March 1920 the unit disbanded and Freiston aerodrome closed that same year.

It was not used during the Second World War but the site has since been used as HM Detention Centre, North Sea Camp.

Fulbeck, Lincolnshire

121/SK895510. 8 miles W of Newark, W of the A17(T) road

This south Lincolnshire airfield was well sited about three miles west of the village of Fulbeck and bounded on the west and east by country roads.

Fulbeck opened in 1940 as an RLG for Cranwell in order to relieve the congestion caused by the increase of Oxfords by the College FTS, and they used Fulbeck until May 1942. During September and October 1941, 11 SFTS equipped with Oxfords used the station and in 1942 and 1943, 1485 Bomber Gunnery Flight and Air Bomber Training Flight were also stationed here, both units also being equipped with Oxfords.

From April 1943 until April 1944 the airfield was used to store 32 Airspeed Horsa gliders which were looked after by No 2 HGMU and were then handed over to the Allied Airborne Forces. During this period the airfield was developed and three concrete runways were laid to the standard pattern and joined by a perimeter track. The station was then transferred to the USAAF on October 1 1943 for the use of the American IXth Air Force.

Fulbeck was designated Army Air Force Station 488 and several American ground units arrived during the early days of October. During the second week of October the 434th TCG, under Colonel Fred D. Stevens, arrived at Fulbeck fresh from the USA.

The squadrons were equipped with C-47 and C-53 type transport and cargo aircraft and, as was common with each group, had four squadrons. During their stay at Fulbeck the units were only engaged in local flying and transporting supplies. The only action they saw was on the morning of December 7 1943 when Halifax EB187 of No 1664 CU landed at the airfield because of fuel shortage while on a training flight. The aircraft was refuelled and, as it attempted to take off, it swung to one side and the undercarriage collapsed.

On December 10 1943 the ground and air units of the 434th TCG began to move to Welford Park for a training exercise with Allied paratroopers and did not return until January 10 1944. Then, on March 3, they moved out completely to Aldermaston (now the Atomic Weapons Establishment).

For a few weeks during March Fulbeck was without any resident flying units, until the 29th when the 442nd TCG, under Colonel Charles M. Smith, arrived straight from the USA. It was a new group, also with four squadrons, and was assigned to the 50th TCW. The Americans were put through their training and by May they appeared to be ready. On D-Day they were in action—operation 'Boston', the 82nd Airborne's task, was on—and 45 transport aircraft took off and headed for Drop Zone 'T', two miles south-west of Ste-Mère-Église. They dropped the 1st Battalion 507th Paratroop Infantry Regiment and the Regiment headquarters at 02.40 hours. Three aircraft were shot down and 28 received minor damage.

The following day 56 aircraft of the 442nd then took part in operation 'Memphis', the re-supply mission for the American 101st Airborne Division, but this was their last mission from Fulbeck and on June 12 1944 the 442nd moved to Weston Zoyland in Somerset. By the end of the month all American units had departed from Fulbeck and the station prepared for handing back to the Royal Air Force and was used during the last week in June by No 1660 CU for circuits and bumps.

However, there was a change of plan and the Americans returned to Fulbeck with the arrival of the 440th TCG on August 30 in preparation for operation 'Comet', the forerunner of 'Market', but this was cancelled and the Group returned to its base in Exeter only to return to Fulbeck on September 11 as part of the 'Market Garden' force. On Sunday morning, September 17 1944, the 90 aircraft of the 440th TCG, with the 376th Parachute Field Artillery on board, took off from Fulbeck and headed for March to join the main force, then took the southern route across the Wash and turned at North Foreland. Their drop zone was near Nijmegen and many of the Group's aircraft were shot down, including that of the Group CO, Colonel Frank Krebs, who returned to his unit via the Dutch Resistance. On September 18 and 23 the 440th flew two glider missions during the Battle of Arnhem and on the 24th returned to transport duties in France.

This time the Americans had gone for good and Fulbeck returned to the Royal Air Force and opened in No 5 Group, Bomber Command. On October 17 1944, No 49 Squadron, equipped with Lancaster Mk Is and IIIs, arrived from Fiskerton and at long last the station was to be operational, albeit very briefly. The squadron took part in a raid on the German Baltic Fleet at Gdynia in December and in March 1945 helped to pulverise the defences of Wesel. In April 1945 No 49 Squadron moved to Syerston, Nottinghamshire.

Another brief operational life was that of No 189 Squadron which flew in on November 2 1944 having formed two

The derelict control tower at Fulbeck, photographed in May 1980.

weeks previously at Bardney. From here the unit took part in the bomber offensive alongside No 49 Squadron. On March 2/3 1945, Lancaster EE136, named 'Spirit of Russia' made its 109th and last mission while with 189 Squadron. Then, on April 25/26 1945 it was the squadron's turn to make its last operational mission when 14 Lancasters took part in a raid on the Vallo oil refinery. During its brief, mayfly-like, wartime career, No 189 Squadron flew a total of 652 sorties against the enemy, 647 from Fulbeck. The squadron helped to drop food to the starving Dutch and to ferry British troops home from Italy. In October 1945 No 189 Squadron moved to Metheringham where it disbanded the following month.

During 1945 the airfield was used for a short period by an experimental unit, the Automatic Gun Laying Turret Flight, but their Lancasters soon departed and the airfield closed to flying later that year.

The site was retained and used for storage purposes, and then, in 1953-54 the runways were rehabilitated and the airfield opened as a RLG for Cranwell until about 1970 when the airfield again closed to flying. By the beginning of 1980 most of the facilities had been dismantled, apart from the tower that looked 'wide-eyed-and-legless' and one 'T2' hangar that was in a semi-derelict state. The runways that once vibrated to the roar of the 'Lanc' engines now sighed under the phut-phut of the go-kart engine. The site is still MOD property but a proposal to use it as a military training area aroused local feeling; why, I cannot think, for it was conceived in war, so what better memorial for those who flew from here and never returned to have their own wartime base in a peace-keeping role. In September 1980 manoeuvres associated with exercise 'Crusader 1980' were carried out here and the wartime control tower had the prime role. Let us hope that it remains so in the future.

Gainsborough, Lincolnshire

112

In the First World War the German Zeppelin L13 dropped bombs at Gainsborough, but little damage was done. However, because of these raids the War Office established several Home Defence squadrons. These squadrons were based in a convenient small town and had each of its three flights operating from aerodromes within the district.

One of the HD squadrons was No 33 equipped with FE2b and FE2d aircraft which had its headquarters at Gainsborough where there was also a small landing ground which opened in December 1916. The precise location of this is uncertain but it is known to have been a small field on the west (Nottinghamshire) bank of the River Trent into which the squadron aeroplanes flew when they were due for overhaul or repair at headquarters maintenance shops. The three flights were stationed at sites that were relinquished after the war but were to be reactivated a few years later in the Second World War, Scampton, Kirton-in-Lindsey and Elsham for 'A', 'B' and 'C' Flights respectively.

The headquarters of 33 Squadron was transferred to Kirton-in-Lindsey in June 1918 and the field at Gainsborough does not appear to have had any further connection with military aviation. Today there are no records and no trace of any airfield.

Gamston, Nottinghamshire

120/SK695765. 2 miles S of Retford, N of the A1(T) road at Elkesley

Situated just north of the main road at the village of Elkesley, Gamston was one of the few Nottinghamshire sites selected as a bomber station and was constructed to the usual wartime pattern of three runways with the main runway parallel to the B6387 road.

However, when it opened in December 1942 it was as a satellite of No 14 (P) AFU, Ossington, which was in Flying Training Command equipped with Oxford aircraft and it was not until this unit moved out in May 1943 that the station transferred to Bomber Command, although it was in No 93 Group, a training group, again as a satellite of Ossington, which had similarly been transferred.

So, built as an operational bomber station, Gamston was only to play a role in operational training for Bomber Command. On June 1 1943, 'C' Flight of No 82 OTU arrived with their Wellington Mk IIIs and Xs and the Martinets which would be used for drogue towing plus Hurricanes for fighter affiliation. A year later this unit was re-designated No 86 OTU for the role of night bomber crew training, but still only with the twin-engined Wellington. This was to be for only a few months and in October 1944

Above *Gamston control tower as it is today. Fire Tender shed to the right.* **Below** *A Nissen hut lurking in the undergrowth. Gamston 1979.*

the unit was disbanded and all the personnel at Gamston were posted to form No 22 HGCU at Keevil and Fairford.

Gamston was then transferred to No 7 Group, Bomber Command, and November 1944 saw the arrival of No 3 AS from Sheperds Grove. This was a personnel holding unit and the only flying at the station was by the Wellingtons of No 93 Group Disposal Unit that arrived at the same time. These two units remained at Gamston until they disbanded in January 1945. The following month No 30 OTU arrived from Hixon, and this unit was also equipped with Wellingtons.

Gamston was then transferred to No 91 Group and No 30 OTU was disbanded on June 12 1945. The station was now to house No 9 ACHU, an aircrew holding unit, and Gamston was at last to play an important role for it was to be a major holding unit. On July 1, 401 surplus

RAAF aircrew arrived to await repatriation to Australia, but this was easier said than done and was to prove a great problem as the run-down of the RAAF came to a standstill as aircrew moved into holding units and by September 1 there were 1,841 at Gamston. All training ceased on September 7 and men were immediately posted to Gamston so that, by October 25, all squadron RAAF members had arrived here for repatriation. It was very poor treatment to suddenly thrust aircrew, still under the nervous strain of operations, into the shambles and discomforts of stations like Gamston. It is sad that within a few months of VE-Day nothing remained of the bombing units as those history-making aircrews passed through Gamston and by the end of 1945 the station had closed.

For many years the station lay idle then, in May 1953, it re-opened as a satellite to

Worksop for No 211 AFS, later No 4 FTS, flying Meteors and Vampires.

Gamston finally severed its links with the Royal Air Force, when in 1957 it closed down and became an inactive station. Today, a number of the wartime buildings still remain, the large hangar on the far side being used by Bridon Ltd for their Dornier Skyservant. The control tower is now a house but still retains its wartime appearance, and a few Nissen huts are still visible along with the Fire Tender Shed that is now used to store machinery.

Goxhill, Lincolnshire

113/TA115210. Approximately 16 miles NW of Grimsby, W of Goxhill

Goxhill, the most northerly of the Lincolnshire sites, for it was almost on the desolate south bank of the Humber, and certainly one of the most isolated airfields, was a place of mystery which records do not solve. It was never operational yet it had a decoy airfield at Burnham, a few miles to the west of the airfield.

The airfield, built just west of the village of Goxhill, was bounded by the railway and the East Halton Beck. It was a standard bomber station, with three concrete runways, the main one on an axis north-east, south-west. The technical site, two 'T2' and one 'J' type hangars were on the west side of the airfield close to the minor road. The control tower was sited just forward of the 'J' hangar.

It opened on June 26 1941 as a bomber station in No 1 Group, Bomber Command, but received no bomber squadrons. On September 18 1941 the No 1 Group Towed Target Flight formed here with an establishment of nine Lysanders, the first two arriving on October 25. This role was shortlived for, in December 1941 the bomber station was transferred to No 12 Group Fighter Command and it became a fighter station in the Kirton-in-

Above right *Handsome and rugged, even in wartime—Captain Clark Gable, who spent some time at Goxhill, was part of Hollywood's war effort but during his time in England he went on five missions while working on a movie that tells the story of two gunners. He began as a buck private, went through gunnery school, then came to England.* **Right** *Inside the radio room in the control tower at Goxhill. The floors have rotted away and ammunition boxes litter the ground floor.*

Lindsey Sector and was used by Spitfires of No 616 Squadron from that station during January 1942. No 15 (P) AFU from nearby Kirmington then used the airfield from May 15 to June 4 1942.

The mystery of the ex-bomber station takes another turn for in June 1942 it became a station of the USAAF VIIIth Air Force. Most peculiar for Goxhill was a long way from their stamping ground which was in East Anglia. However, this was to be the role of the airfield, now Station 345, and it was to receive newly arrived Fighter Groups from the USA which trained here to acclimatise themselves in English weather and operational techniques. The first Americans to arrive were the USAAF 1st FG in June 1942 with P-38 Lightning aircraft. The Group comprised of three squadrons, the 27th, 71st and 94th, but only the 71st was based at Goxhill. They remained until August 24 1942 when they then moved to Ibsley but the following day the 52nd FG moved in and made Goxhill their home until the following October. They were equipped with Spitfires and these made an unusual sight in their American markings.

On October 8 the 81st FG arrived, or part of it for only 93 Squadron and HQ Flight came to Goxhill with their P-39 Airacobras. This unit moved out on November 15 1942. For the Americans, Goxhill, which they named 'Goat Hill', must have been a very bleak posting and those arriving in the winter of 1942/43 with the cold easterly winds must have received an everlasting impression of England. These were the 78th FG which

arrived on December 1 with its component squadrons, 82nd, 83rd and 84th. The 78th received its P-38 Lightnings at the end of the month and began a training programme. The Americans quickly acclimatised themselves to the Lincolnshire customs, and of course won the hearts of the local female population. Being Christmas, the Americans held several parties for the local children.

By the end of February the Group had re-equipped with P-47s for all P-38s and most of their crews were transferred to North Africa. The pilots preferred the P-38 Lightning. On April 1 1943 the 78th Fighter Group began to move to Duxford, its permanent wartime base, and by the 3rd they had all gone from Goxhill.

The next to arrive was the 353rd FG with its three squadrons, the 350th, 351st and 352nd, on June 7. This unit was assigned with P-47s but they did not arrive until July. Meanwhile, the Group had a great welcome from the Luftwaffe who announced on the German radio programme 'Axis Sally' that they would pay the Group a visit. On their second night at Goxhill the Germans came in low over the sea and attacked the airfield. Records do not show if any damage was done. On August 3 the 353rd FG moved to Metfield.

During the latter part of 1943 Goxhill saw two more fighter groups, both equipped with P-47D Thunderbolts. These were the 356th FG that arrived on August 27 and moved to Martlesham Heath on October 5, and the 358th FG that arrived on October 21 and departed on November 29.

Goxhill in June 1980. Control tower on left with fire tender shed and floodlight and tractor shed. 'J' type hangar.

Lockheed P-38 Lightning of the VIIIth Air Force coming in for a landing at Goxhill.

By the end of the year the build-up was complete and in December 1943, the 496th Fighter Training Group (FTG) was formed with two squadrons, the 554th specialising in training for the P-38 Lightning and the 555th which flew P-51 Mustangs. The Group CO was Colonel Harry W. Magee and the unit was set up as a Fighter Training Combat Crew Replacement Center and served both the VIIIth and IXth Air Forces. At first the unit had many problems, one being the poor mechanical condition of the aircraft supplied to the Group which in the main were battle-weary 'cast-offs' from front-line squadrons.

The training proceeded and by the end of October 1944 there had been 118 accidents, with 53 aircraft lost, 23 pilots killed and seven injured.

The 496th FTG left Goxhill during December 1944 and the airfield was then transferred to RAF Fighter Command on January 20 1945. Flying then ceased and on May 27 it transferred to Maintenance Command and until it became inactivated on December 14 1953 the site was used for bomb storage by No 233 MU, Market Stainton.

On January 29 1962 the airfield and technical site buildings were sold to Mr John Faulding who had farmed the area, and built a bungalow on the site in the late 1950s. However, the three hangars were not included in the sale and were retained by the Ministry of Supply (later the Ministry of the Environment) and

were used for storage of Green Goddess fire-engines and other items. The site was finally evacuated in mid-1977 and, today, the runways remain intact along with the hangars, control tower and operations block that, sadly, never knew the meaning of the word.

However, it is a good example of a wartime airfield that had been protected by its inaccessability, and I trust Mr Faulding will continue to preserve that little piece of history for all runways and perimeter track are in reasonable condition.

Grantham, Lincolnshire

130/SK925351. On the SW side of Grantham just off the A52

Grantham was the original name for the airfield which was renamed Spitalgate in 1944 and the airfield is dealt with under that name. This section deals with Grantham—St Vincents.

In October 1937 the Air Ministry took over a large house, just east of the airfield, at the foot of Spitalgate Hill in Grantham. The house was called St Vincents and from October 1937 to November 1943 it was the HQ of No 5 Group, Bomber Command. At the outbreak of war No 5 Group was commanded by Air Vice Marshal A.T. Harris.

After No 5 Group moved out to Morton Hall, near Swinderby, St Vincents then became HQ 9th Troop Carrier

Command, USAAF, from December 2 1943 to 1945. On June 6 1945 the 61st Troop Carrier Group of the USAAF made a gift of two plaques to the Mayor of Grantham, and one is now hung in the Sessions Hall at the Guildhall. After the Americans departed St Vincents was placed on C & M and in 1977 it was sold to Grantham Borough Council who now use it for their offices.

Greenland Top, Lincolnshire

113/TA180115. W of Grimsby and NE of Keelby

A site that was used in the First World War although today there is no trace of any kind. It opened in 1918 and housed 505 Flight, 251 Squadron, equipped with DH6 aircraft. The role of the unit was to patrol the Humber estuary on anti-submarine operations and after the unit disbanded in 1919 this primitive airfield closed.

Grimsby (Waltham), Lincolnshire

See Waltham

Grimsthorpe, Lincolnshire

130/TF015215. 4 miles NW of Bourne, S of Swinstead and W of the B1176 road

Like many of the large houses and park-lands, Grimsthorpe Castle, the home of Lord Ancaster, was used by both the Army and the Royal Air Force in both World Wars.

In World War 1 there was an ELG on the Grimsthorpe Estate, but no buildings were ever attached to it. It was sited on the highest ground just south of the village of Swinstead and west of the Swinstead to Creeton road. It was very well sited but could never be extended for the River Glen was on the western boundary and the Swinstead village only a short distance to the north. Lord Ancaster can remember seeing a few aircraft use the field, but only a few times.

In World War 2 the estate had a dual role. Grimsthorpe Park was used as a bombing range and was used in the main by RAF Cottesmore and its satellites. The range, with a small pill-box at the north and south boundaries, the south one of which still remains today, was sited in the centre of the park just south of the lake. It was a good bombing range and the only damage done by the RAF was one cow, killed in action. This was one of the sites that the Ministry wished to maintain after the war but were not able to do so. The ELG was never reactivated during the Second World War for it was not practicable to extend the site for reasons previously mentioned. The Deer Park was used as a tank training ground by various Army regiments which were camped in the grounds, and some even billeted in the castle itself. One Army officer insisted a guard should be placed on the castle roof, not just as a lookout, but to patrol along one side, and by so doing the soldier wore the lead away from the roof. Today, the castle is back in a peaceful setting and during August each year is open to the public.

Harby, (Langar), Nottinghamshire

See Langar

Harlaxton, Lincolnshire

130/SK902325. 2 miles S of Grantham

This was one of the early training aerodromes built for the RFC in the First World War. It was equipped with wooden hangars of the 1916 RFC pattern and the usual hutted accommodation.

In November 1916, No 44 Reserve Squadron moved in as the station opened. This unit was equipped with Avro 504s, BE2s and RE7s and remained at Harlaxton until November 1917, having been re-styled No 44 Training Squadron in May.

The aerodrome continued to be used by a series of training units, No 68 from January 30 1917 to September 1917 with DH5s; No 54 Reserve Squadron, re-named 54 Training Squadron, in May, with DH6s and 504s from March 17 1917 to 1918; No 98 with DH9s during August 1917 and 1918; and Nos 26 TS, 64 TS, 20 TS and 53 TS with a mixture of RE8s, DH6s and 504s. Also during 1918 there was a general reorganisation and the flying training establishments were redesignated Training Depot Stations and Harlaxton became No 40 TDS in the summer of 1918, before closing in 1919. It was one of the many aerodromes in the United Kingdom not required for the tiny post-war RAF.

The site soon reverted to agriculture but the marking circle remained clearly visible from the air as it had been laid out with chalk which did not become over-grown.

In the 1930s this was one of many former aerodrome sites that were surveyed with a view to being reactivated to serve

Harlaxton aerodrome in 1917.

the expanding RAF, but it was not immediately required. However, by 1941 it had become obvious that the circuit at nearby Grantham, another airfield dating back to World War 1, was congested, so work was put in hand to prepare Harlaxton as a Relief Landing Ground. So, a once busy training station in World War 1, Harlaxton opened on April 4 1942 as a RLG for No 12 SFTS with Anson and Battle aircraft.

Harlaxton, as a satellite of Spitalgate that housed No 12 SFTS, later renamed 12 (P) AFU, was extensively used and when the unit was equipped in September 1943 with Blenheims, the heavy work load and bad weather were too much for the grass surfaces and by November 1943 they began to break up. The parent station, also grass, was in the same state, so the Blenheims used Balderton airfield. But the situation did not improve and the aircraft moved to Cheshire and Lancashire until steel tracking was laid in early 1944.

The position in June 1944 was RLG for 12 (P) AFU, Spitalgate, with Oxford, Blenheim and Anson aircraft of No 21 Group. This unit remained at Harlaxton until February 1945 and continued in use by the successor unit at Spitalgate, No 17 SFTS, for a few months before finally closing later in the year.

Today few traces remain of the former airfield which played such a vital part in training pilots in two World Wars, and the Grantham bypass of the A1 Great North Road passes very close to the site just to the north of Little Ponton.

Harringworth (Spanhoe), Northamptonshire

See Spanhoe

Hemswell (Harpswell), Lincolnshire

112/SK940910. Approximately 13 miles N of Lincoln, N of Harpswell, W of the A15 road

First used during World War 1 when it was called Harpswell, after the small hamlet that lay at the southern end of the airfield, Hemswell was one of many airfields built on the top of the Lincoln Cliff just west of Ermine Street. These locations made ideal sites for training stations and this was the role of Harpswell when it opened in June 1918. It was one of the last airfields to open and soon closed. It housed No 199 TS which was established to train pilots and observers for night operations but it was shortlived and the unit disbanded in June 1919. Harpswell became redundant and closed. The site was promptly reclaimed for agricultural use and all traces of the airfield were soon eradicated.

In the early 1930s the site was surveyed to assess its suitability for reoccupation to serve the expanding Royal Air Force. It was selected and work began on developing it into one of the earliest of the Expansion bomber bases. The airfield is bounded on the south by the A631 road and its western boundary is the B1398 road. On the eastern side, towards the A15 road, it had an arc of four 'C' type hangars and behind these were grouped the workshops, barracks and other buildings.

It was an important airfield and a KQ site was set up as a decoy airfield at Toft Grange, some six miles south-east of Hemswell, in the early part of 1940.

The new bomber airfield, known as Hemswell after the village immediately to its west, possibly also because it was built on Hemswell Cliff, opened in January 1937 in No 5 Group, Bomber Command,

Station HQ Wing, Hemswell, June 1945.

and was the third of many to come. The first unit to arrive was No 144 Squadron in February 1937 with Audax Biplane bombers. This was soon joined by a second squadron, No 61, that had just re-formed and had the badge with the Lincoln Imp. The squadron first had Audax aircraft, then both squadrons received Ansons and by early 1938 both had been re-equipped with Bristol Blenheim Mk Is. However, the Handley Page Hampden was chosen to be the main bomber and at the outbreak of the Second World War both squadrons were flying Hampdens.

No 61 Squadron (whose code letters now changed to 'QR'), was the first to bomb a German land target when, on March 19/20 1940, five Hampdens were despatched to the seaplane base at Hörnum. The first bombing attack by No 144 Squadron was not until the war was three weeks old when, on September 29 1939, three Hampdens bombed enemy ships. But these early bombing raids were fruitless and costly. Both squadrons remained at Hemswell until July 1941 when they then moved to North Luffenham. During their operational life at Hemswell they had taken part in many raids, including the first bombing raid on Berlin on August 25/26 1940.

Next to arrive were two Polish squadrons, No 300 and No 301, both equipped with Wellington Mk Ics, and neither of the squadrons had a badge authorised. Both units arrived during July 1941 and that same month Hemswell was transferred to No 1 Group which had taken over the bomber stations in north Lincolnshire and set up headquarters at Bawtry.

No 300 Squadron continued operations with their Wellingtons and attacked a wide range of targets before moving a few miles south to Ingham in May 1942. No 301 Squadron remained and continued its offensive, still using the Wellington right up until the squadron disbanded on April 7 1943. The last operational mission as a bomber squadron came on March 29/30 1943 when five Wellingtons were despatched for Bochum.

After No 301 (Polish) Squadron had disbanded here, the personnel were posted to other Polish squadrons, two of which still remained at Hemswell: No 305, which had arrived in July 1942 equipped with Mk IIs and IVs; and No 300 that had returned in January 1943, now equipped with Wellington Mk IIIs, and had just started to receive the first of the Xs when in June 1943 the squadron returned to Ingham along with No 305 Squadron.

Hemswell then closed and was inactive for several months while runways were laid. These were three concrete runways to the standard bomber pattern, the main one on a north-east axis, and one of the two auxiliary runways being in direct line with Hemswell village. The airfield re-opened in January 1944 with the arrival of No 1 Group LFS and remained non-operational until November 1944 when 1 LFS moved out to be replaced by two Lancaster squadrons.

In the October changes, when it was decided to transfer Scampton to No 1 Group as No 15 Base, Hemswell became a satellite of Scampton. No 150 Squadron arrived on November 11 and No 170 Squadron on November 30, both having just re-formed as heavy bomber squadrons equipped with Lancasters. Subsequently, both units took part in many major raids. Between November 11 1944 and April 1945, the last mission of the war on Berchtesgaden, No 150 Squadron flew 827 sorties from here and in so doing lost eight aircraft and 40 aircrew. The squadron then took part in food drops to the Dutch people and transporting ex-PoWs home to England before it disbanded at Hemswell on November 7 1945.

No 170 Squadron flew over 900 sorties from Hemswell and during its operational life from October 19/20 1944 to April 25 1945, its last mission also Berchtesgaden, the squadron had flown a total of 980 sorties and dropped 4,322 tons of bombs. 13 aircraft and 62 aircrews were missing. Before it disbanded on November 14 1945 the squadron also took part in operations 'Manna', 'Exodus' and 'Dodge'.

The end of the war meant rapid closures for many bomber stations, but Hemswell was retained as a permanent station, and the graveyard of many more squadrons. No 1687 BDTF flew in from Scampton with Spitfires and Hurricanes on April 2 1945 and disbanded on October 30 1946. On November 4 1946 the Mosquitoes of No 109 Squadron (having arrived the previous November) and 139 (Jamaica) Squadron (having arrived the previous February), departed for Coningsby.

During October and November 1946, three squadrons arrived, Nos 100, 97 and 83, all equipped with Avro Lincolns. Hemswell was now established as a Lincoln airfield and from July to December 1947 housed a detachment of Lincolns from 61 Squadron and from October to December 1947 a detachment from 57 Squadron. The other Lincoln squadron was No 12 from January to March 1948. No 100 Squadron was the first of the resident units to leave and moved to Waddington in March 1950. In April 1952, No 199 Squadron made a brief visit back into Lincolnshire, having been transferred from Watton to Hemswell and from 90 Group to Bomber Command, and arrived with Mosquito NF 36 aircraft, but moved in October to Honington, Suffolk. Then, in December 1955, both remaining Lincoln squadrons departed. No 83 eventually went to Waddington after being re-named Antler Squadron with effect from January 1 1956. During 1953 it had been based abroad for five months operating against the Communist terrorists in Malaya. Finally No 97 ceased to exist and became known as Arrow Squadron. It also had been detached abroad for a few months.

The station still remained a bomber airfield, but now only housed two squadrons, Nos 109 and 139 both arriving on March 31 1950 equipped with Mosquito B35 aircraft and during 1952 and 1953 converting to Canberra jet bombers. Both units moved to Binbrook in January 1956 and with their departure the station ceased to be a bomber base.

Site limitations made it unsuitable for development into a V-bomber base and it was closed for flying. The site was then used as the headquarters for the American Thor ICBM complex, 97 Squadron being based on the airfield as one of the five dispersed sites in addition to the headquarters, and each of the squadrons housed three missiles. These were flown in from the USA in Globemaster transport aircraft. The site was also occupied by support units of the USAF during the period 1958 to 1964.

From 1964, Hemswell was occupied by No 7 School of Recruit Training, and this unit remained until 1967 when the airfield was then vacated by the Royal Air Force with the exception of the married quarters which were retained for Scampton, the rest of the station going on to care and maintenance. The airfield was then used by a flying club for several years but in 1973 took on a very different use when thousands of Asians were expelled from Uganda and Hemswell became their temporary home. By 1979 it was derelict, the four 'C' type hangars had been converted into grain stores and the 'T2' type, erected at the end of the arc early in the war, was advertised for sale. Go-karting and other sporting activities have used the runways but the Property Services Agency is now trying to dispose of them and return the land to its former owners.

Hibaldstow, Lincolnshire

112/SE980010. SW of Brigg, S of Hibaldstow and E of A15

Hibaldstow airfield had not been a World War 1 site like so many others in the area but it was the most northerly of the airfields situated on either side of the A15, Lincoln to Brigg, road.

Construction work started in 1940 and the airfield was laid out with the standard three paved runways linked by a perimeter track with the control tower on the western edge of the airfield, near the A15.

From its layout it is obvious that Hibaldstow was destined for greater things but in fact had only a brief operational life and was one of the first airfields to close. The station opened in May 1941 and was thought important enough to have two decoy airfields, one at Cadney and a QX site at Thornton Le Moor. However, it was only to be a satellite for nearby Kirton-in-Lindsey and the first occupants were No 255 Squadron which moved in from the parent station

Control tower at Hibaldstow which has now been made into a dwelling.

that same month with Defiants and began to re-equip with the twin-engined Beaufighter II. During this changeover period there were many accidents as the squadron took on a night fighter role. By September the unit was operational and on the 20th of the month moved to Coltishall.

This squadron was replaced by No 253 from Skeabrae equipped with Hurricane IIs which operated largely at night as the satellite squadron for the Turbinlite Havocs of No 538 Squadron, which also arrived in September but was then called 1459 Flight. Although the Turbinlite experiment was superseded by AI radar, one German aircraft *was* shot down by the squadrons on May 1 1942, but this turned out to be the only success. A few days after the 'kill', No 253 Squadron moved to Shoreham in support of the Dieppe raid but had returned by the end of May. It then moved to Friston for a few weeks in June and July and again for three weeks in August, but by the end of the month it was back at Hibaldstow.

Another Turbinlite Havoc unit, No 532 Squadron, arrived in September 1942 but only two months later the fighter squadron, No 253, moved to north-west Africa. On January 25 1943 No 538 Squadron disbanded, rapidly followed by No 532 on February 1, which brought to an end the operational life of the airfield. The night defence of Lincolnshire and the North Midlands now rested with Coleby Grange—a weak link that was never exploited by the Germans.

In May 1943 the airfield became a relief landing ground for No 53 OTU based at the parent station of Kirton-in-Lindsey and was used by their Masters and Spitfires until May 15 1945 when the unit disbanded. While at Hibaldstow one of the OTU's Spitfires, the famous AB910, took off with ACW Margaret Horton sitting on the tail, the pilot not noticing her until he was airborne! Fortunately, the Spitfire and its back-seat passenger landed safely after a complete circuit of the airfield.

Hibaldstow then closed to flying in 1945 and was one of the many unwanted airfields. Over the years the buildings have been dismantled, except the control tower, which has been converted into an attractive two-storey home, retaining the front walk-round balcony. The runways are also in fair condition.

Holbeach, Lincolnshire

131/TF450310. On the mud flats of the Wash near Holbeach St Matthew

Holbeach opened as a bombing and gunnery range in 1928. A small landing ground did exist but this cannot be traced. It is a range that has always been extensively used and which still serves today as an Air Weapons Range for the Royal Air Force, American and NATO air forces.

Holbeach (Sutton Bridge), Lincolnshire

See Sutton Bridge

Aerial view of Hucknall from the north, circa 1935. A Westland Wallace of No 504 Squadron is taxiing off.

Hucknall, Nottinghamshire

129/SK525470. On the outskirts of Hucknall, S of the B6009

In the early days of the First World War it was first thought that the aerodrome should be on Papplewick Moor but this was abandoned because the ground was waterlogged. It is ironic that Papplewick Moor should later have become a RLG for Hucknall.

However, the Hucknall site was decided upon by the experts and the land was purchased from the Duke of Portland. The contractors were a firm from Blackpool, Parkinsons, who set about the job in earnest and used hundreds of men on the contract. An extensive landing ground, hangars and other buildings made up the aerodrome.

Hucknall opened during the First World War as a training ground and remained such throughout the whole of the war. Very few records exist for this period, although some Americans, flying Curtiss Jennies, are known to have been trained here during this period. After the 1914-18 war it was thought that the site would be made into a permanent aerodrome for Hucknall but, like many other projects, it was not taken up and as a result, the buildings, that had been produced at great cost, were offered for sale by the Ministry. One of the hangars was occupied and some of the buildings were made into dwellings. The 107 acres were eventually sold to George Elkington,

a Hucknall farmer. The landing ground had little use.

However, all was not lost and, with the birth of the Nottingham Aero Club, the Ministry decided to purchase the land and the 107 acres from George Elkington. It also purchased 20 acres of adjoining land from the County Council and Bulwell Wood Hall, which has since been demolished.

A rebuilding programme was undertaken with Laing, the main contractors having the task of bringing the aerodrome buildings up to standard with a view to future use. On March 26 1928, No 504 (County of Nottingham) Squadron was formed here as a cadre unit of the Special Reserve. It converted to an auxiliary squadron on May 18 1936 and had a day bomber role, equipped with Hawker Horsleys up to early 1934 then with Westland Wallaces until May 1937, when it re-equipped with Hawker Hinds. On October 31 1938 its role changed to 'fighter' and the unit re-equipped with Hurricanes and moved out in August 1939 to Digby.

Meantime, in December 1934, Rolls-Royce moved into two of the hangars and set up what was to become the centre of Rolls-Royce engine test-flying. By the end of 1935 the company had developed the PV-12, later to become famous as the Merlin—and who at that time would have thought this would be an engine to play such a major part in World War 2?

Above *Hawker Horsleys of No 504 Squadron from Hucknall flying over Nottinghamshire in 1933.* **Below** *Spitfire AB910, which is now in the Battle of Britain Memorial Flight at Coningsby, seen at Hucknall circa 1963.*

During the expansion of the RAF in 1936 many squadrons were brought back in the Order of Battle. No 98 was one example, moving into Hucknall in August equipped with Hawker Hinds. The local people got to know them well as many made forced landings in the district. During the autumn of 1937 several Hinds landed anywhere but at the airfield. K6718, piloted by Flying Officer Plant, overturned in a field at Broxtowe; another, K6719, piloted by Pilot Officer Grindon, forced-landed at Gunthorpe Bridge; while K6721, piloted by Flying Officer Dowson, landed on a hill at Hobsie Farm, Pinxton, Nottinghamshire. The field was so small the aircraft could not take off and had to be dismantled and returned to Hucknall by road. Another

squadron to re-appear was No 104 (Bomber) Squadron which had re-formed at Abingdon early in 1936 and moved to Hucknall in August. This unit was equipped with Hawker Hinds and remained here until May 1938.

At the outbreak of the Second World War the airfield was in Fighter Command, but no Fighter Command units appeared. In September 1939 the units were No 98 Squadron with the Battles they had re-armed with in 1938, and No 1 (RAF) Ferry Pilots' Pool in Maintenance Command. 98 Squadron were the main occupants and served as a reserve unit until moving to Scampton in March 1940.

On March 14 1940 a Polish training unit formed with 31 Battle aircraft and flying commenced the following month but, in

Above *VC 10 Flying Test Bed for RB 211 engine (on the left) taking off at Hucknall, March 1970.* **Below** *Tyne Lincoln at Hucknall.*

June 1940, the unit moved to Bramcote. That same month No 1 Group Headquarters was evacuated from France and was established at Hucknall, remaining until July 1941.

An interesting event occurred in 1940, when the Rolls-Royce Experimental Unit was repairing Spitfires and Hurricanes during the Battle of Britain. An attempt was made by a German to steal a Spitfire which was parked on the tarmac waiting for its ferry pilot to take it to a squadron. At the time it was rumoured in the town that a German spy had come to steal a Spitfire. However, it was not until after the war that the true story emerged. It was an escaped German PoW who called the airfield for transport, claiming to be a Dutch pilot who had forced-landed. He was brought to Hucknall and initially the

adjutant believed his story but, while the German was sitting in the cockpit, the adjutant got suspicious and ordered him out—it was a good try.

In January 1941 the Poles returned and No 1 (Polish) FTS formed, equipped with Tiger Moths, Battles and, from April, with Oxfords. In June 1941 the unit was redesignated No 16 (Polish) SFTS and the following month moved to Newton. It was replaced by another Polish unit, No 25 (Polish) EFTS, that moved in from Peterborough on July 16 1941 and remained for the duration of the war.

Hucknall, being only a grass airfield was unable to operate jet aircraft, so in 1943 the flying of jets by Rolls-Royce was transferred to Balderton *(qv)* where hard runways were available. But, after only a year it became necessary to move to

Church Broughton in Derbyshire and remained there until 1946.

The station continued in a training role and its status on June 6 1944 was No 25 (Polish) EFTS, of No 21 Group, with a RLG at Papplewick Moor; plus No 12 Group Communications Flight, ADGB, which continued to use the airfield after the hostilities had ceased; along with No 504 Squadron that was now equipped with Mosquito T3, NF30 and Spitfire F22 aircraft; Headquarters No 43 Group, Nottingham UAS; No 664 Squadron with Austers, and No 54 MU.

With the end of the war, military projects were curtailed and Rolls-Royce turned to engine development for more peaceful purposes. A Lancaster Mark III—EE134 'Y' Yoke—which had become a veteran of 99 sorties while with No 619 Squadron, after the finish of operations moved to No 5 LFS where it was coded 'CE-O'. From here it found its way to Rolls-Royce at Hucknall where it served as a power-plant fire extinguisher ground test-rig. Not the sort of role one would expect with such a fine war record. 'Y' Yoke was often the subject of pyrotechnic displays as its Merlins were purposely set on fire whilst running. These tests led to the erection of the Fire Tunnel. This was a more versatile rig within which complete installations with their respective wing sections from a variety of aircraft had their fire prevention systems fully developed.

By July 1952 the only unit still at Hucknall was 1970 Flight of No 664 Squadron, Home Command, which was flying a few Auster AOP5 and AOP6 aircraft. In 1954 Rolls-Royce made aviation history with the 'Flying Bedstead' which became the first aircraft in the world to make a vertical ascent and landing assisted only by the thrust from its two Nene engines. The Flying Bedstead had originally begun its tests tethered to a gantry in July 1953.

In 1957 RAF involvement was terminated at Hucknall. Rolls-Royce Flight Development Establishment continued at Hucknall with a programme of flight and ground testing and, with the acquisition of the Gazelle free turbine, helicopter flight development was transferred here. This increased the test fleet to include Wessex and Belvedere helicopters. By 1958 the development of supersonic engines commenced with the arrival of a Lightning fighter and up to 1969 tests were carried out with five such aircraft. In 1971 test flying came to an end and, although today Rolls-Royce remain in strength, the RAF hangars and other buildings have been taken over by private industry.

Immingham, Lincolnshire
113/TA183140. On S bank of Humber

Immingham was first used for military reasons in World War 1 when action was taken to set up a defence system for the Royal Navy fuel storage tanks. The outcome was that the RNAS set up No 8 Kite Balloon Section, the kite balloons used being similar to the observation balloons used by the RFC. These were flown at about 3,000 ft and the observer looked for submarines, mines etc.

From April 1918, Immingham became part of the Royal Air Force and was briefly re-named Royal Air Force 8 Balloon Station, being disbanded in 1919. In the Second World War the area around Immingham and the Humber Estuary was designated a barrage balloon area, the balloon used being a 'lethal' barge-borne type.

Ingham (Cammeringham), Lincolnshire
121/SK965835. Approximately 7 miles N of Lincoln, W of the A15 and E of the B1398 roads

Sited just west of Ermine Street, this was one of the many sites surveyed during the 1930s and early 1940s for possible development into airfields for Bomber Command. Only a small percentage were selected and some of these were found to be unsuitable during the early construction stages and were then abandoned. Ingham somehow passed all the paperwork, but never made the grade as an airfield.

It was situated on the top of the Lincoln Cliff immediately above the village of Ingham with the A15 as the eastern boundary and the B1398 as the western. Work started on constructing the airfield in 1941 and by the end of the year it was pressed into service as a Relief Landing Ground for 11 SFTS at Shawbury, even though work was still in progress. The tower and a 'T2' hangar were on the west side of the airfield near some farm buildings which were left in position on the site. A 'B1' hangar was on the eastern side near the A15 and a further hangar was in the north-east of the site. Much of

Cliff House, Ingham, which was used as an Officers' Mess during the war. (June 1980.)

the hutted accommodation was dispersed along the western side of the airfield, some of the huts in a small thicket at the side of the B1398. Paved runways were not laid, which was most unusual for an anticipated bomber station, although there was a perimeter track and three 'pan-type' hardstandings. The surface of the landing area was fairly level but was very bumpy and full of potholes.

Ingham, known also as Cammeringham after another neighbouring village, opened in May 1942 in No 1 Group, Bomber Command, as a satellite for Hemswell, but as a bomber airfield it left much to be desired. In the middle of the airfield sat Cliff House Farm in a grove of tall trees, another of the peculiarities of the site. The house itself was used as a Mess during the war years. The first unit to take up residence was No 300 (Polish) Squadron, equipped with Wellingtons, which arrived in May and operated until January 1943 when it was moved to Hemswell.

The Poles were replaced by No 199 Squadron the following month from Blyton. Equipped with Wellington Mark Xs, this unit moved to Lakenheath in June 1943 in order to re-equip with the four-engined Stirlings. As 199 Squadron moved out two Polish units moved in, No 300 Squadron again with 305, both from Hemswell, but the latter did not remain very long and in September moved out with its Wellingtons to Swanton Morley in order to re-equip with the North-American Mitchell.

This left No 300 Squadron the resident unit, remaining at Ingham as if for some kind of punishment, although the unit re-equipped in January with Wellington Mark IIIs. But as these became obsolete No 300 had to leave Ingham since its muddy, bumpy grass-surface and restricted site was unable to operate the heavy four-engined Lancasters so, in March 1944, the squadron moved to Faldingworth.

With the departure of the Polish squadron Ingham became non-operational but it was still used for flying and during 1944 housed the Martinets of 1481 Bombing and Gunnery Flight for a few weeks and 1687 BDTF equipped with Spitfires and Hurricanes. This latter unit continued training, which involved giving practice in evasion techniques to the operational bomber crews, by way of mock fighter attacks. In December 1944 the unit moved to Scampton and in early 1945 the airfield closed to flying and was reduced to care and maintenance.

The site soon returned to agriculture and most of the facilities dismantled. However, the fire tender shed, pyro store, signals room, crews' rooms, rest rooms, MT workshop with pit and original shelving and several other buildings are still in good condition. Some even have their original painted legends on the doors. The 'T2', albeit in a modified condition, is still being used by a local farmer. The control tower is still complete except for glass panes in the window frames. Cliff House has been restored and turned into two dwellings.

Kelstern, Lincolnshire

113/TF260920. NW of Louth between the A631 and A16 roads

Situated high on the Lincolnshire Wolds, Kelstern was a bleak site which was used during World War 1 as an Emergency Landing Ground by Home Defence squadrons of the Royal Flying Corps. Lieutenant A.R. Kingsford from No 33

Aerial view of Kelstern taken in March 1980. Although now largely returned to agriculture, its former outlines are still visible. The water tower is in the top left-hand corner.

Squadron, Scampton, thought that he had come down in 'No Man's Land' when he had cause to use the ELG, and his log book records: 'October 18th 1917— crashed on forced landing at emergency landing ground in fog, FE 2B 5636. Got teeth knocked out, Observer minor injuries. I left him with two mechanics and went to a farmer's home nearby, he was irate, being wakened at 3 am, offered no help!'

After the First World War the site was discarded. However, during the Second World War as demand increased for more and more bomber airfields the site was surveyed and found to be suitable, but using a much larger area than the original landing ground. Construction work started in the winter of 1942/43 and in September 1943 Kelstern opened as a heavy bomber station in No 1 Group, Bomber Command, as a satellite for 12 Base Station, Binbrook, the other satellite for this base being Waltham.

The airfield conformed to the standard pattern of the wartime airfield, the usual runway layout surrounded by a perimeter track around which were hardstandings for the aircraft.

The unit for which the airfield had been planned, No 625 Squadron, formed at Kelstern on October 1 1943 from a nucleus provided by 'C' Flight of 100 Squadron based at Waltham. The squadron was equipped with Lancaster Is and IIIs whose first operation was on the night of October 18/19 when nine aircraft participated in a raid on Hanover.

On the morning of February 19 1944 the news had just been received that operations that night were on. It was very cold, with the ground snow-covered, and at 15.00 hours the crews filed into the large blacked-out Nissen hut for their briefing. The red tape on the map stretched deep into the heart of the Father-land to Leipzig, 113 miles south-west of Berlin and 70 miles north-west of Dresden.

At 20.00 hours Squadron Leader Barry Douetil taxied his Lancaster from dispersal and, at the appropriate signal, 'T' for Tommy, JA862 was thundering down the runway on its mission of death. Take-off was always a worry, having to go up to two miles between dim blue lights with the brake pressure diminishing much faster than the engines could build up and if the aircraft left the perimeter track with a full bomb and fuel load it would immediately bog down.

Take-off was uneventful though and they climbed, very slowly due to the heavy bomb load, through ten-tenths snow clouds with clear skies at about 12,000 ft. At Cleethorpes they joined up with other aircraft taking part—two searchlights made a 'gate' through which they flew, so the bomber stream started coherently. They then set course for the Dutch coast.

In the region over Hanover, still on course for Leipzig, 'T' Tommy was attacked twice by a Focke-Wulf FW190; on the second attack cannon shells hit the starboard wing, setting it alight. Barry Douetil:

'I could feel the impact of the hits through my hands on the control column and at the same time could hear the rear gunner's four guns firing back, but by this time I could also hear the noise of the flames over the noise of the engines. Following the usual drill, whilst I was still controlling the aircraft, the flight engineer undid my seat belt and clipped the chest type parachute pack on to the harness, we did not fly with parachutes attached. A short while afterwards the aircraft went over onto its back and I fell on to the roof which seemed to give way and I found myself at about 20,000 ft falling rapidly through the darkness.'

Squadron Leader Barry Douetil landed heavily in a frozen field on the outskirts of Hanover. For him the war was over and he became a Prisoner of War in Stalag Luft 3 in Silesia until it was overrun by the Russians. He was the only crew member to survive.

On the fateful Nuremberg raid of March 30/31 1944, No 625 Squadron despatched 13 aircraft and one failed to return.

On October 15 1944, No 170 Squadron, which had previously been an Army Co-Operation squadron, re-formed here as a heavy bomber unit equipped with Lancasters (code letters 'TC'). The squadron moved that same month to Dunholme Lodge.

No 625 continued to operate from

Kelstern water tower standing at the cross-roads. Photographed June 1980.

Kelstern until April 1945 when the unit then moved to Scampton where it was finally disbanded on October 7 1945 after a brief but hectic life of slightly over two years. The squadron took part in many major raids, dropped food to the starving Dutch people and brought home ex-Prisoners-of-War from Belgium.

The departure of No 625 Squadron left Kelstern without a resident squadron. It was a bleak site with primitive facilities and suffered circuit overlap problems with other nearby airfields, notably Binbrook and Ludford Magna, so it was hardly surprising that it closed shortly before the

The last few remains of Kelstern. A Nissen hut with two carts and rusty farm machinery stand exposed on the bleak Wolds.

war ended. The site was returned to agriculture and most of the facilities were completely dismantled, leaving few traces of the former airfield.

The only remains are the ops block that is used as a store for hay, one small hangar-type workshop, two Nissen-type workshops, the electricity sub-station, some parts of the runway and perimeter track and the water tower.

Kelstern has a strange silent atmosphere which you can feel as you stand on the one-time main runway. It is not possible to kill the airfield by taking down the huts and as the mists began to roll in you cannot help but wonder what the tired crews thought as they returned from their missions to such airfields as this.

At a remote road junction just beyond the western perimeter of the site a small monument has been erected in memory of the casualties suffered by the aircrew of No 625 Squadron, a last remaining link with those wartime days.

King's Cliffe, (Apethorpe)
Northamptonshire

141/TL030980. SW of Stamford, W of the A1(T) road

King's Cliffe is situated to the south of the old Roman Road that joins King's Cliffe and Wansford and served as the northern boundary.

Work started in 1940 and it was laid out as a standard fighter station with grass surface runways and designed to accommodate two fighter squadrons on dispersal. The station offices were located to the west of the airfield, near to King's Cliffe village, while the administrative and technical sites were on the eastern side.

King's Cliffe opened in 1941 as a satellite for Wittering and had its own decoy airfield at Alwalton, to the south-east of the station near the main A1(T) road. The first unit to arrive was No 266 Squadron equipped with Spitfires, which moved in from the parent station at Wittering during October 1941 and remained until the end of January 1942 when the squadron then moved to Duxford. It was immediately replaced by the Spitfires of No 616 Squadron from Kirton-in-Lindsey and, at the end of July, having been to West Malling for two weeks at the beginning of the month, the squadron moved to Kenley while No 485 Squadron, which was at Kenley, moved to King's Cliffe. This unit finally moved out to West Hampnett in January 1943 after

having been to West Malling in August for a few weeks and Kirkston during October.

The station had now received its first American units, which had arrived in December 1942. These were a few P-39 Airacobras of the 347th Fighter Squadron. January 1943 saw further American units, including the 56th Fighter Group with P-47c Thunderbolts. The object of the unit was to train with these aircraft and at the same time learn Royal Air Force fighter tactics. By April this unit was operational and it moved to Norfolk. The airfield was again used by Wittering and on June 29 1943 a detachment of 349 Squadron moved in with Spitfire Vas but, when the Americans returned in August 1943, the squadron moved to Wellingore.

During this period three hard-surfaced runways and a perimeter track were constructed by W & C French Ltd. The main runway was 1,700 yards long and on an east-west axis, while the two intersecting ones were 1,350 and 1,100 yards. 12 Blister hangars were dispersed around the perimeter and other buildings were erected but, by the time the Americans returned to King's Cliffe, now designated USAAF Station 367, in August 1943, there was still a shortage of accommodation. The 20th Fighter Group, comprising three squadrons, the 55th, 77th and 79th, moved in with P-38H Lightnings and such was the accommodation problem that the 55th Squadron had to be billeted at Wittering. The squadron moved to King's Cliffe as soon as the barracks were ready and in December 1943 the Group commenced operations. The role of the Group was to give much needed fighter cover to the bombers of the VIIIth Air Force.

In July 1944 the Group re-equipped with P-51 Mustangs and, as history has proved, it became one of the greatest piston-engine fighters of the Second World War. With a speed of 440 mph and a range of 2,300 miles, with external fuel tanks, it could escort bombers all the way to Berlin and back. By the end of the war the 20th FG had flown 312 combat missions, the last of which was on April 25 1945. The 20th Fighter Group had a credit of 449 enemy aircraft destroyed during operations.

With the war now over in Europe the Americans made only local flights and on August 1 they held an air show at King's Cliffe for the local people who were able

Top *P-38 Lightning being refuelled at King's Cliffe.* **Above** *P-38 at King's Cliffe. Many of these aircraft were lost due to engine failure which was a common problem.* **Below** *Lieutenant Heiden congratulates his ground crew at King's Cliffe.*

Aerial view of King's Cliffe with the Roman road to the north. RAF Photograph, January 16 1947 (Crown copyright).

to see at close quarters the men and their machines, which included three B-17s. The following month the Americans began to move out and on October 20 1945 the Group said farewell to their wartime home and returned to the USA.

King's Cliffe then returned to the Royal Air Force but it was badly sited for any future development and from February 6 1946 the station was used as a German PoW Holding Unit, being able to accommodate up to 2,800 PoWs at any one time. Difficulty was found in communication and control and on November 4 Deene Thorpe was taken on as a satellite until July 16 1947. During September 1947 King's Cliffe closed down but was used for armament storage until being abandoned on January 1 1959 and sold later that year.

Today, all hangars are gone and most of the runways and perimeter destroyed and the land put back to farming. However, as a reminder of its wartime past, the control tower still stands in perfect isolation and there are a few Nissen and Maycrete huts dotted around the once-busy fighter station.

Kirmington, Lincolnshire
112/TA095103. E of Brigg, S of A18 road

Situated a few miles from Brigg and south of the Brigg to Grimsby road, Kirmington was one of the airfields in north Lincolnshire that was constructed for No 1 Group, Bomber Command, during the early part of the Second World War.

It was a standard pattern heavy bomber airfield with the usual three 50-yard-wide concrete runways and widely dispersed accommodation. Work started in the latter part of 1941 and during construction the site was used as a relief landing ground for the Oxfords of 15(P) AFU, based at Leconfield, just across the Humber in Yorkshire. This use terminated in October 1942 when the airfield opened and was accepted by Bomber Command.

That same month saw No 150 Squadron arrive from Snaith, flying Wellington Mark III aircraft and playing their part in the strategic bombing offensive. This squadron was joined in the latter part of December 1942 by the home echelon of No 142 Squadron which moved in from Waltham and was also equipped with Wellington Mark IIIs.

Just before the unit arrived, 13 tropicalised Wellington Mark IIIs, along with all crews and ground crews of No 150 Squadron, had moved out to Blida in North Africa. The home echelon remained at Kirmington and flew two operations, then, on January 27 1943, the home echelons of Nos 150 (B) and 142 (B) Squadrons merged to form No 166 (B) Squadron (code letters 'AS'). This was an old squadron that had first formed in 1918 and had now re-formed as a bomber squadron. The squadron badge was a bulldog affrontée and was very Churchillian. The unit remained at Kirmington throughout the remainder of the war, its first bombing mission being on January 29/30 1943 when 12 Wellingtons were despatched to bomb Lorient. Flying Wellingtons and then Lancaster Marks I and III, the squadron participated in many major raids including the fateful Nuremberg raid of March 30/31 1944 when the station despatched 20 bombers and lost four. The last mission of the war was on April 25 1945 when 24 of the 33 squadron Lancasters bombed the SS barracks at Berchtesgaden. The squadron disbanded on November 18 1945.

During its operational life at Kirmington No 166 Squadron dropped 27,287 tons of bombs. The squadron had also seen the re-birth of a night fighter squadron as a bomber squadron for, on October 7 1944, No 153 Squadron re-formed from a nucleus of 27 aircrews from No 166 (B) Squadron. Equipped with Lancasters (code letters 'P4'), the unit made its first bombing mission on the night it re-formed when 11 Lancasters bombed Emmerich. A week later the squadron moved to Scampton.

Kirmington closed in December 1945 and the station was put on a C & M basis on February 8 1946. However, over the next few years the runways were kept in service to provide diversion facilities for Binbrook. During the late 1940s several Ministry Disposal Sales were held on the airfield and in 1953 the whole site was transferred to the Ministry of Agriculture, Fisheries and Food. The land now returned to farming and the A18(T) crossed part of Runway No 1. Runway No 3 was in two parts, 540 NW and 810 SE.

By the early 1960s the excellent runways were beginning to deteriorate but the airfield was being used by various crop spraying and other light aircraft. Then, in 1966, it was decided that Kirmington was the best site for the proposed Regional Airport. Services started from Kirmington about 1967 when a firm called Air Links Chauffeurs started to use part of the disused runway with a Cessna 172, and in February 1968 they became Humber Airways Ltd. After a Piper Aztec and Aztec C, two Islanders, G-AXRM and G-AXRN joined the Kirmington scene. In 1970 Lindsey County Council bought the ex-wartime bomber base for some £85,000 with the intention of developing it into an airport. The estimated expenditure for developing the airport facilities in order for the airfield to be licenced was £160,000. The first job was to resurface the main 1,600-yard runway and then work started on the terminal site. The airport opened in March 1974, a few days before local government changed the county boundaries and by so doing removed Kirmington from Lincolnshire into the new county of South Humberside from which it then took its name and became known as Humberside Airport.

Today it is a growing airport and Eastern Airways and Lease Air both operate out of Kirmington with a fleet of aircraft which includes an HS 125 jet, two Chieftains, five Aztecs and, not out of place on the tarmac, even in the 1980s, three DC-3 Dakotas, G-AMRA, G-AMYY and G-AMPO. There is also a resident flying club and it is heartening to see the old wartime bomber base keeping its past alive.

Below left *Plaque in St Helen church in Kirmington village.* **Below right** *The apron Marshal directs in a RAF Hercules to its parking position at Humberside Airport in June 1980.*

Kirton-in-Lindsey, Lincolnshire

*112/SK945972. N of Lincoln W of the
A15 road*

Another Cliff site, just west of Ermine
Street, Kirton-in-Lindsey was first used as
a landing ground in World War 1 when
'B' Flight of No 33 Squadron moved here
in December 1916. This was a Home
Defence squadron whose HQ was at
Gainsborough until June 1918 when it too
moved to Kirton-in-Lindsey. This unit re-
equipped with Bristol Fighters and Avro
504 night fighters and remained here until
it disbanded in June 1919. The airfield
quickly returned to agriculture.

During the Royal Air Force Expansion
period in the mid-1930s the site was
surveyed and found to be suitable for
development into a fighter airfield. The
site was just south of the village of Kirton-
in-Lindsey and was contained within three
roads. To the west the B1398, the B1205
forming the southern boundary and the
B1400 defining the northern and eastern
boundaries. The airfield buildings were
sited to the north where the two roads join
and three 'C1' seven-bay hangars were
erected in an arc in this area, together with
the brick-built accommodation, some of
which was on the opposite side of the
B1400 road.

Kirton-in-Lindsey opened in May 1940
as a fighter station with a decoy airfield at
Cadney, approximately six miles to the
north-east. The role of the station was to
give fighter cover to the northern sector,
fly convoy patrols off the east coast,
support Circus operations and provide for
battle-weary squadrons to rest up and re-

group. The Kirton-in-Lindsey squadrons
were to play an important part in the air
fighting over the English Channel and
France. The first three squadrons to arrive
in May were Nos 222 and 65 with Spitfires
and 253 with Hurricanes. These only
remained a few weeks and by July all the
units had departed only to be replaced in
August by Nos 264 with Defiants and 74
with Spitfires. The turn around was fast
and furious and as 74 Squadron departed
in the early part of September, No 307
(Polish) Squadron with Defiant night
fighters and 616 Squadron with Spitfires
took its place. No 264 departed for
Rochford in October.

On October 23 No 85 Squadron arrived
with their Hurricanes but the following
month they departed along with 307
Squadron. On November 23 No 255
Squadron was formed here with Defiants
to join the resident squadron and No 71,
the first American Eagle Squadron which
had just arrived with Hurricane IIas.
America was still officially neutral, but
these brave men had volunteered to join
the Royal Air Force and had formed No
71 (Eagle) Squadron at Church Fenton.
The Eagle squadrons were made up of all-
American pilots and by the time America
had entered the war, three such
squadrons, namely Nos 71, 121 and 133,
had been formed and served with the RAF
before being transferred on September 29
1942 to the USAAF's VIIIth Air Force as
the 4th Fighter Group at Debden where
they became Nos 334, 335 and 336 Fighter
Squadrons respectively.

The station now housed three squadrons but only for a short period as, early

*A Boulton Paul Defiant of No 264 Squadron that was at Kirton from July until October
1940 when the unit then moved to Rochford.*

in the New Year, No 616 departed. However, the station was again brought back to three-squadron strength with the arrival of No 65 in February 1941, flying Spitfires.

Within the planned expansion of Fighter Command three RAAF squadrons were formed during 1941. The first, and what was to become the most distinguished, was formed here on April 8 1941; No 452, with an establishment of 12 + 4 Spitfire Mark Is. The following day No 71 Squadron left and the Australians settled down to the tasks ahead of them. By May 10, 20 newly trained RAAF pilots had arrived straight from OTUs and a vigorous training programme got under way. The Commanding Officer, Squadron Leader Dutton, and the two Flight Commanders, Flight Lieutenants Douglas and Finucane (the latter killed in action on July 15 1942), were all RAF. No 452 became operational on May 22 1941 and began operational patrols. By the end of the month the squadron had re-equipped with Spitfire Mark IIas and the Defiants of 255 Squadron had moved to

the newly opened airfield at Hibaldstow, which Kirton-in-Lindsey had taken on as a satellite. The second Eagle Squadron had also formed, No 121, equipped with Spitfires.

This left only day fighters here and minor routine patrols continued from the resident squadrons. To give an indication of the work load, during the period May 22 to July 11, No 452 carried out 189 operational patrols and from those early raw-recruit days, which now seemed a million years ago, they had been welded into an experienced fighter unit. On their last mission from here on July 11 the unit, along with No 65 Squadron, was part of a No 12 Group Wing on a Circus operation. Having refuelled at West Malling they crossed the French coast at 14.45 hours near Dunkirk. At 15.00 hours No 452 was approaching St Omer when they were attacked by eight Bf 109s. Finucane shot down one but the rest of the squadron split up and could not get into an attacking position. Meanwhile, Sergeant Roberts, who was out of formation, had been shot down. He walked into Calais where he

Above *Tiger Moths at Kirton-in-Lindsey, July 1952.* **Below** *Kirton-in-Lindsey as at June 1980. The airfield deserted, the control tower empty.*

received help from the Underground movement only later to be caught by the French police and handed over to the Germans. However, he escaped and again contacted the French Resistance. Taken over the Pyrenees into Spain, then Gibraltar, he was back in England by October.

With the bit between their teeth, No 452 Squadron wanted action and on July 21 they were transferred to Kenley in No 11 Group, where they would be in constant action. This unit was replaced by No 136 Squadron which formed here with Hurricanes on August 20. This was to be the squadron's only British base for in November it moved to the Far East where it remained until it disbanded. The previous month had seen No 65 Squadron depart and the return of No 616 Squadron. To bring 1941 to a close, No 121 Squadron, having re-equipped with Spitfires, moved to North Weald and was replaced by the Spitfires of the third Eagle Squadron, No 133.

On January 30 1942, No 616 Squadron departed to King's Cliffe and on March 3 was replaced by No 486 (RNZAF) Squadron, equipped with Hurricane IIbs, and this unit was to herald a year of many different nationalities at Kirton-in-Lindsey. No 486 Squadron departed in April, followed on May 3 by No 133 Squadron. The new arrivals in May were two Spitfire squadrons, No 306 (Polish) and No 457 (RAAF). In June No 306 Squadron departed only to be replaced immediately by another Polish unit, No 303 Squadron, also with Spitfires.

At this period of the war it did appear that Australia might be invaded and to help with the air defences of her country, No 457 Squadron left Kirton for Australia on June 21 and was joined on the journey home by No 452 (RAAF) Squadron. Meanwhile, the Americans had arrived on the tenth of the month in order to gain operational experience. The unit was the 94th Squadron of the 1st Fighter Group, USAAF, equipped with P-38 Lightnings. This unit remained until August 24 1942 and was replaced the following month by No 43 Squadron, equipped with Hurricane IIcs. This was a famous pre-war unit, 'The Fighting Cocks', and was only at Kirton to re-group before departing in November for Gibraltar, from where it took part in the North Africa landings.

On October 9 another American unit, the 91st Squadron of the 81st Fighter Group, had arrived with P-39s. This unit pulled out just before the end of 1942 to leave No 303 Squadron in sole charge. No 303 Squadron departed in February 1943 and was replaced by Nos 317 and 302 Squadrons, both equipped with Spitfire Mark Vb aircraft. By now the writing was on the wall and there was little need for a fighter station in this area so, in April 1943, the two resident Polish squadrons, Nos 302 and 317, left and brought to an end the fighter era of the station. The station's role now changed to the training of fighter pilots and on May 9 No 53 OTU arrived from Llandow with a full complement of Spitfires plus a few Masters. The station now took on Hibaldstow as a satellite and its status at June 6 1944 was 53 OTU of No 9 Group. No 53 OTU remained the resident unit and flew training sorties from both airfields until it disbanded in May 1945.

In May 1946, No 7 SFTS moved in with their Oxfords from Sutton Bridge when that airfield closed, but it had moved out of the frying pan into the fire for the axe was about to fall on Kirton's restricted, grass-surfaced airfield. However, it did manage to linger on for a few years after the School moved to Cottesmore during the spring of 1948.

The next few years were to see non-flying units, the Central Synthetic Training Establishment and Aircrew Transit Unit, 1948 to 1949, followed by the Aircrew Educational School, 1949-1950 and the Link Transit School, 1950 to 1952.

In 1952, No 2 ITS equipped with Tiger Moths moved in and in 1954 this unit became No 1 ITS with the role of very basic training for aircrew officers. This unit moved out in 1957 when the airfield closed to flying and was put on C & M. The airfield re-opened in 1960 to house a Gliding School and No 7 School of Technical Training. Then, in December 1965, the station was finally vacated by the Royal Air Force and transferred to the Army, housing the Royal Artillery.

The airfield is still used as a gliding centre for a civilian club and Army Air Corps helicopters are seen to use it from time to time. The hangars and tower that lie at the northern end of the airfield are very close to Kirton-in-Lindsey village and all this area is now enclosed by a tall wire fence for these, and the adjacent living quarters, are occupied by No 16 Air Defence Squadron of the Royal Artillery and are now named Rapier Barracks.

Above *Aerial view of Langar, circa early 1950s.* **Below** *Lancastrian Mark 4 VH742 fitted with Rolls-Royce Nenes. It was delivered to Langar on August 8 1945 and moved to Hucknall in October 1946.*

Langar (Harby), Nottinghamshire

129/SK740335. 15 miles SE of Nottingham, SE of Bingham on the A52 road

Sited between the villages of Langar, after which it was named, and Harby, the one it was most known by. Work started in early 1940 on the bomber station that was built to the usual design of the period and had the normal three runways with the main one almost on a north-east axis.

The airfield opened in No 5 Group, Bomber Command, and was first used as a satellite for Bottesford. A.V. Roe workshops on the west side of the airfield opened during September 1942 and they carried out major repairs and reconditioning on Lancasters during the war years. Langar was to see very little operational life and the only operational squadron to use the station was No 207 that arrived in September 1942 from Bottesford. Equipped with Lancasters, the unit took part in many major raids. On October 17

1942 the squadron despatched 14 Lancasters for the famour low-level raid on the vast French Schneider works situated at Le Creusot, near the Swiss border. With all the bomber force under 1,000 ft, they crossed the English Coast at Land's End, then flew south-westward over the Bay of Biscay before turning over the French coast for the 300-mile run to target. However, at this point one of 207's Lancasters had to turn back on three engines and was attacked by three Arado seaplanes, just off the coast near Brest. The Lancaster gunners put up a brave fight, shooting down two and damaging the third, which turned tail leaving the now crippled Lancaster to make its way home to Langar. The bomber reached base safely but the flight engineer had been killed during their fight with the Arados.

The squadron continued with its raids on enemy territory with targets as far afield as Italy and Poland. In May 1943 the

squadron lost their CO, Wing Commander T.A.B. Parselle, who failed to return from a raid on Dusseldorf.

During the summer of 1943 Langar, and approximately 20 other bomber-sized airfields in the Midlands and Eastern England, were used to store Airspeed Horsa gliders in preparation for the planned invasion of Europe. These were now being produced in great quantity by the Ministry of Aircraft Production for the Allied Air Forces. During this build-up No 207 continued to operate, but it was obvious that Langar had been ear-marked for an American base and in October 1943 the squadron moved to Spilsby and the station was reduced to a C & M basis while the airfield was prepared for use by the American IXth Air Force Service Wing.

Langar was now Army Air Force Station 490 and the American Service Units began to arrive on October 18 1943. By the end of the month 10 Service Group and the 27th Mobile Repair and Reclamation Squadron had arrived. The 435th TCG arrived during November with their C-47 transport aircraft but little was achieved and they moved out at the end of January 1944.

These were replaced by the 441st TCG equipped with C-47s and C-53s. This unit began a concentrated training programme of day and night formation flying which they maintained until departing to Merryfield on April 25 1944. During this period Langar was not opera-tional, its role being as a transport base and also as somewhere to build the

Canadair 'North Star', serial No 17511, of No 426 Squadron, RCAF, at Langar in September 1959.

American Waco Hadrian gliders from the parts supplied directly from the States. Over a short period of time several hundred were built and issued to the operational troop carrier groups of the IXth AF. By the middle of May their task was complete and the majority of the American units had departed.

It was planned to hand the station back to the Royal Air Force by the end of July 1944, but this was delayed and the reason became obvious when, in September, Nos 99, 100, 301 and 302 Squadrons of the 441st TCG arrived back at Langar with 90 C-47s. From here they would fulfil their part in operation 'Market', the airborne element of 'Market Garden'.

On September 17 1944, two serials of 45 aircraft took off for Drop Zone 'T' just west of Nijmegen. The aircraft carried 1,922 American paratroopers, the 'Screaming Eagles'. After their drop the aircraft returned to their permanent base at Merryfield and Langar's brief opera-tional life was again at an end. The airfield was placed under C & M until No 1669 HCU arrived in early October. The role of this unit was to convert pilots to bomber aircraft. The unit used Halifaxes and Lancasters but by the end of March 1945 the unit disbanded and Langar was again put on to C & M. In May No 53 RU (P) was formed and moved the following month to a PDC. Part of the airfield was then handed over to the MAP. On December 18 1946 the airfield closed down completely.

For five years the airfield was left to decay then, in 1951, it was surveyed and found to be suitable as an air materiel base for the RCAF. Langar had a new lease of life and was to become RCAF Langar, part of Canada's contribution to

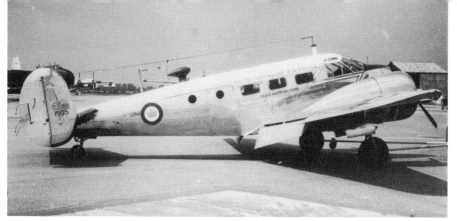

RCAF Beech UC-45, 1595, of 30AMB at Langar on July 7 1962.

NATO. Work began immediately on the airfield and No 30 Air Materiel Base moved in during October 1952. Three main sites were available and made ready, the technical site which comprised the aerodrome and the three runways, the main one 6,000 ft long and the two intersecting ones of 4,000 and 4,250 ft, the latter being used only for taxiing aircraft. There were also 44 buildings, 25 being new ones. The domestic site had 11 buildings while the PMQ site was situated at Radcliffe-on-Trent and comprised 41 houses. A further 200 married quarters were completed in January 1958 on a 27-acre site just off the main road in the village. To the locals it was known as 'Little Canada'.

Royal Canadian Air Force Langar came under No 1 Air Division HQ at Metz, Moselle, France, and was the only UK base. No 30 AMB was made up of Base HQ and four different sections, integrated to form an efficient unit. These were the 312th Supply Depot, that covered 7½ acres of warehousing and held 80,000 different items, needed to support the operations of the Air Division as well as F-86 Sabre spares for the air forces of Turkey and Greece and CF100 spares for the Belgian Air Force. An emergency demand made at 08.00 hours could be delivered the same afternoon.

This efficiency necessitated close liaison with the second section, 137 (Transport) Flight, equipped with five Bristol Freighters and one Beech C-45 passenger aircraft. The third section was the 314 Technical Services Unit which was responsible for getting repairable items to the UK and assisting in the supply of spares. The fourth section, 5 Movements Unit, co-ordinated all passengers and material both in and out of Langar. The other unit at Langar was the Langar Detachment of 426 Transport Squadron that serviced all visiting Dakota, North Star and Comet aircraft, but this did not come under the control of No 1 Air Division.

The Canadians were very much liked in the Nottinghamshire countryside and towns and became an integral part of the Nottinghamshire community. In 1960 a maple tree was planted in Granby, Nottinghamshire, presented by the people of Granby, Quebec. For 11 years the base throbbed with life, then, with a rundown of 30 AMB, closure was inevitable and in 1963 RCAF Langar, that had spread over 377 acres, closed down.

In September 1968 A.V. Roe also closed down and today Langar is just another disused airfield. Post-war years had seen Yorks, Lancastrians, Shackletons and Meteors pass through A.V. Roe's. However, there is hope for the airfield, which is owned by Roland Gale, who lives at Langar Lodge and who would like to see the airfield retained and put to use in the aviation field. At the moment the control tower is used by the British Parachute Schools and has received a coat of paint. The runways are in fair condition but mosses are covering much of them. There are still many derelict wartime buildings and installations on the west side of the airfield. A.V. Roe workshops to the west of the Harby/Langar road are now used as an industrial estate.

Langtoft, Lincolnshire

130/TF138113. S of Bourne, E of the A15 road

Sited to the south of Langtoft village but in fact nearer to the village of Market Deeping, the actual camp was built on North Fields, between Five Houses and Towngate. This was one of the two GCI radar stations constructed in Lincolnshire, opening early in the Second World War and closing in the 1950s.

Leadenham, Lincolnshire

121/SK960520. E of Newark-on-Trent

Sited to the east of the village of Leadenham, this was just a large grass field turned into an airfield and had only the basic facilities. It opened in September 1916 and housed 'C' Flight of No 38 Squadron, whose HQ was at Melton Mowbray. The unit flew FE2bs on Home Defence duties but, like the rest of the squadron, it never achieved anything. In May 1918 the unit was replaced by 'A' Flight of No 90 Squadron, flying Avro 504s, but in June 1919 it disbanded and the airfield closed. It was never reactivated and no trace can be found of it today. However, only a mile or so further north on the heath, Wellingore opened as an air-field during the Second World War.

Leicester (Braunstone), Leicestershire

See Braunstone

Leicester (Desford), Leicestershire

See Desford

Leicester East, Leicestershire

141/SK015660. E of Leicester between the A6 and A47 roads

One of Leicester's many airfields, it was a standard wartime airfield with the usual three concrete runways and encircling perimeter track off which were 'spectacle'-type hardstandings for 36 aircraft in 13 doubles and ten singles. The airfield also had four 'T2' hangars.

Leicester East opened on October 15 1943 and housed units of 38 Group. The first flying unit, No 196 Squadron, arrived on November 18 1943 from Witchford with Stirling Mark IIIs. The squadron was awaiting conversion to Stirling Mk IV glider-tugs, and after re-equipping moved to Tarrant Rushton on January 7 1944.

On November 23 1943 No 620 Squadron arrived from Chedburgh with their Stirling IIIs. Mk IV glider-tugs arrived during February 1944, being then used to drop supplies to the French Resistance for a few weeks before moving to Fairford on March 18 1944. They were soon followed by No 190 Squadron on March 25. This unit had re-formed at Leicester on January 5 1944 with an establishment of 16 Stirling IVs plus four in reserve and

became a glider tug unit with Horsa gliders.

On May 3 1944 No 107 (T) OTU was formed, their duties being to convert crews to C-47 Dakotas and glider-tug duties. For their training the unit also used the satellite airfield at Melton Mowbray. On March 26 1945 the OTU was redesignated No 1333 Transport Support Conversion Unit. The role of the unit still remained the same and on October 25 1945 it moved to Syerston.

This was the last RAF flying unit to be based at Leicester East and, with the departure of No 1333 TSCU, the station was placed on a care and maintenance basis but, on December 31 1947, this was withdrawn and the airfield was officially abandoned.

Today, it is still in use as a civilian airfield and Leicestershire Aero Club, on behalf of Leicestershire City Corporation, operates from here. In 1977 the wartime airfield was renamed Leicester Airport. The original control tower has been renovated and is in use along with the main runway, 28/10, which is 3,000 ft in length. A large Decca radar trials installa-tion now occupies the west side of the field.

Loughborough, Leicestershire

129/SK208548 (World War 1). E of Loughborough between old Great Central Railway line and River Soar. 129/SK525215 (World War 2). NW of Loughborough, N of the A6(T) road

Loughborough had two airfields and both were connected with Brush Coachworks Ltd. The one used in the First World War was known as Loughborough Meadows. It was a private field and was used exclu-sively by the Brush Electrical Engineering Company, to test-fly their aircraft. The grass field was used from October 1915 until April 1919 and during that period Brush built 87 Farman Longhorns, 350 Avro 504As, Js and Ks, one experimental Henri Farman Astral twin-engined bomber, 20 Short 827 seaplanes and 142 Short 184 seaplanes at their Lough-borough factory. All these aircraft, except, of course, the seaplanes, were test-flown from Loughborough Meadows. After the First World War the field fell into disuse and there is no record of it being used after that period.

During the Second World War the Loughborough factory was again involved in aircraft production. The airfield was

Above *Short 184 seaplane N9089 built by Brush in 1918. This is a late production machine, recognisable by the bomb beam below the fuselage, between the float struts and the Scarf ring for the observer in the rear cockpit.* **Below** *Construction shop of Brush Coachworks Ltd at Loughborough during World War 2—DH89A Dominie Is.* **Bottom** *Hampden repair shop of Brush Coachworks Ltd.*

now sited to the north-west of the town and was a grass field with a maximum length of just under 2,000 ft. It was used by Brush Coachworks Ltd to test-fly the DH 89 Dominie. In the three years from March 1943 to March 1946 they produced 335 aircraft. To test them, they were towed to the field, tail first, and the wings were then fitted on. It is interesting to note that this small factory was on the Luftwaffe list and by 1941 the Germans had detailed aerial photographs of Loughborough with Brush Electrical Ltd marked out in detail. After the war the airfield closed and it has now completely disappeared, the site being an industrial estate with one section being used by Riker Chemicals.

Ludford Magna, Lincolnshire

122/TF200880. S of the village

A sign above the door, a name on the wall of the few remaining buildings, this is all that is left of the people who lived here. Today, the wheat is returning to this English field, but it was a very different story in 1943.

Ludford Magna opened in June of that year with the roar of Lancaster engines as No 101 Squadron flew in, and it was to be their home for the rest of the war years. Situated in the rolling Wolds countryside, the airfield was constructed early in 1943 by contractor George Wimpy. It was completed in 90 days and the runways were built on Magna and the dispersed sites on Parva, adjacent to the village after which it was named.

It was a standard heavy bomber station with three concrete runways, the main one being 5,850 ft and the intersecting ones 3,600 and 4,290 ft with the usual encircling perimeter track and hardstandings. It was a bleak setting, but even the cold winds blowing across the Wolds, and the heavy rains, could not dampen the spirits of the crews or groundstaff. The rains did, however, earn the airfield the nickname of 'Mudford' Magna.

Soon after their arrival at Ludford Magna a fresh task fell to the squadron when it was chosen to carry special equipment to confuse enemy R/T frequencies. The special duties seemed appropriate to their squadron motto 'Mens Agitat Molem' (Mind over Matter).

Known by the code name 'Airborne Cigar', or ABC for short, it was first used on October 7/8 1943 and the special

Aerial view of Ludford Magna taken in March 1980. All runways are gone but still clearly visible. Ludford village is at the top of the photograph. Three Thor sites are in the middle.

Photograph of 'Y'-Yeoman and crew after they had just arrived at Ludford Magna. They went missing on June 25/26 1943. From left to right George Hay (Pilot), Bill Bush (Engineer), Jock MacLeay (Navigator), Ian Hill (Mid-Upper Gunner), Yorky Millns (Rear Gunner), Keith Smith (Bomb Aimer) and Bert Scott (Wireless Operator).

Lancasters with their two large dorsal masts carried an eighth crew member and extra VHF equipment. To compensate for the additional equipment the bomb load was reduced by 1,000 lb. The Special Duty Operator, as he was known, was specially trained and German-speaking, and all were volunteers from various aircrew trades.

No 101 Squadron carried out the radio counter-measures from their Ludford Magna base, and their task was so important that ABC aircraft flew on every major raid from October 1943 to April 1945. Their Radio Counter-Measures (RCM) role was top secret and even today little more can be revealed about them for the information is still classified. Also, because of the nature of its work with ABC aircraft, Ludford Magna was one of the 15 stations that was equipped with FIDO.

Not all the squadron Lancasters were equipped with ABC. However, the ones that were ABC-equipped carried out their duties on top of their normal bombing. Their targets were those of the Main Force of Back-up Crews, facing the same enemy and sharing the same risks. In fact, greater than average risks for, when the ABC aircraft operated their special equipment at night over enemy territory, the German ground stations were able to vector their night fighters on to the 'jamming signal' they were transmitting. Thus, ABC aircraft were more vulnerable than the other aircraft in the bomber stream. This was made very clear on the night of the fateful Nuremberg raid of March 30/31 1944. 101 Squadron put up the largest squadron effort with 26 ABC Lancasters. Seven aircraft and 56 men failed to return to Ludford—almost one-third of the squadron.

On August 17 1943 the squadron took part in the famous attack on the German experimental station at Peenemünde. They also made attacks on railway communications and airfields in the preparations for assault on North-West Europe. Also, they played an important part in Operation 'Overlord' and, on the night of June 5/6 1944, 21 ABC Lancasters rolled down the runway on a mission solely to use their 'Spec. Op' to jam enemy W/T and so prevent night fighters being directed against the airborne invasion forces.

In the early weeks of 1945 there was heavy snow on the Wolds and crews had the pleasure of clearing the runways during the day before their night mission. Sergeant van Geffen was a Special Duty Operator with No 101 Squadron and he wrote in his diary at the time:

'2nd February 1945—Target Wiesbaden —aircraft H—How, DV302—Mission Abortive. Navigator reported 'GEE' u/s over base immediately after take-off. Checked 'ABC' equipment which was also u/s. Proceeded out over North Sea and jettisoned bombs before returning to base. Four other aircraft from 101 Squadron failed to take-off, two were bogged down, another unable to pass them and the fourth had magneto trouble

Above *Ludford Magna in June 1980. The barber's shop and WAAF hairdresser can still be seen above the door of this Nissen hut.* **Below** *The gym at Ludford Magna in June 1980. Today it is used for farm storage but is still referred to as the gym.*

—From the previous night's raid on Ludwigshafen, three 101 aircraft failed to return—included in the crews were Frank Smith who came up with me, Pilot Officers Kenny and Fenske and Flight Lieutenant Harrison. Breach of security was responsible for our losses.'

On March 3 1945 night intruders shot up the airfield and village with no opposition. Then, gloom really settled over the station on March 23 1945 for Lancaster III DV245 'S' Sugar, or 'The Saint' as it was better known, failed to return from a daylight raid against Bremen while on its 119th sortie.

On April 25 1945 came the last of No 101's bombing missions during World War 2 when 24 Lancasters attacked Berchtesgaden. From October 1943 to April 1945, 101 squadron had flown 2,477 sorties from Ludford Magna in support of the main bomber force.

During October the squadron moved to Binbrook and in the latter part of 1945 the station closed down and was put on a C & M basis. During the late 1940s and early 1950s the hangars were used for storage,

particularly in the case of the 'Ground Nut Scheme'.

Then Ludford Magna was re-activated and in July 1959 No 104 Squadron was formed with the American Thor ICBM, three missile pads being built in the middle of the runways. However, the Thor forces did not last very long for by early 1963 it was evident that Thor was vulnerable to air attack. In May 1963 the unit disbanded and that same month Ludford Magna closed down.

During the early part of the 1970s the runways were removed and the hard core used in building sites, some even being used in the construction of the Humber Bridge. Over the years the hangars have disappeared and apart from the missile bunkers and the perimeter track the airfield has reverted to agricultural use. On the Parva site some of the huts are still standing, these being Maycrete huts of varying sizes, one or two having a new lease of life and being used for local business firms and the local farmer. Dominating the skyline is the water tower, a piece of furniture from wartime days

Above *Bombing Leaders' Course at Manby, June 1943.* **Below** *Valetta C1, VW825, at Manby on August 14 1960.*

which stands to remind the sleepy village that it was once a hive of activity.

On Sunday July 16 1978 the village returned to that wartime spirit when a memorial to airmen who never returned from bombing raids was unveiled at the side of the main road in the centre of the village. A Book of Remembrance to the fallen aircrews is kept in the village church. Ex-airmen travelled from far afield, even Canada, to relive those war years spent at Ludford Magna.

Manby, Lincolnshire

113/TF385866. E of Louth adjacent to the B1200 road

This was another of the sites surveyed during the mid-1930s and found suitable for development into an armament training station. Construction work started in 1936 and during this period a steel framework, 50 ft high and 500 yards long, was erected across the landing area and covered with metal sheeting to create a screen to act as a wind-break. The object of this device was to enable aircraft to make cross-wind landings and after it had

been completed in April 1937 the theory was tested by a 63 Squadron Battle, a 10 Squadron Whitley and a 114 Squadron Blenheim.

With the strong off-shore winds along the east coast the aircraft had plenty of chance to put the theory into practice, making many landings throughout August and September, and proved that the screen was feasible. Further trials were then carried out by a Harrow of 215 Squadron during October and a Wallace from North Coates in January 1938. However, by February it was not practicable to continue here, as Manby was now nearing completion, so the screen was dismantled and moved down to Rollestone Camp in Wiltshire where the experiments continued. However, none of the RAF Commands were able to find use for the screen and the project was eventually abandoned.

Manby, situated on the south side of the B1200, was equipped with substantial brick-built accommodation, typical of the Expansion period and neatly grouped on the eastern side of the airfield behind the hangars. These were unusual as they

Top *Manby water tower photographed in June 1980.* **Above** *Manby as at June 1980, the substantial brick-built accommodation, now empty.*

comprised three 'C' type (Hipped) seven-bay hangars and two aircraft repair sheds, a unique combination.

The airfield opened in August 1938 in No 25 Group, Flying Training Command, RAF, as No 1 Air Armament School, and was undoubtedly the home of the Royal Air Force armament training the day war was declared. The station had by now taken over the bombing and gunnery range at Theddlethorpe and had started courses for armament officers, bomb aimers, air gunners and armourers with a variety of aircraft including Battles, Wallaces, Hinds and Wellingtons. Manby was also considered important enough to have a decoy airfield at Mablethorpe from the outset of war.

The station was extremely busy from the beginning and the intake increased each month. Because the Manby circuit was getting congested the small airfield at

Caistor was taken over as a Relief Landing Ground from December 1942. Many new training techniques were developed here and in July 1944 the school was renamed Empire Central Armament School which remained as such until November 1944 when it was then renamed Empire Air Armament School. The training was kept to a very high standard, the main courses being— Advanced Armament, Specialist Armament, Air Bombing Instructors' and Bombing Leaders' courses.

The school was now equipped with Wellington, Martinet and Hurricane aircraft. The station had also seen changes and Manby now had two paved runways. These were intersecting, the main one being 1,448 yards and the other 1,232 yards long. Both were of the standard 50-yard width and had a tarmac surface.

Post-war, Manby was retained as a

permanent station and continued training, but in a more sophisticated atmosphere. July 1949 saw many changes. During the middle of the month, the former wartime bomber airfield at Strubby, a few miles south-east of Manby, was brought up to standard and re-opened as a satellite landing ground, its runways being much longer than those of the parent station. Then, on the 31st of the month, the RAF Flying College formed, taking over the previous school and being equipped with Valetta, Meteor and Canberra aircraft.

Over the years the college became well established and, in 1958, No 4 Squadron was formed with Jet Provosts of the Refresher Flight while in July 1962 a further change in name resulted in the College of Air Warfare. During this period the school had become a separate unit and in 1964 their Varsity aircraft were replaced by Jet Provosts. The respective roles were for the college to deal with electronic warfare while the school retrained aircrew.

During the mid-1960s, Airwork Services Ltd took over many of the airmen's duties. In 1965 the last Meteor was withdrawn and the following year the last Canberra.

During the early 1970s there were many rumours and, in September 1972, Strubby was closed down. Then, in January 1974 after several false alarms, the College of Air Warfare, the main resident unit, moved to Cranwell. The School of Refresher Flying moved to Leeming in Yorkshire and Manby finally closed on April 1 1974, a victim of the defence cuts. The closure of the station caused great hardship in an area that had become dependent on the RAF stations for their way of life. The situation had been made more difficult with the increase of the civilian work force over the previous two decades.

In the years that followed the five hangars were converted into grain stores and much of the main site, including the Station HQ, SSQ, Guard Room and the Post Office, was sold to East Lindsey District Council for £100,000 and they now have their main offices in Tedder Hall. The rest of the station is empty, and although the original tower on the main site is still intact, the new one built in the 1960s has been vandalised. The final chapter was written in July 1980 when the former air base was sold to Mr Paul Toynton for £415,000.

Air gunners under training at Manby in 1943. Clay pigeon shooting from a power turret.

Market Harborough,
Leicestershire

141/SP710890. Approximately 1 mile NW of Market Harborough, W of the A6 road

The airfield lies immediately outside of Market Harborough, near the village of Foxton, after which it was known locally. Construction work started in 1942 on a standard airfield with the usual paved runways and dispersed accommodation.

The airfield opened in No 92 Group on May 1 1943 but the first resident unit did not arrive until August 1. This was No 14 OTU from Cottesmore, now flying Wellington, Ansons and Oxfords. A satellite was established at Husbands Bosworth, which had been intended as a satellite for Bruntingthorpe but now came under the control of Market Harborough.

This was retained until June 15 1944 when that part of 14 OTU based there formed into a new unit, No 85 OTU, with an establishment of Wellington aircraft. The parent unit now became a '¾' OTU but continued to provide operationally trained aircrew. This was done with a further resident unit, No 1683 Bomber Defence Training Flight, which had been housed here since August 1943, and operated obsolete Hurricane fighters which they used to provide simulated attack experience for the bomber crews.

No 1683 BDTF moved out during the autumn of 1944 but No 14 OTU remained here until after the war and disbanded on June 24 1945. The airfield then closed to flying and was later taken over by Maintenance Command to re-open in February 1946 as No 113 Sub-Storage Depot, parented by No 273 MU, Polebrook. The main task of the unit was to dismantle Airspeed Horsa gliders. During this wrecking period part of the airfield was used for a time by Miles Aircraft Ltd for storing Queen Martinets and Monitors. This continued for just over a year, after which the Sub-Storage unit began to depart and on April 27 1947 all remaining personnel were withdrawn, the 62 Horsa gliders still on the airfield being taken over by No 6 MU, Brize Norton, and the station was closed down.

After the site had been vacated by the Royal Air Force the airfield facilities were dismantled and it was converted into a prison. However, to the west of the A6(T) road one or two general purpose huts pertaining to its wartime history can still be found.

Market Stainton, Lincolnshire

122/TF230802. S of the A157 road between the villages of Benniworth and Market Stainton

Market Stainton was established as No 233 MU and opened in January 1943 as a bomb dump for the airfields in the eastern part of Lincolnshire.

The camp did not get underway until the spring and LAC Jones VR of Valley, Anglesey, was one of a hundred men posted to RAF Market Stainton to start the bomb dump. When they arrived there were only one or two billets. The bombs were dispersed along the roadsides and covered many miles of grass verges. About a dozen lorries were used to carry the bombs in from the railway and about a two mile stretch of one road was closed-

off, with gates at each end for stacking the gas bombs. These were very dangerous and guarded day and night in case of any leakage. They were four gallon drums of different gases. Over 250 airmen manned the unit and the first Tallboys arrived in April 1944. Bombs arrived by both road and rail. The site closed in 1948.

Melton Mowbray, Leicestershire

129/SK750155. Just S of Melton Mowbray on the B6047 road

Sited between the southern outskirts of Melton Mowbray and the village of Great Dalby, work started on constructing an airfield here in mid-1942. For this purpose the B6047 road was closed for it passed right through the centre of the airfield and today it is part of it. It was a hilltop site built a short distance from an airfield in use during World War 1 which housed No 38 Squadron's HQ with 'A', 'B' and 'C' Flights at Stamford, Buckminster and Leadenham respectively. The squadron's role was Home Defence duties around the Midlands. However, the new airfield was not built on this World War 1 site.

It was built to the standard pattern with three standard 50-yard-wide concrete runways, the main being 5,400 ft and the two intersecting runways 4,350 and 4,020 ft long with an encircling perimeter track around which were 15 'spectacle' loop concrete hardstandings and four 'T2' hangars.

It was built originally as a station for Maintenance Command but, by the time it opened on August 1 1943, control had been taken over by No 44 Group of Transport Command and the first unit to arrive was No 4 Overseas Aircraft Preparation Unit which handled many types of aircraft—Spitfires, Mosquitoes, Corsairs, Vengeances, Hellcats and even Halifaxes.

In October 1943 the station took on another role with the arrival of two Ferry Training Units, No 306 FTU from Long Kesh, equipped with Beaufighters and Beauforts, and No 307 FTU from Finmere with Bostons. Many changes took place in January 1944: on the 13th, No 304 FTU arrived with Beauforts, Beaufighters, Bostons and Wellingtons and by the end of the month had taken over the other two units in an amalgamation.

The status as at June 6 1944 was No 304 FTU and No 4 Overseas Aircraft Preparation Unit, both flying various aircraft and

Nissen hut of the former SSQ site at Melton Mowbray. The brick chimney is a post-war addition.

still within 44 Group. However, on November 25 1944 both these units disbanded but No 12 Ferry Unit then formed and was equipped with one Proctor, two Oxfords, two Bostons, three Beaufighters, two Ansons and two Wellingtons. The unit had the role of ferrying aircraft from Melton to overseas units.

With the closure of the APU the station was able to accept from November 1944 part of a training unit, No 107 OTU, from its parent station at Leicester East. This unit was equipped with Dakota and Halifax aircraft, plus a fleet of Horsa and Hadrian gliders. The unit was engaged in the training of Transport Command crews, chiefly in the art of glider towing and troop carrying. The link with Melton Mowbray is carried further in the fact that Boulton & Paul Ltd had an assembly plant on King Street where Horsa gliders were erected.

During September and October two Heavy Freight Flights, Nos 1588 and 1589, were formed. Both units were equipped with Stirling Mark Vs and departed overseas in mid-October. November 1945 saw No 107 OTU, now retitled 1333 (T) SCU since the previous March, depart from Melton Mowbray and that same month No 12 Ferry Unit disbanded, leaving the station with no resident flying units.

The airfield then closed and was reduced to care and maintenance. For many years it was left to decay then, in 1958, it was selected as a satellite for

North Luffenham and a Thor missile site was constructed in the middle of the former airfield. The Royal Air Force returned with No 254 Squadron, but their stay was shortlived and the station closed again in August 1963 and was finally vacated by the Royal Air Force in 1964.

Most of the facilities were dismantled including the hangars, but the control tower survived in a derelict condition until about 1970 when it was then demolished. The runways have been shortened and the main one now forms the B6047 road. A former domestic site to the east is still in use as an industrial complex and the former sick quarter site near the cross-roads is also in use by a private company. Several other buildings still stand, albeit in a dilapidated condition, to the north and east of the airfield. Leicestershire County Council has a highway maintenance depot on the wartime airfield.

Metheringham, Lincolnshire
121/TF105610. SE of Lincoln between the B1189 and B1191 roads

One of the many Lincolnshire airfields constructed for No 5 Group, Bomber Command, Metheringham was unusual because it was situated in the Lincolnshire Fens and this type of ground was considered to be too unstable to take the weight of concrete runways under a heavy work-load.

However, work began during the winter of 1942/1943 and by October yet another bomber station was ready for action. It was built to Class 'A' specifications with three concrete runways, the main being lined almost north-south. The main and the usual two subsidiary runways were all

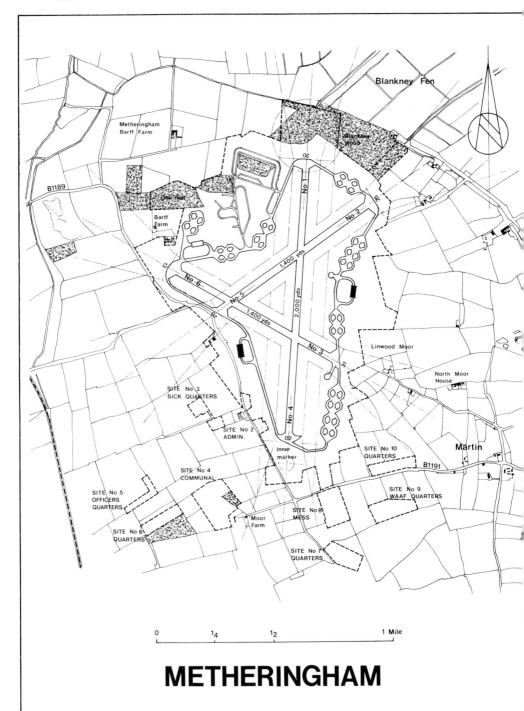

METHERINGHAM

Above left *Water tower at Metheringham which still remains today.* **Above right** *Metheringham—the few remaining huts are just ruins but above the door 'Armament Orderly Room' was still just visible when photographed in June 1980.*

linked by a perimeter track on the western side of which was the control tower. The airfield was bounded to the north and east by Car Dyke, an old Roman Canal. The northern end was wooded with Fox Covert and Blankney Wood and use was made of this natural cover. Martin was the nearest village but for some reason the airfield was named Metheringham after the much larger village two or three miles to the west.

The airfield opened in October 1943 and the following month the Lancasters of No 106 Squadron arrived from Syerston. This squadron was to be the resident unit and will be the one always to be associated with Metheringham. It had re-formed as a bomber squadron in June 1938 at Abingdon, Oxon, and was then equipped with Hawker Hinds. It had come a long way since those early days and had now graduated to the four-engined Lancasters. With these bombers the squadron carried on the war from Metheringham and bombed many targets, among which were the coastal gun battery at St Pierre du Mont and the V-1 storage sites.

On April 26/27 1944 No 106 Squadron took part in a raid against Schweinfurt.

As Lancaster ME669 'O' Orange was leaving the target area it was attacked and hit by a night fighter. A fire broke out on the starboard wing and between the fuselage. Also, the inner engine burst into flames. Sergeant Jackson, the flight engineer, opened the escape hatch and climbed out along the top of the fuselage to the starboard wing with a hand fire-extinguisher. As he climbed out his parachute opened and spilled into the cockpit. Undeterred, he carried on while the front crew members gathered it together and let out the rigging lines. But Sergeant Jackson slipped and while he hung on to an air-intake on the leading edge of the wing his face and hands were severely burnt.

He fell, dragging his parachute behind him, which had caught fire in a number of places. He landed very heavily and sustained a broken ankle. However, he was alive but in a pitiful state, and crawled to the nearest village where he was taken prisoner. He withstood the intense pain and spent ten months in hospital. For his action he was awarded the Victoria Cross for conspicuous bravery. This amazing story did not come out until after the war for, despite Sergeant Jackson's outstanding efforts, the aircraft crashed. Flying Officer Mifflin, the pilot, and Johnson both died in the aircraft while the other crew members, Toft, Higgins, Sandelands and Smith, parachuted out and were taken Prisoner of War.

No 106 Squadron remained at Metheringham until February 18 1946 when it then disbanded. It had won a total of 267 decorations including the Victoria Cross and had lost 187 aircraft, three of these on the fateful Nuremberg raid out of 17 despatched. Its last mission of the war was on April 25/26 1945 when 14 Lancasters were despatched to bomb the Vallo oil refinery.

During 1945 there were two other Lancaster squadrons here. On June 15 No 467 arrived and began training for Far East operations but was soon declared redundant and disbanded on September 30 1945. The other was No 189 Squadron which arrived during October just 12 months after it had formed, only to be disbanded on November 20 1945.

After No 106 Squadron had disbanded on February 18 1946 the station closed to flying and was vacated by the Royal Air Force shortly afterwards. Today, the hangars have gone and only a ruin marks the position of a once-busy operational tower. One runway and all of the eastern section of the perimeter track have been converted into public roads. Very little remains of this busy wartime bomber airfield. But, pausing on the perimeter track on a summer's evening, it is not hard to imagine them as they taxi out from their dispersal and, with a gentle breeze in the long summer grass one might even seem to hear that familiar roar of Merlin engines.

Netherthorpe in 1979.

Netherthorpe, South Yorkshire

111/SK538804. W of Worksop between Shireoaks and Thorpe Salvin

Situated a few miles to the west of Worksop just south of the A57 road, this was an airfield of little significance during the Second World War.

The site was first licenced as an airfield on April 12 1935 and was then used by Sheffield Aero Club. During December 1938, M & H Mining Contractors took over control of the airfield and except for the war years, when the airfield was only used for a few months in 1940 by the Lysanders of No 613 Squadron, an Army Co-Operation unit, and in 1945 by No 24 Glider School for a few months, the airfield remained in their hands until October 1951.

The airfield, with its two small grass runways only 480 and 417 yards long, was then taken over by the Netherthorpe Flying Club, using a Miles Messenger and an Aiglet Trainer in 1961. Today, the airfield is still in use for club flying.

Newton, Nottinghamshire

129/SK680415. 7 miles E of Nottingham between the A52 and A6097 roads and E of the A46(T)

It is ironic that the only RAF airfield in Nottinghamshire still in use today should be one with grass runways, but that is the case and Newton is the airfield.

Newton does have a long association with flying, an airfield first being established here in 1936 and becoming operational in July 1940 in No 1 Group. Group Captain G.Y. Tyrrell was the Station Commander and the first operational sorties were flown by Fairey Battles of Nos 103 and 150 Squadrons commanded by Wing Commanders T.C. Dickens and

Above *A Dakota of No 12 Group Communications Flight at RAF Newton in 1951. This aircraft was the Allied work-horse of World War 2.* **Below** *Bulldogs operating from Newton, March 22 1979.* **Bottom** *Police Dog Training Flight on exercise at Newton in June 1978.*

Aerial view of RAF Newton with a clear view of the five 'C' type hangars and control tower at the top and the 'H' blocks and brick water tower on the left of the photograph. Taken by the RAF on April 6 1978.

Hesketh, DFC, respectively. During October 1940 the squadrons were re-equipped with Wellingtons which were used against targets in Germany and against the *Gneisenau* in Brest harbour.

In July 1941, the station was transferred from Bomber to Flying Training Command, and No 16 (Polish) SFTS, with Group Captain J.L. Kepinski as Commanding Officer, moved from Hucknall that same month. The Poles were to set up a lasting tie with the station. So strong was the connection with the Free Polish Forces that the station's crest today incorporates the Polish Eagle. Of the Polish airmen trained at Newton, 42 had won British decorations by the end of the war. During their training they used a variety of aircraft including Battles, Oxfords, DH 60 Moths, Moth Minors and Master IIIs.

In November 1942 DH 82 Moths arrived at the station and in April 1943, Magister Is and Avro Ansons came into service with the school. During this period the station commander was Group Captain E.B. Grenfell, AFC, who remained in that position until August 31 1944.

Newton had a hectic training programme but after three years the grass strips paid the price and, owing to the unserviceability of the airfield, Head-quarters No 21 Group ordered Sutton Bridge to be taken on as a satellite in order to maintain the training programme.

By the end of March 1944, Newton airfield was considered serviceable again and the status on June 6 was No 16 (Polish) SFTS and No 1524 BAT Flight, both units in No 21 Group, Flying Training Command, with a satellite at Orston and a RLG at Tollerton. The first Harvard IIB trainer arrived in August 1944.

The school continued after the war until October 1946 when the FTS then disbanded and Newton transferred to Fighter Command. No 12 Group made it their headquarters and flying was continued by No 12 Group Communications Flight and the following year by Nottingham University Air Squadron (renamed East Midlands Universities Air Squadron).

In August 1958 the role of the station changed and it was transferred to Technical Training Command as No 9 STT while, at the end of 1959, its guided weapons courses were transferred from Yatesbury. After additional electrical and instrument ground training was transferred from Melksham in 1964, Newton became a busy centre.

Again the wind of change swept

through the station and in September 1973 all electrical and instrument training was transferred to Halton. This left only the guided weapons training courses at Newton and in 1974 this section was absorbed by the Engineering Training and Support Squadron after No 9 School of Technical Training ceased to exist. In October 1974 the Royal Air Force School of Education, the Royal Air Force Police School, the Management Training Squadron and the Air Cadet Training Centre arrived.

There were again further changes during 1975 and 1977 with many units. These involved No 644 Gliding School which arrived in 1975 and operates from Syerston. Cadets attend from three ATC Wings: South Midlands, East Midlands and Lincolnshire. The Management Training Squadron merged with the Support Command School of Civilian Management to form the RAF School of Management Training. The last to move in was the Air Cadet Central Gliding School Detachment from Swanton Morley in August 1977 when it amalgamated with its parent unit at RAF Syerston.

Today, the three grass runways, two of which are 2,400 ft long and the other 3,700 ft long, are active, and there are five 'C' Type hangars, which were built in 1938 and still in use.

North Coates, Lincolnshire

113/TA375025. S of Grimsby between Northcoates Point and Horseshoe Point

This flat piece of land lies immediately behind the sand-dunes on the Lincolnshire coast and an aerodrome called North Coates Fitties was opened on this site in 1918. The resident unit was No 248 Squadron, 404 Flight, equipped with Short 225 aircraft, and this unit flew coastal patrols during the latter part of the First World War. In March 1919 it disbanded and in June the aerodrome was abandoned.

The Lincolnshire coast was perfect for armament training and in 1927 the Air Ministry bought 88 acres of the First World War site with the intention of using it for annual summer armament practice camps for bomber squadrons, and the site was re-opened in that role. It continued in that capacity until 1934 when, during the Expansion period of the Royal Air Force, it was then decided to upgrade the site into a permanent airfield.

The station opened in 1935 as No 2 Armament Training Camp and in January 1936 the Air Observers' School was formed. The following year these two units, equipped mainly with Wallace aircraft, merged to become 2 Air Armament School and in March 1938 this unit was renamed No 1 Air Observers' School. No 1 AOS, now flying Battles, remained here until the outbreak of war in September 1939 when it was then hastily moved to a quieter area in North Wales and the station was transferred to Coastal Command.

The station became RAF North Coates at the start of World War 2 but during the first few months of the war had no resident flying units either because of fear of attack or because no squadrons were available, and housed only ground units. These included No 2 Recruit Training Pool and No 1 Ground Defence School, the forerunner of the RAF Regiment, whose role was to train airmen for airfield defence. Then, in late February 1940, the

Bloodhound Mark 1 missile at North Coates in 1958.

first squadron arrived flying Blenheim IVfs and a few Battles. This was No 235 Squadron which was followed in March by two more squadrons, Nos 236 and 248. Both of these were equipped with fighter versions of the Blenheim and these long-range fighter squadrons of Coastal Command patrolled far out over the North Sea.

The airfield had by now been extended and the single runway was 1,400 yards long. This pointed towards North Coates village and the sea, ending almost on the beach. A piece of perimeter track was laid to link each end of the runway to the buildings that were all grouped at the northern end of this very isolated outpost.

When the Germans invaded Denmark and Norway in April 1940, Nos 235, 236 and 248 Squadrons moved south to join Fighter Command. That same month No 22 Squadron arrived equipped with the new Bristol Beaufort. This unit was accompanied in May by No 812 Squadron, Fleet Air Arm, whose Fairey Swordfish looked very out of place alongside the Beauforts. However, these aircraft did their task well. Together with No 22 Squadron they attacked enemy shipping and it was this role that the station assumed for the remainder of the war. During April No 22 Squadron sent a detachment to St Eval, Cornwall, and from there they attacked the German battlecruiser *Gneisenau* in Brest harbour. For his part in this operation Flying Officer Keith Campbell was awarded a posthumous Victoria Cross.

Over the next three years many units operated from North Coates. In April 1941, No 42 Squadron arrived, equipped with Beauforts. One of their members was Pilot Officer Philpott, DFC, who later became one of the escapees in the now famous 'wooden horse' breakout, for which he was awarded the Military Cross. The following month, No 816 Squadron, FAA, took over its sister unit, No 812 Squadron's commitment. June saw the departure of Nos 22 and 42 Squadrons together with the Swordfishes of No 816, and the arrival of No 86 equipped with Beauforts.

On July 9 Lincolnshire saw the arrival of another Canadian squadron when the Lockheed Hudsons of No 407 (Canadian) Squadron moved into North Coates. This unit was engaged on anti-shipping strikes which were carried out almost at sea level, making the operation highly dangerous. However, the Canadians, with the help of their Commanding Officer, Wing Commander Styles, soon became experts in their task and were most successful during their period at North Coates, damaging 150,000 tons of Axis shipping.

During October the pace slowed down when two non-operational units arrived at the airfield, these being No 6 Anti-Aircraft Co-Operation Unit flying Lysanders and an Air-Sea Rescue unit, No 278 Squadron, equipped with Lysanders and Ansons. A Walrus amphibian was later added for pick-up work. The role of these units was air-sea rescue along the Lincolnshire and Yorkshire coasts and involved dinghy drops and spotting missions. The ASR unit worked in conjunction with 22 Motor Launch Unit based at nearby Grimsby. With the arrival of these units the station was again congested and many of their aircraft had to use the airfield at Donna Nook a few miles down the coast.

Through the winter months the station continued operations then, in February 1942, Nos 86 and 407 Squadrons departed to be replaced by Nos 53 and 59 Squadrons. Both units were equipped with Hudsons and a high proportion of the pilots were Australian. On the 24th of the month Flight Lieutenant R.C. Guthrie attacked a convoy which consisted of seven merchant ships and four naval escorts. His Hudson attacked the largest ship with his four 250 lb bombs but in the process he was repeatedly hit and under great difficulty managed to crash-land at Bircham Newton.

No 217 Squadron, equipped with Beauforts, also arrived in February and this unit stayed a short time before moving to Ceylon. February also saw the arrival of a second-line FAA unit, No 776 Squadron, equipped with the standard Blackburn Roc fighters. Also, 6 AACU was replaced by a detachment from 7 AACU.

By the end of March 1942, No 59 Squadron had become operational and was sharing operational duties with 53 Squadron, but in May both units were replaced by the Hudsons of Nos 206 and 224 Squadrons which remained for the summer months. On June 5 No 415 (RCAF) Squadron arrived equipped with Hampdens which were being used as torpedo bombers. This was the only Canadian Torpedo Bomber squadron formed overseas and on July 30 1942 it moved to Wick in Scotland.

Coastal Command continued attacking enemy shipping but the German ships

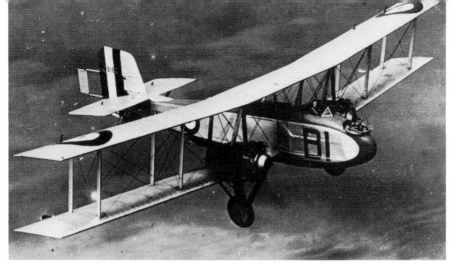

Sidestrand B1 at North Coates in 1929—Pilot, Flight Lieutenant G.N.P. Stringer, DFC. On bombing practice—duration 2 hours 25 minutes.

were well armed with anti-aircraft guns and even though the anti-shipping strike units had proved fairly successful, other and more effective means had to be discovered. North Coates was selected to try out some new tactics and, in August 1942, No 143 Squadron arrived, equipped with Beaufighters. The following month Air Ministry agreed to nominate this aircraft as the standard strike machine for Coastal Command. September saw the arrival of two further Beaufighter squadrons, Nos 236 and 254. Of all the many units operated from North Coates, the station was to become best known for these squadrons, which formed the 'North Coates Wing'.

This was a strike wing based on the pattern which had proved successful at Malta, in which a squadron of fast torpedo bombers was accompanied by one or more squadrons of equal performance that could concentrate on suppressing enemy anti-aircraft fire with their cannon fire and bombs. No 254 Squadron was to be the Beaufighter torpedo squadron while Nos 143 and 236 were the two Beaufighter 'anti-flak' squadrons.

By the end of the year the Wing had made its first sortie but it miscarried badly and the squadrons were immediately withdrawn for intensive training until April 1943 when they once again became operational. During June the rocket-armed Beaufighter became available and the Wing was a huge success. This led to the formation of a second Wing at Leuchars. In August No 143 Squadron departed but the Wing continued to operate with the remaining two squadrons and it was so successful that the enemy had to curtail

trade from Rotterdam and route the iron ore and associated cargoes through Emden.

In February 1944, No 143 Squadron returned but in May it moved to Manston, Kent, to take part in operation 'Overlord'. The status of North Coates on June 6 was No 236 and 254 Squadrons, both equipped with Beaufighter X aircraft and in No 16 Group. The North Coates Wing continued to inflict crushing blows on the enemy shipping with their underwing rocket projectiles and in September was rejoined by No 143 Squadron. Its stay was brief, however, for in October it moved to Banff in Scotland to help form a new Strike Wing.

The North Coates Wing continued with its successful tactics and, in 1945, No 254 Squadron began to partly re-equip with the Mosquito Mark XVIII which had been produced specifically for Coastal Command carrying a 57 mm (6 pr) Molins gun. However, very few saw any operational service for only 27 were produced.

During the first week in May 1945, Nos 236 and 254 Squadrons were credited with five U-boats sunk but their war days were nearly over and towards the end of the month the Wing disbanded. That same month No 236 Squadron moved out, followed in June by 254 Squadron. During operations from North Coates 97 decorations had been won and 484 airmen had lost their lives.

After the war the airfield was occupied by various non-flying units, No 15 School of Technical Training, No 1 Initial Training School, No 54 MU and No 5131 Bomb Disposal Wing, whose task it was to make the Lincolnshire area safe from unexploded bombs. This unit remained until the mid-1950s and by this time all the other units had gradually moved out.

In 1956 a detachment of Sycamore helicopters from 275 Squadron arrived, their duties being search and rescue. Meanwhile, top VIPs were thick on the ground and towards the end of the year work started on converting the airfield into Fighter Command's first missile site. In 1958 it re-opened as the first station to be equipped with Bloodhounds and their associated radar tracking sets with the arrival of No 264 (SAM) Squadron in April. This unit disbanded in 1962 but 17 Joint Services Trials Unit arrived to introduce the Bloodhound Mark 2 into service and to look after the weapons. During October 1963, No 25 (SAM) Squadron formed and became the resident missile unit, remaining at North Coates until February 1971 when it then moved to Germany. The station was then reduced to care and maintenance. It was re-activated in 1976 as a Bloodhound 2 Missile Site and 'B' Flight of 85 Squadron moved in with missiles that had been withdrawn from Cyprus and Singapore. The station is still active today.

North Killingholme, Lincolnshire

113/TA130170. NW of Grimsby

Killingholme was first associated with military aviation as early as August 1914 when a seaplane station was opened at the northern end of Killingholme Marshes on the Lincolonshire side of the Humber bank. This site was used by the Royal Navy and aeroplanes were engaged on the usual coastal patrols. Killingholme remained predominantly a seaplane base but a few landplanes were also based here and the DH 6s of 252 Squadron, based at Redcar, and other Yorkshire-based squadrons, often used the airfield in the latter part of 1917 and early 1918. In July 1918 the site was transferred to the US Navy but in January 1919 was returned to the Royal Air Force and in October of that year closed down completely.

Almost two decades later the area along the Humber bank was again surveyed for possible airfield sites and two were selected a few miles inland from the former Killingholme site. The two were Goxhill, a few miles further north, and North Killingholme.

Construction work started in late 1942 although, in many ways, North Killingholme was a restricted site, being bounded on all sides by roads, railways and Skitter Beck. The airfield was built to the standard pattern with three concrete runways with an encircling perimeter track off which were the usual concrete hardstandings. The technical site was to the east of the airfield and contained a 'T2' hangar and on the southern boundary near the railway lines to Immingham Docks there was a further 'T2' hangar. A third 'B1' hangar was sited at the northern end and the living accommodation was dispersed around the site.

North Killingholme opened in November 1943 in No 1 Group, Bomber Command, but it did not receive a squad-

Lancasters of 550 Squadron on dispersal at North Killingholme.

This oblique photograph shows what little thought has been given for these excellent runways. Taken in March 1980 looking west towards Skitter Beck.

ron until early in the New Year. On January 4 1944, No 550 Squadron moved in from Waltham where it had formed the previous November. The squadron was equipped with Lancaster Mark Is and IIIs plus the Oxford used by the Commanding Officer, Group Captain McIntyre, and this was to be the only operational squadron resident here. For its part in the Nuremberg raid of March 30/31 1944, No 550 Squadron put up 17 Lancasters of which two failed to return.

The pace increased throughout 1944 and Flying Officer Bud Stevenson, a Canadian pilot, now living in London, Ontario, recalls the pace of operations. 'The Duisburg raids I remember very well for one morning at 04.30 I was arranging my 'chute in the seat prior to take-off, the next morning at 04.30 I was removing the 'chute—after TWO trips to Duisburg in 24 hours.'

These October raids were part of the terrible onslaught on Duisburg when two separate attacks were launched on the city within 24 hours. The first was on October 14 when 1,063 bombers were despatched with 4,782 tons of bombs. Since it was a daylight raid 15 aircraft were lost. For the second wave on the night of October 14/15, 1,065 aircraft were despatched with 4,547 tons of bombs and six aircraft were missing. It is interesting to note that Duisburg received in 24 hours almost the equivalent total of bombs dropped against *all* British targets during the worst month of the Luftwaffe Blitz, September 1940.

The last operational mission of the war

for 550 Squadron was on April 25 1945 when 23 Lancasters bombed Berchtesgaden. The squadron then took part in operations 'Manna', 'Exodus' and 'Dodge' before disbanding on October 31 1945.

During its wartime career, No 550 Squadron made 192 operational missions and lost 61 aircraft. The casualties were 150 aircrew killed and 189 of which no news was received. The awards gained were one DSO, 73 DFCs, two bars to DFCs, 12 DFMs, one CGM, and one Croix de Guerre. The squadron also had three outstanding Lancasters, all Mark IIIs, which passed the 100-sortie mark. These were EE139 'B' Baker, named 'The Phantom of the Ruhr', and previously with No 100 Squadron, with 121 sorties; ED905 'F' Fox, ex-'Press on Regardless' and previously with Nos 103 and 166 Squadrons, with over 100 sorties; and PA995 'V' Victor, named 'The Vulture Strikes', which had completed over 100 sorties at the time it went missing on a raid against Dessau on March 11 1945.

After 550 Squadron had disbanded the airfield closed to flying in 1945 and does not appear to have had further use by the Royal Air Force. All three hangars are still standing and look to be in very good condition, but those and a few Nissen huts are all that remains. The airfield is now an industrial estate and cluttered on the runways are buildings of all shapes and sizes. The only thought that anyone gave to it is in the name for the road into the estate which is called Lancaster Approach.

North Luffenham, Leicestershire (Rutland)

141/SK940050. Approximately 6 miles W of Stamford, N of the A6121 road

This hilltop site lay between the villages of Edith Weston in the west and Ketton to the east. North Luffenham village was at the southern end of the airfield. It was chosen for development into a bomber airfield and work started in 1940. It was constructed as a grass airfield and designed according to the current standards with a technical site containing 'J' and 'T2' type hangars. These, with all the other accommodation buildings, were sited in the north-west corner near the village of Edith Weston. The airfield also had a decoy at Pickworth but this cannot be traced, nor indeed is there evidence that it was ever used.

North Luffenham opened in December 1940 and within a few weeks nearly a thousand people were housed on the station. The first occupants were No 17 EFTS that formed here on January 6 1941. The school gave basic flying instructions to Royal Air Force pilots on Tiger Moths, Miles Magisters and Ansons. In mid-July No 17 EFTS moved to Peterborough and the station was transferred to No 5 Group, Bomber Command, for it was now decided that the airfield was capable of supporting operations. By the end of July Nos 61 and 144 Squadrons had moved in from Hemswell. Both units were equipped with Hampden bombers and the early operations were minelaying and against naval targets. However, as the pace of operations increased, the North Luffenham squadrons attacked shipyards at Kiel and a variety of other German targets. In October 1941, No 61 Squadron began to convert to Manchester aircraft and the following month it moved to North Luffenham's satellite airfield at Woolfox Lodge.

No 144 Squadron continued to operate from here with the Hampdens which it retained throughout its stay at North Luffenham. In November 1941 one of the squadron's aircraft bombed from low level a 10,000-ton merchantman and was responsible for the death of Major General Felix Varda, the German Anti-Aircraft Defence Commander, who was on board this ship. The squadron also took part in minelaying and bombed the docks at Dunkirk and Le Havre.

From January 27 to March 17 1942 an operational echelon of No 408 (Goose) Squadron, Royal Canadian Air Force, was detached to North Luffenham from Balderton. After the Canadians had left, 144 Squadron took part in the devastating raid on the Renault factory, just outside Paris. But the squadron's operational role was coming to an end and, on April 6 as the Hampdens took-off for Essen, it was to be their last sortie. It was also to be the end of the squadron's association with Bomber Command for at the end of April it was transferred to Coastal Command and moved to Leuchars, Scotland.

On March 27 1942, No 61 Squadron Conversion Flight was formed at North Luffenham with Manchester Mk I and Lancaster Mk I aircraft (code letters 'QR') but, on May 5 1942, the unit moved to Syerston. The station was now transferred to No 92 Group and, on April 25 1942, No 29 OTU was formed. This unit (code letters 'NT' and 'NF'), had an establishment of Wellington Ias and IIIs, Ansons, Lysanders and Defiants. Their role was to provide the final stage of training for bomber crews.

Sometimes the OTUs supplied crews, made up from instructors and senior pupils, when a heavy raid was mounted. One such occasion was on June 26 1942 when 29 OTU despatched eight aircraft to take part in the 1,000-bomber raid on Bremen. The airfield was also used during this period as a RLG for the Oxford trainers of 12 (P) AFU from Spitalgate. In June 1943 No 29 OTU moved to Bruntingthorpe so that the runways could be rebuilt.

That same month the airfield closed for reconstruction work and North Luffenham became inactive. During this period, in January 1944, modifications to Hamilcar gliders was carried out by MAP at the station. The following March the work was completed and the station reopened in No 23 Group, Flying Training Command. The airfield now had three concrete runways, one main and two intersecting ones, with an encircling perimeter track. At some stage the airfield also acquired a 'B1' hangar on the southern boundary and a row of 'T2s' on the northern edge.

Opposite page, top to bottom *North Luffenham. Horsa glider of No 21 HGCU in May 1947; Halifax of No 21 HGCU in 1947; Sabre 2 BT164 of 441 Squadron in 1954; Brigand T5 of No 238 OCU in June 1958.*

During March 1944, No 21 HGCU arrived from Brize Norton. The unit's function was to train glider pilots on the Airspeed Horsa troop-carrying glider. These were towed by Whitleys which were replaced by Albemarles in September 1944. Gliders became a familiar sight over the Rutland countryside and many of them took part in the D-Day airborne operations. As these blunt-nosed plywood craft skidded safely to a halt in the Normandy fields many of the Airborne Division had reason to be grateful for the thoroughness of the training received by the glider pilots at North Luffenham. No 21 HGCU moved back to Brize Norton in October 1944. The following month the station became No 73 Base in No 7 Group with Woolfox Lodge as a sub-station for No 1651 HGU and Spanhoe a sub-station for No 1657 HCU, but the latter was not taken up for the airfield was still being used by the USAAF.

The next unit to arrive was No 1653 HCU on November 27 1944 from Chedburgh with an establishment of Stirling Mk IIIs, Lancaster Is and IIIs, Spitfire Mk Vs, Hurricane Mk IIs, Beaufighter VIs and Mosquito XIXs. This unit's role was to train bomber crews which involved long cross-country flights, but the station was not operational and no missions were flown from here.

After the war the station began to run down and in September 1945 the airfield was opened for the first time to the general public when over 13,000 attended the Battle of Britain Day celebrations.

The following month, on October 28, No 1653 HCU moved out to Lindholme. This unit was replaced with the return of No 21 HGCU that arrived from Elsham Wolds in December 1946. The unit was equipped with Dakotas, Horsa gliders plus Halifaxes and their Hamilcar gliders. In the following year it was joined by two more training units, No 1333 TSCU flying Dakotas and Oxfords, which arrived from Syerston during July, and 1382 (T) CU flying Dakotas, Ansons and Oxfords that arrived from Wymeswold in the early part of December.

However, by the end of the year No 21 HGCU had disbanded and in the first week in January 1948 the other two units were both disbanded. From these units No 240 OCU was re-designated with an establishment of Anson, Dakota, Devon and Valetta aircraft. The unit's role was to train transport Command crews and many of their aircraft took part in the Berlin

Airlift during 1948/49. In April 1951, No 240 OCU moved to Dishforth and was replaced by No 102 Flying Refresher School which formed here the same month. The School used Spitfires, Vampires, Meteors and Harvards to train pilots of the Royal Air Force Reserve.

No 102 FRS remained at North Luffenham for only six months and in November the station was handed over to the Royal Canadian Air Force as a fighter base for NATO No 1 Fighter Wing, RCAF (NATO) formed here on November 1 1951. For the next three years, F-86E Sabres of Nos 410, 439 and 441 Squadrons flew from this airfield as part of Canada's contribution to NATO's defensive air shield. All three squadrons had been in Lincolnshire during World War 2 as part of No 12 Group and took part in the air defence of Great Britain.

During this period the station received occasional visits by North Star, Bristol Freighter and Expeditor aircraft from Langar but, by the end of 1954 the squadrons began to move out and on November 14 No 410 moved to Baden-Soellingen, Germany. This unit was followed on December 20 by No 441 Squadron which moved to Zweibrucken, Germany. On March 31 1955 No 439 Squadron moved to Marville, France, and brought to an end the Canadian era at North Luffenham.

In April the station was handed back to the Royal Air Force and the Night and All Weather Operational Conversion Unit was formed with the function of training Meteor crews in all-weather flying. The NF 14 Meteor at the main entrance was a reminder of this role. In April 1956 a dispersal from Leeming arrived so that runway repairs could be made at their station and until the end of the year Meteor NF 11 aircraft of 228 OCU used the airfield. In January 1957 the Night and All Weather OCU amalgamated with 238 OCU, which arrived from Colerne with Brigand T.5s (the last in RAF service), Balliol T.2s and Valetta T.3s and C.1s. Because of runway repairs at North Weald, Hunter F6 aircraft of the renowned 111 ('Treble-One') Squadron used the airfield from mid-February until March 1958 and were the last RAF operational aircraft to do so. In June 1958, 238 OCU disbanded and the station was placed on C & M.

However, by the end of the year work started to convert the station into a Thor IRBM complex. North Luffenham was to be the Thor Intermediate Range Ballistic Missile HQ and launch emplacements were constructed here and at its four satellites, Folkingham, Harrington, Melton Mowbray and Polebrook. The station re-opened in October 1959 under No 3 Group, Bomber Command, and the Thor missiles were brought in by USAF Cargomasters during 1960. Americans from the Douglas Aircraft Company came to establish the missile base and a large colony lived in caravans. By May the towering white columns of 15 Thors stood sentinel against the skyline.

Concurrently with the formation of the Thor base, No 151 (SAM) Wing HQ and Technical Site was established to operate and control two Mark 1 Bloodhound Squadrons, namely No 62 (SAM) Squadron at Woolfox Lodge and No 257 (SAM) Squadron at Warboys. In mid-August 1963, North Luffenham became the last of the Thor complexes to close and the last fixed-wing aircraft left the airfield with a Thor surface-to-surface missile on September 27 1963.

In November 1963 the Radio Technical Publications Squadron moved to North Luffenham from Upwood. This unit's role was to produce documents used in servicing the sophisticated electronic equipment. The following year the Bloodhound squadrons were disbanded and by the end of 1964 all missiles and launch emplacements had been dismantled. The station then came under the control of Signals Command and became the home of Midlands Radar Unit. From the Ketton–North Luffenham road you can still see the complex radar disk sweeping the sky from its perch on the white blockhouse. In 1969 Signals Command became No 90 (Signals) Group within Strike Command but in 1972 was transferred to Maintenance Command which in turn was re-titled Support Command. In 1971 the station also housed No 63 Squadron, Royal Air Force Regiment, Rapier (Ground to Air) Missiles, but this unit moved to Germany in 1974.

In the early 1970s fixed-wing aircraft returned when Chipmunk trainers operated from the airfield during the summer months for the ATC and CCF air section cadets. In 1972 the station became part of Support Command but by the mid-1970s a rundown was in the wind. However, in 1977 the rundown was delayed and today the future of the base seems assured. Let us hope so for since being opened in 1941, North Luffenham

has featured in many roles and, although now non-operational, it still has an important part to play in the modern Royal Air Force and makes a substantial contribution to employment in the Rutland, Leicestershire, area.

Today, the station is home for the Aero Medical Training Centre and courses are also held for Medical Officers, Flight Sisters, Decompression Chamber Operators and Air Ambulance Attendants. North Luffenham is also home to the Ground Radio Servicing Centre (GRSC), RAF Language School and the Midland Radar unit which provides an operational air traffic service for all off-airways aircraft from the Thames estuary to Tyneside, covering airfields in Lincolnshire, East Anglia and the Midlands. Millions of pounds worth of computers and electrical apparatus back up the skilled controllers. A far cry from those wartime days when 1,000 bombers at a time took to the air and returned only by the grace of God and the skill of the pilot.

North Witham, Lincolnshire

130/SK945225. S of Grantham, W of the A1 road

During the latter part of 1943 the 9th Tactical Army Air Force moved to England from Italy in order to support the US Army in operation 'Overlord'. However, many airfields were not completed and the units moved around while awaiting their final assignment orders. By January 4 1944, the 9th Air Service Command had been assigned six airfields for Tactical Air Depots, the equivalent to the RAF Maintenance Unit, and the 1st Tactical Air Depot was established at North Witham. South Witham, with No 100 MU, had opened in March 1942 with three officers and 90 men and was a very busy bomb dump with ammunition being brought in by both road and rail.

The airfield was one of many that was hastily built in order to accommodate the expanding Allied Air Force and was the first one to be taken over by the Americans. The airfield covered an area of 742 acres and the main runway was 2,000 yards long and 50 yards wide. On December 14 1943 the first personnel began to arrive at the station, these being RAF men of the newly formed 9th Troop Carrier Command Substitution Unit, and the airfield officially opened the following day. For the next 12 months it was

On the eve of D-Day, a final check before loading from these Pathfinder paratroops. Note their blackened faces and the daggers on their legs. This is at North Witham even though the aircraft code of '8Y' was one from the 98th Squadron of the 50th Wing.

officially termed the 9th Troop Carrier Service Wing. Also, it was given the American identity, Army Air Force Station 479.

The first commanding Officer, Squadron Leader G.F. O'Brian, assumed command on December 24. On the last day of 1943 the personnel arrived from the Army Air Force Station 489, Cottesmore, where they had been billeted during the completion of their accommodation.

The first American units began to arrive on January 5 1944 and for the next two weeks they came in dribs and drabs. The main force of 75 officers and 1,256 men of the 33rd and 85th Air Depot Groups did not arrive from Cottesmore until the end of the month. On February 16 1944 the 85th Air Depot Group was re-designated the 29th ADG.

The units were very busy, preparing new Dakotas for issue to operational Groups, supplying Troop Carrier Command with spares, performing major repairs and services to aircraft which could not be done on their own airfield.

During March, a special American unit arrived from Cottesmore. This was the Pathfinder School and when they arrived a large number of the Air Depot personnel had to move into tented accommodation at the northern end of the airfield on a 71-acre site which became known as 'tent city'. With 86 RAF personnel and nearly 3,600 Americans, accommodation was very crowded. During this period six Butler hangars were built at the Air Depot

area, just north of the 'T2' hangar, the remaining 'T2' adjoining the technical site being used by the Pathfinder School whose role was to train small groups of pathfinder paratroops. These parachutists would be the advance party of an airborne assault and would set up portable radio signal devices to guide in the main force to the drop zones. The unit also trained aircrews in the use of their special radar aids.

It was an intensive training programme and June 5 1944 saw the culmination of their efforts. North Witham was the first Lincolnshire USAAF base to mount an operation when, at 21.30 hours, 20 C-47s of the 9th Troop Carrier Command Pathfinder Group started to take-off. Captain of the leading aircraft was Lieutenant Colonel Joel Crouch, the School Commandant. There were approximately 200 American pathfinder paratroopers aboard. Their task was to prepare the drop zones of the 82nd and 101st Airborne Divisions for D-Day. At 00.15 hours the parachutists landed in Normandy, to start the greatest invasion the world has ever known. The drops were successful and all but one aircraft returned safely to base.

For a short period the Pathfinder School also trained a detachment of the 1st Independent Polish Airborne Brigade but, by the middle of September, the school was renamed the Pathfinder Group Provisional and it then moved to an airfield in the south of England.

As at all airfields, the crash crews were frequently on call, the first occasion being on February 21 1944 when a Lancaster Mk

A peaceful summer's evening as day turns to night. As far as it is able to detect from the official US records these are the Pathfinder paratroops at North Witham. Many of the aircraft are uncoded and one or two have '9X', '6Z' and '8Y' codes of the 440th TCG, 50th Wing, that did training at Bottesford. These could have been used to bring the unit's aircraft up to strength. It is interesting to note that in the background there is a Lancaster.

III, ND419 of No 460 Squadron from Binbrook, crashed under a mile just SSE of the airfield into Beaumont Wood at 06.45 hours. All the crew members were killed. Another near miss was on February 3 1945 when Halifax NP757 of No 408 Squadron crashed just 400 yards from 'G' dispersal, midway between the airfield perimeter and the bomb dump of No 100 MU at South Witham.

With bases now being firmly established on the continent, the Air Depot Units began to move out during December 1944 and, by April 1945, the Americans had completely gone from North Witham. The airfield was placed under C & M and reallocated to Maintenance Command, No 40 Group, on May 7 1945. On the 9th No 100 MU started to use the runways and hardstandings to store its bombs and within a few weeks they were piled high on every available bit of concrete.

On July 1 the airfield was handed over to No 259 MU under the control of Headquarters 55 Wing, No 40 Group. No 259 MU, under the command of Wing Commander S.A. Byrd, was an aircraft stores depot and North Witham was being used as an Equipment Disposal Depot. During September 1945 No 4 Personnel and Despatch Unit took over the station for a few months until June 5 1946. The role of the unit was to place RAF Regiment personnel into categories for early release as they returned from overseas. While awaiting release many were given duties guarding German Prisoners of War.

No 259 MU moved out during May 1946 and No 100 MU and its bombs vacated the airfield during 1948. For the next few years very little is known about the airfield and it became an inactive station in April 1956. The rundown was then rapid and the land was sold off in February 1960.

North Witham had not been liked by everyone who had served there, particularly the Americans under canvas and the Air Depot personnel who had to work in muddy conditions because of lack of storage buildings and paved roads. Notices were all around the airfield proclaiming 'Mud Control—Walking off the concrete paths is forbidden' during the war years.

Today, much of the airfield land is owned by the Forestry Commission and a new Twyford Forest now grows on the western side of the site. The sole surviving 'T2' hangar near the technical site is surrounded by new factory buildings. The only other remains from those wartime days are a few Nissen huts at the bottom section of the main runway and further south on the Swayfield road near Hall Farm a few living site buildings are visible. Parts of the runways and hardstandings also remain, along with the control tower, standing as a silent reminder of the past.

Nottingham (Tollerton), Nottinghamshire

See Tollerton

Nuneaton, Leicestershire

140/SP375965. N of Nuneaton and adjacent to the main A5(T) road E of the A444 and W of the village of Higham on the Hill.

Nuneaton opened in February 1943 as a satellite for No 18 (Polish) OTU at Bramcote and was a standard bomber training airfield with three concrete runways, 1,850 yards, 1,540 yards and 1,430 yards long with an encircling perimeter track. But its role as a training satellite was very short. The following month No 18 OTU moved to Finningley and both Nuneaton and Bramcote were transferred to No 44 Group, Transport Command, during April with the arrival of No 105 OTU.

The Wellingtons of No 105 (Transport) OTU took up residence and the airfield remained a satellite of Bramcote until August 1945 when the unit moved out. The airfield was then put on a care and maintenance basis and a small work force went daily from the parent station at Bramcote. In September 1946 the airfield closed down completely and today it is used as a proving ground by the Motor Industry Research Association and entry is prohibited. The control tower and one 'T2' hangar plus some perimeter track and the runways still remain.

Orston, Nottinghamshire

129/SK780405. E of Nottingham and Orston village, N of the main A52 road.

This small airfield opened during 1941 in No 21 Group as a satellite for 16 (Polish) SFTS, Newton, for their Oxfords and Masters. It was a grass strip with a maxi-

mum length of just over 1,200 yards and after any heavy rain the ground was unserviceable. The airfield was used only by Newton and had very primitive facilities. It closed after the war and was soon under the plough. Today, the only main building has been re-roofed and is being used by a local farmer, while there is no trace of the former wartime airfield.

Ossington, Nottinghamshire

120/SK745645. 8 miles NW of Newark, W of the A1(T) road at the Carlton-on-Trent junction and just W of the village of Ossington

Construction work started here in 1941 and the North Wood in the north and the High Wood to the south of the airfield were turned into natural cover. The village road leading to Kneesall ran right through the centre of the airfield.

The airfield was originally selected as a bomber station in No 5 Group and had a decoy airfield at Upton. It was a standard bomber airfield with the usual three concrete runways, 4,980 ft, 3,600 ft and 2,770 ft long with the normal dispersed accommodation. But it never became a front-line bomber station for soon after opening in January 1942 it was transferred to Flying Training Command. On January 19 it became the home of No 14 (P) AFU equipped with Airspeed Oxford aircraft, the unit's role being pilot training.

No 14 moved to Banff, Scotland, in May 1943, after which the station was returned to Bomber Command, No 93 Group, with Gamston as a satellite. On June 1 1943, No 82 OTU was formed here with an establishment of 54 Wellington Mk III and X aircraft and five Martinet TTs that were used for drogue towing. The role of the station, with Gamston as a satellite, was operational training of all

Ossington—the few remaining huts on the Living Site in 1977.

Ossington in 1977. The Admin site—pathway to nowhere.

types of aircrew, ie, pilots, wireless operators, navigators and air gunners. The status of the station on June 6 1944 was No 82 OTU with Wellington and Hurricane IIc aircraft and No 1685 (B) DTF equipped with Tomahawks. Both units were in No 93 Group, Bomber Command.

With the tide now turned in Europe, the need for aircrews was not as demanding and the role was changing. On January 9 1945, the station was transferred to Transport Command and No 82 OTU was replaced by No 6 LFS. This school was operated jointly by Transport Command and British Overseas Airways Corporation with the immediate role of training 72 aircrew to operate Lancastrians on the England to New Zealand route. On November 1 1945 the unit was renamed No 1384 Heavy Transport Conversion Unit. Its function was to train Lancaster crews in the transport role but in November it converted to Yorks, using some of the first BOAC civil-registered aircraft, and the primary purpose then became conversion of aircrew from Lancasters to Yorks.

In May 1946 the unit completed its flying commitment and its aircraft departed. The station then closed to flying and in August 1946 closed down.

By 1979 all the runways had been broken up and disposed of for hardcore. Almost all the airfield buildings have also disappeared. Part of the former MT Section still remains and is used by the local farmer. Large sections of the perimeter track are used as service roadway. All that now remains of the domestic and administrative sites are a few concrete pathways leading into the fields with a pile of broken concrete to mark the site of a former building.

Papplewick Moor, Nottinghamshire

120/SK550510. Approximately 7 miles N of Nottingham at Papplewick crossroads S of the B6011 and W of the B683 roads

After being turned down as a possible site for Hucknall, Papplewick was established in 1918 as a RLG for No 15 Training Depot Station at Hucknall. This formed on April 1 1918 but disbanded the following year and Papplewick Moor was abandoned. It was a single grass strip some 3,000 ft in length and laid out on the Moor after which it was named. In the late 1920s local inhabitants recalled seeing one or two aircraft but the field was never put to any regular use.

On June 4 1937, an Avro Anson of the School of Air Navigation, RAF Manston, was engaged on a navigational exercise involving a trip to Northern Ireland. The aircraft was piloted by Sergeant Underhill, and the observer was Pilot Officer C. Lamb. On the return flight they encountered phenomenal thunderstorms over the Irish Sea, which persisted over the mainland. The aircraft became icebound in the dense cloud and navigation became very difficult.

Upon taking the decision to descend in order to check bearings, the aircraft broke cloud at about 2,000 ft and it was established that the lights of two towns which became visible were Nottingham and Derby. The pilot circled the area in which he estimated Hucknall to lie, but evoked no response from the ground. He then spotted what he took to be a large obstruction-free field, and kept it in his view while he tried to get a closer look at it. The visibility was restricted to brief glimpses in the lightning flashes which were fortunately pretty regular. The pilot made five attempts to land, slowing down his approach and flattening his gliding angle at each successive attempt, but he decided that the landing speed would be too great to pull up in the short run available.

On the sixth approach, he came in very low, lifted his nose over the boundary hedge, and dropped the tail into the hedge. The result was a very quick stop; the fuselage just aft of the gun turret broke in half, and the nose tipped forward, digging into the soft ground. No one was injured, and the crew was entertained at the 'Griffin's Head' until transport could be arranged to take them to Hucknall. Upon visiting the site of the crash the following morning, the pilot was able to observe a row of hills which were in the line of approach and which he had been completely unaware of, while along the edge of the field itself was an electric power line suspended from a row of poles. Each time an approach was made, the Anson had passed between two poles and underneath the line! The pilot was mercifully unaware of the unseen dangers surrounding him and what he thought was Hucknall had in fact been Papplewick Moor.

During the Second World War the field was again brought into service and the site was administered by No 21 Group Flying Training Command as a RLG for the Tiger Moths of 25 EFTS based at Hucknall. But, things had changed since it was first used for between the wars the nearby village of Papplewick had spread along the south side of the field and now made landing approaches somewhat hazardous. Therefore, the Tiger Moths merely made dummy runs at the field

Auster D4/108, G-ARLG, at Rearsby in September 1963.

without actually landing. There do not appear to have been any facilities other than a temporary duty crew at Papplewick and what few huts there were have all disappeared except two that are used by a farmer.

Ratcliffe, Leicestershire

129/SK630160. NE of Leicester

This was just a small grass strip situated to the north of the village after which it was named and was built in 1930 by Sir Lindsey Everard who operated his private aircraft from here. On May 3 1939 the first flight by aircraft G-AFWN, known as Model Plus C, the forerunner of the famous Auster, took place from this airfield. With the outbreak of war the airfield was requisitoned and became No 6 Ferry Pilots' Pool of the Air Transport Auxiliary. It remained in this role for the duration of the war and closed in 1945.

Rearsby, Leicestershire

129/SK650140. NE of Leicester, SE of Rearsby village and the A607 road

This small grass site opened as an aerodrome just before the outbreak of the Second World War. During the early days Leicestershire County Flying Club operated from the aerodrome. In 1938 Taylorcraft Aeroplanes (England) Ltd was formed and work began on their first aircraft, which had its first test flight at nearby Ratcliffe on May 3 1939. By the outbreak of war in September a total of 23 were complete.

However, with the outbreak of war private flying was banned and in order to keep the team together the company started sub-contract work for the major aircraft firms. Fortunately their aircraft,

which had been loaned to the RAF and RAFC to test its possible use for artillery observation duties, was accepted by the Army for the AOP role and the remaining 22 civil aircraft were impounded and re-engined with the Cirrus Minor. These became the Model Plus D and were delivered in 1940/1941, a few of them seeing service in France prior to the Dunkirk evacuation. A further order for 100 Plus Ds with larger Perspex windows was ordered in 1941. With this order underway the Ministry of Aircraft Production requested a name for the aircraft, and the Auster was born. The Plus D became known as the Auster Mark I, 'Auster' being a Roman name for a warm southerly breeze.

Meanwhile, MAP had asked the company to repair Tiger Moths and later in 1940 it also took on Hurricane repair work. Four new hangars were built and the aerodrome was extended to cope with flight-testing the repaired Hurricanes. Much-needed labour was recruited from the surrounding factories in Leicester, Syston and Melton Mowbray.

During the war many models of the Auster were produced and used on all fronts in the Far East and Europe. After the war the Auster was further developed for military purposes and used in the world's trouble spots, but the helicopter was gradually taking over this role. On March 8 1946 the company name was changed to Auster Aircraft Ltd and Rearsby was made the main factory. However, by 1947 the aircraft production began to slow down and the Auster Company had to diversify its interests, only just surviving a slump in light air-craft sales brought about by over-production and the dumping of large numbers of ex-military training aircraft on to the market.

Aircraft production continued on a reduced scale and in 1959 the company tried to enter the helicopter market but failed. In the early 1960s Auster Aircraft were taken over by British Executive and General Aircraft Ltd (Beagle) and the Rearsby branch became Beagle-Auster. The production of aircraft continued until 1964, the last one to be turned out being a Beagle Husky (G-ASNC) which was granted its C of A on April 23 1964. In 1968 Beagle-Auster was sold to Hants and Sussex Aviation at Portsmouth and the following year it closed. Today the site is used by light industry and nothing remains of the airfield.

Douglas C-47 crew members of the 314th TCG pose in front of their aircraft at Saltby on May 21 1944. Note the 'Bugs Bunny' nose insignia which was unusual on the C-47.

Saltby, Leicestershire

130/SK865265. 11 miles S of Grantham, W of the A1

Situated just east of the village of Saltby and bounded on three sides by country roads, this site started life as a grass air-field. It opened in August 1941 under the control of No 7 Group, later retitled 92 Group of Bomber Command, as a satellite for Cottesmore, a few miles to the south. Sections of No 14 OTU moved in equipped initially with Hampdens and a few Ansons, but these were replaced by Wellingtons towards the end of 1942. Within weeks of the airfield being opened it was bombed on three occasions by the Luftwaffe, although no damage was done.

During the expansion of bomber air-fields the site was selected for develop-ment and, in August 1943, No 14 OTU moved to Husbands Bosworth so that concrete runways could be constructed here and other enlargements made in order to bring the airfield to class 'A'

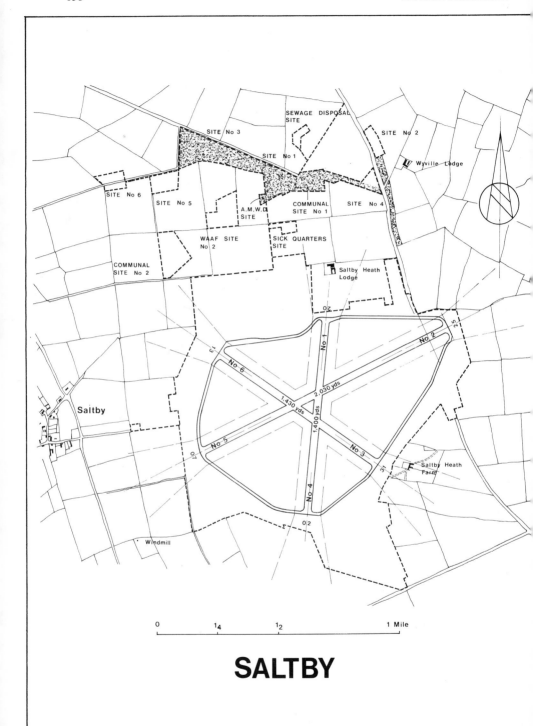

SALTBY

Saltby, June 6 1944. Airborne infantrymen await the signal to board their gliders.

bomber status. One main runway was built, almost on a west-east axis and 2,000 yards in length with two intersecting runways and an encircling perimeter track and hardstandings.

There were four 'T2' type and one 'B1' type hangars, two sited on the west of the airfield, one on each side of Herring Gorse in the north and one on the east side. Accommodation and other buildings were around and in Herring Gorse which gave natural cover. During this period, a section of No 2 HGMU moved in from Snailwell and stored 32 Horsa gliders at the airfield for MAP. Like many other airfields in this area these were here in readiness for the planned invasion of Europe and were transferred to the USAAF in February 1944.

The Americans were already building up their airborne forces in this part of England in readiness for the forthcoming invasion and on December 18 1943, Saltby was transferred from No 5 Group, Bomber Command, to the IXth AFTCC substitution unit whose HQ was at St Vincents, Grantham.

When the runways were completed in February 1944 Saltby, now officially known as USAAF Station 538, received the 314th TCG of the IXth Air Force. This Group consisted of four squadrons, Nos 32, 50, 61 and 62 under the command of Lieutenant Colonel Clayton Stiles and

were equipped with Dakotas and C-53 aircraft, plus the 32 Horsa gliders which were already stored here.

This Group had been part of the XIIth Air Force and had nine months of combat experience behind it having operated in North Africa and taken part in the airborne Sicilian landings. During April and May full training operations were carried out, including towing Waco CG-4A and Airspeed Horsa gliders in both day and night formation.

Then, on the evening of June 5 1944, it was for real and 51 C-47s and nine C-53s of the 314th TCG, loaded with 1,007 men of the 508th Parachute Infantry Regiment, including the 2nd Battalion Regimental HQ, plus 42,838 lb of ammunition and equipment, vibrated the very earth as they took off and headed for Dropping Zone 'N', north-east of Ranville, which they reached just after 02.00 hours on June 6 1944. 18 aircraft were damaged and one shot down over the target area. The next day a re-supply was flown with 50 C-47s and two C-53s but, due to bad weather, 13 aircraft returned to Saltby with their supplies. Heavy flak damaged 30 aircraft.

Between June and September aircraft flew supply missions from Saltby to the continent and on September 17 1944, 72 aircraft of the 314th TCG took off as part of the Arnhem Force. Loaded with 1,015 paratroopers and 248 parapack loads of

Above *Major-General Stanislaw Sosabowski, the 52-year-old leader of the First Polish Parachute Brigade, confers with a colleague. All bases in this area had been fogged-in and take-off was cancelled until 13.00 hours on Thursday, September 21 1944. The Poles jumped into a holocaust just as Sosabowski had feared.* **Below** *The last wartime relic is the water tower, photographed at Saltby in May 1980.* **Above right** *Decontamination centre at Saltby in June 1980.*

equipment, the force used the northern route and, leaving the English coast at Aldeburgh, headed for Dropping Zone 'X', Renkumse, on the south side of the Utrecht-Arnhem railway line.

The following day, D + 1, 72 aircraft again took off from Saltby and headed for Arnhem. This time they had 1,217 paratroopers including part of the 4th Parachute Brigade and 219 parapacks of equipment all bound for Ginkel Heath, Dropping Zone 'Y'. Many of the force were hit and four aircraft were shot down by heavy fire from the drop zone.

Throughout their stay at Saltby the 314th TCG took part in all the airborne landing operations and flew many transport missions to and from the continent but by early March 1945 the Group had moved to a new base in France.

With the Americans gone, the Royal Air Force once again controlled the airfield and, during the last week in March, No 1665 HCU moved in from Tilstock. The unit was equipped with Stirlings and Halifaxes plus a few Oxfords and Spitfires whose role it was to convert crews on to heavier aircraft in the transport role. But they were not to stay and left for Marston Moor during early August 1945.

However, during this period the station was also used by both the Royal Air Force and the Americans. These were C-46s of the 349th TCG and their duties included transporting men and equipment of the British 1st Airborne Division to Stavangar. During this period numerous Stirling and Commando aircraft used Saltby and at 23.50 hours on May 29 Stirling 'T', PW386, swung on take-off and crashed

into a line of C-46s. The Stirling and one C-46 burst into flames and Flight Sergeant Nettleton, the pilot, received cuts and burns. An American who was asleep in one of the aircraft was killed.

On May 30, 33 C-46s departed from Saltby having completed 73 operations, 224 lifts, and carried 1,163 personnel of the British 1st Airborne Division and over 1,700,000 lb of freight. Saltby then went on to a C & M basis and was parented by Melton Mowbray, then Wymeswold, but its active flying days were over. The site was later used for storage by Maintenance Command and housed Nos 216 and 255 MUs until October 26 1948. It was finally de-requisitioned in September 1955.

Today much of the airfield is back to agricultural land and both the early RAF design watch office and the standard austerity-type control tower have been demolished. The water tower is the only major item still standing. A section of the main runway is being used by the Buckminster Flying Club for their gliders. The club has a small hangar and wooden club-house on the site.

The perimeter track is overgrown and deteriorating. All the huts have gone, the only remains being the gun butts and decontamination centre. Now, it looks as if these few remains will be bulldozed away for the black gold beneath, if the proposed new coalfield that is planned for the Vale of Belvoir goes ahead. It certainly looks as if it will and, if so, Saltby would become a dumping ground for mine waste, being earmarked as a colliery site. The defunct ironstone line would be re-activated. This once busy wartime airfield would be gone for ever.

Scampton, Lincolnshire

112/SK965795. N of Lincoln, between the A15 and B1398 roads

Another of the Lincoln Cliff sites but destined to become the best-known of all the many wartime bomber stations, Scampton is sited just north of Lincoln and to the west of Ermine Street. The site was first used in the First World War when it was known as Brattleby.

Built on land belonging to Aisthorpe Farm, Brattleby opened in November 1916 and as it was only intended as a training station the buildings were merely temporary wooden huts although the six hangars were rather more substantially built. The units at Brattleby were initially 49 Reserve Squadron which moved to Grantham in November 1916 when 37 RS arrived for six months.

In December 1916 a detachment of No 33 Squadron arrived with FE2 and FE2b aircraft. One of the those World War 1 pilots and a member of 33 Squadron was Major A.R. Kingsford, who recalls: 'Our job was night patrols hunting for Zeppelins, my patrol was Spurn Head to south of Lincoln for three hours duration and we literally froze.' Night flying at this time was in its infancy and not very popular. The patrols were pointless for they had no hope of destroying the Zeppelins, which came over at 18,000 ft, since the FE2bs only had a ceiling of approximately 12,000 ft.

No 60 Reserve Squadron arrived in April 1917 with Avro 504s and RE8s. This unit was renamed 60 Training Squadron in May. In July No 81 Squadron was formed as a fighter unit but it only had a role as a training unit. No 11 TS arrived from Grantham on September 15 1917, this unit later being commanded by Captain Robert Saundby who, during World War 2, became deputy to Harris at Bomber Command HQ. The unit had a variety of aircraft which included BE2s, Avro 504Js and Ks and the Martinsyde Elephant.

In July 1918 the three squadrons that had been at the station during the past 12 months were combined to form No 34 Training Depot Station and by this time the airfield was operating Sopwith Camels and Dolphins, in addition to many other obsolescent types. No 34 TDS, along with No 46 TDS at South Carlton, formed the 23rd Training Wing with their HQ being located at the latter. Scampton was administered by South Carlton throughout World War 1 and did not have its own Commanding Officer.

After the Armistice, training came to a halt almost overnight and in April 1919 the remaining aeroplanes and personnel were transferred to No 46 TDS at South Carlton. The station was not retained in the post-war Royal Air Force and closed in 1919. By 1920 all the buildings had been removed and Aisthorpe Farm was back under the plough, leaving no trace of the former aerodrome.

Because of the situation in Germany in the 1930s many schemes were started to re-equip and enlarge the armed forces. There was a demand for new airfields for the expanding bomber force and Brattleby was one of the many sites surveyed. It was found to be suitable and the land re-purchased.

When it was announced in 1935 that there was again to be an airfield at Scampton many local people were against the project. However, the contractors arrived and work went ahead to construct a grass-surfaced airfield. The airfield occupied the same site as it had in the First World War, plus some land to the south of the original airfield and Aisthorpe House, on the airfield boundary, which was occupied by Mr R. Fieldsend. This was an obvious obstruction to flying but, with the need to rush through the airfield plans, no-one bothered in the early stages. However, it was soon made very clear when, on the night of August 31/ September 1 1937, Pilot Officer Torkington-Leech of No 9 Squadron was attempting to land his Heyford, when he crashed into the house. Fortunately no-one was killed but the outcome of the accident did mean the house was

demolished and the land to the north was absorbed into the aerodrome. The buildings on the new aerodrome included an arc of 'C' type hangars in the south-east corner of the landing area plus substantial brick-built barrack blocks, workshops and messes. However, the squadrons were initially housed in tents with much of the accommodation and the messes in huts for the first few years.

The new airfield opened as RAF Scampton on August 27 1936 as part of No 3 Group, being transferred to No 5 Group on March 10 1939 under whose control it was to remain until 1944 when it was then transferred to No 1 Group. At the time of opening the station was still in a very incomplete state. However, in October the first flying units arrived from Aldergrove: No 9 Squadron, flying Heyfords, and No 214 Squadron with Virginia and Harrow aircraft. The latter squadron received its first Handley Page Harrow on January 13 1937 and brought Scampton into the monoplane era. The squadron, having re-equipped with Harrows, left for Feltwell on April 12 1937.

On June 7, No 148 Squadron was re-formed as a long-range medium bomber unit. Initially the unit flew the Hawker Audax but these were quickly replaced by the Vickers Wellesley. In March 1938, Nos 9 and 148 Squadrons moved out with their Heyfords and Wellesleys to Stradishall and were replaced by No 49 Squadron from Worthy Down and No 83 Squadron from Turnhouse. Both units were flying Hinds but by the end of the year had re-equipped with Hampdens.

In May 1939 each squadron's establishment was increased to 16 aircraft with a further five in reserve. By September 1939 the construction programme was complete and when war was declared on the 3rd, the two Scampton squadrons were standing by with fully armed aircraft. However, the operations in the first few months of the war were uneventful and both squadrons continued to be detached from time to time to Newton and Ringway in accordance with the 'Scatter' plan. Scampton also had a decoy airfield at Rand but records are not clear as to what purpose it served.

At the beginning of March 1940 the Fairey Battles of No 98 Squadron arrived at Scampton from Hucknall but after only three weeks they moved on to Finningley. During April Bomber Command's mine-laying campaign got under way. These

Scampton on June 25 1942. Final checks for the 19 Lancasters and Manchesters of 49 and 83 Squadrons before the third 1,000-bomber raid.

minelaying operations, code-named 'Gardening', were carried out exclusively by the Hampdens of No 5 Group until the spring of 1942. The Scampton squadrons helped inaugurate the RAF's 'Gardening' campaign and played a major role in these operations.

On May 27 1940, HM the King paid his first visit to the station. The following month Air Marshal Sir Charles Portal, the C-in-C, paid a visit and presented a number of personnel with decorations.

Throughout June and July the operations increased with attacks made on the *Scharnhorst* at Kiel and on the Dortmund-Ems Canal. The latter was again the target on August 12 1940 when Flight Lieutenant R.A.B. Learoyd of No 49 Squadron won the first Bomber Command Victoria Cross, for his part in this operation. It was a low-level attack by Nos 49 and 83 Squadrons and, as Learoyd's aircraft pressed home the attack at only 150 ft, it was repeatedly hit. He subsequently brought his wrecked aircraft back to Scampton where he waited for dawn before landing to minimise the risk of further damage.

In September 1940, it was the turn of No 83 Squadron, and Scampton had its second Victoria Cross. This was awarded to Flight Sergeant John Hannah for bravery when his aircraft was set on fire by flak during a moonlight attack on invasion barges at Antwerp. Sergeant Hannah remained to fight the fire, and successfully extinguished it, after two crew members had abandoned the aircraft.

He then helped Pilot Officer Connor to navigate and bring the crippled aircraft back to Scampton.

During the winter of 1940/41 the squadrons were in action whenever the weather permitted. On February 9 1941 the Luftwaffe paid Scampton a visit and a stick of bombs fell on the flarepath. The next night an enemy intruder followed home one of 49 Squadron's aircraft after a raid on Wilhelmshaven and shot it down at Langworth, just five miles from the airfield. These enemy raids were usually carried out by single aircraft and were more a nuisance than anything else. On May 12 the score was settled when a Ju 88 was shot down over the airfield. The crew of Leutnant Hanning's Ju 88 were buried in Scampton churchyard on May 14 1941.

During July, both the resident squadrons were enlarged to have 26 aircraft each and were split into three flights. This increased the station strength to 2,300 personnel and accommodation became scarce. During November No 1518 BAT Flight formed with an establishment of Oxfords. In December 1941, the first Avro Manchesters arrived for No 83 Squadron which re-equipped with them early in 1942. By March the squadron was having to abandon a large number of sorties because of engine and hydraulic faults and by May the Manchesters were being replaced by Lancasters. Meantime, 49 Squadron was replacing its old Hampdens for the dying Manchester but within a few months these, in turn, were replaced by Lancasters.

To help in the change-over to the heavies, No 83 Squadron Conversion Flight operated from April 1 to August 21 1942 and 49 Squadron Conversion Flight from May 1942 to October 7 1942, both units flying Manchester and Lancaster Mk I aircraft. But, Bomber Command was coming under fire and the fateful Manchester only added to the doubts that many had about Bomber Command's ability to destroy German industry by bombing. In answer to the many critics, Harris put all his eggs in one basket and mounted 'Operation Millennium'—the first thousand-bomber raid.

This took place on May 30/31 1942, when 1,046 aircraft were despatched for Cologne, 29 of these being Manchesters and Lancasters from Scampton's two squadrons. 40 aircraft failed to return, including two from 49 Squadron and one of 83's Manchesters. The two Scampton squadrons took part in the two other 1,000-bomber raids, the next being on June 1/2 against Essen when the station put up 22 aircraft with a loss of two. On the third raid on June 25/26 against Bremen 1,006 aircraft were despatched, including 19 from Scampton out of which one was lost among the 44 that failed to return. On this last raid No 49 Squadron and, indeed, Bomber Command as a whole, operated the ill-fated Manchester for the last time, the other squadrons being 50, 61 and 106.

In mid-August 1942, No 83 Squadron moved to Wyton and became part of the newly-formed Pathfinder Force. Three weeks later No 57 Squadron arrived from Feltwell but did not join 49 on operations until mid-October. Equipped with Lancasters, both 57 and 49 Squadrons took part in Operation 'Robinson' and many other successful bombing raids.

On November 7, No 467 Squadron, RAAF, formed here as a heavy bomber squadron in No 5 Group, equipped with Lancasters (code letters 'PO'), but by the end of the month the unit had moved to Bottesford. Another brief stay was made by No 1661 HCU ('C' Fight) from the beginning of November until December 31 1942. In January 1943 Scampton was designated No 52 Base of No 5 Group with control of Dunholme Lodge and Fiskerton, the latter being where No 49 Squadron moved to immediately. It was indeed strange that the parent station should still be without concrete runways and the winter weather was causing serious complications with the heavy four-engined bombers. On March 15 a photo-flash exploded in a parked aircraft and set off four other fully laden bombers. The force of the explosion was so great that two of the aircraft completely disintegrated. Miraculously, no-one was injured.

Up until now the airfield had just been another operational bomber station, but in May 1943 it was to become famous and probably the most well known of all wartime bomber airfields. The reason for this flight to glory was No 617 Squadron which formed here on March 21. It now occupies a unique place in the history of the Second World War. The unit was formed under the command of Wing Commander Guy Gibson for a special, highly-secret operation. Gibson was granted the unprecedented privilege of selecting all of his 21 Lancaster crews.

After intensive training which lasted six weeks, Operation 'Chastise' was launched on May 16 1943 and the first Lancaster took off just before 21.30 hours. Only a short time previously 'Nigger', Guy Gibson's pet labrador, was killed outside the camp gates by a car. Gibson gave instructions for him to be buried at midnight, the time the attack should start on the dams. 19 specially modified Lancasters (coded 'AJ') took part in the raid on the Möhne, Eder and Sorpe dams.

The plan was for Gibson's nine aircraft to attack all three, while a diversionary force of five Lancasters attacked the Sorpe and five Lancasters remained in reserve. Dropping their Barnes Wallis spinning mines at 220 mph and at exactly 60 ft, the squadron breached the Möhne and Eder dams. 'Nigger', the code message announcing the success of the operation, was received at Grantham. Nine aircraft were lost, in all 53 brave young men, and the rest is history. Gibson's own account of the raid is told in his book *Enemy Coast Ahead*, in my opinion the best Royal Air Force book of the war. The 'Dam Busters', as they were now known, won 34 decorations on this operation including a Victoria Cross for Guy Gibson. Costly it was, but failure, no. The damage to power stations, factory buildings, houses, roads, bridges and to agriculture was enormous. But what is surprising to me is that, having paid this high price, Bomber Command made no attempt to stop the repair work on the dams.

On May 10, No 5 Group Servicing Flight was established and had the task of assisting all units in the Group with any technical problems. During June No 1518 BATF moved out with their Oxfords. Meanwhile operations continued and Scampton remained in the forefront of the bomber offensive. On operation 'Bellicose' on June 20/21, the station put up 11 Lancasters which landed at Blida in North Africa. This was the first shuttle raid and 617's first operation since the Dams raid.

However, at long last it was decided to develop Scampton's facilities and No 57 left for East Kirkby on August 29 and 617 for Coningsby the next day. Scampton then closed down and work started on runway construction and general expansion which lasted for nine months. During this period Scampton still controlled the operations flown from its two satellites. Also, the station was the home of several training units, one being the Aircrew Commando School that moved in from Moreton Hall.

Work continued throughout the spring and summer of 1944 then, on July 13, the airfield was declared fit for day flying and No 1690 Bomber Defence Training Flight arrived from Syerston under the command of Squadron Leader J.L. Munro. The unit was equipped with seven Spitfires, 12 Hurricanes and eight Martinet target-tugs. The unit's role was to provide fighter affiliation for all squadrons in No 5 Group.

Throughout September the airfield continued to be used by the Bomber Defence Training Flight which was now averaging some 55 sorties a day. On the

Vulcan B2 of No 27 Squadron at Scampton on June 29 1961.

11th of the month No 5 Group NCOs' school was formed for the purpose of drill, administration and organisation courses. By the end of the month the construction work was complete and Scampton fully re-opened. The airfield received a brief visit from the Americans when, on the 23rd, seven C-47s of the 440th TCG were diverted in from Fulbeck.

October 1944 saw many changes. On the 1st of the month No 1690 BDTF moved back to Syerston. On the 3rd, the Aircrew Commando School moved to Balderton followed on the 14th by the 5 Group NCOs' School. A few days later the Lancasters of No 153 Squadron arrived and on the 20th the airfield was again operational when 14 of their Lancasters took part in a raid on Bremen. Scampton was now transferred to No 1 Group and on the 30th of the month No 52 Base moved to Syerston and Scampton became No 15 Base with Fiskerton and Hemswell as satellites.

During December, No 1687 Bomber Defence Training Flight moved in from Ingham with a large establishment of Spitfires, Hurricanes and Martinets. This unit was to provide the training facilities for No 1 Group. However, the winter of 1944/45 posed many problems, not only for flying but also for provisioning of all stores because of the blocked roads. During February 1945, No 153 Squadron operated 11 times and during the Kleve raid on the 7th, Richard Dimbleby of the BBC flew with one of the crews and recorded his impressions of the sortie.

Many of the March operations were daylight raids in support of the advancing Allied ground forces. However, these

were not easy and Scampton lost seven aircraft plus a further four which crashed on landing. On April 2 No 1687 BDTF moved out to Hemswell and on the 5th, No 625 arrived from Kelstern. This unit took part in operations 'Manna', 'Dodge' and 'Exodus' but on October 7 1945 was disbanded. No 153 also took part in the same operations and disbanded on September 28 1945, having flown a total of 1,041 operational sorties.

Post-war Scampton was retained as a permanent Royal Air Force station and when it was opened to the public on September 15 1945 for the first Battle of Britain Day, over 15,000 people attended. In November 1945, No 57 Squadron returned and on December 3 the unit was joined by the Lancasters of No 100 Squadron. Both units took part in operations 'Dodge' and 'Wastage', the latter being the disposal of the bomb stockpile. In January 1946 the squadron strength was reduced from 26 to 16 aircraft and in May of that year both units moved to Lindholme, No 57 Squadron having re-equipped with Lincolns a few weeks earlier.

Scampton was now without a resident flying unit but this did not stop the work of No 1 Group Major Servicing Unit which had returned in May 1946 and had the task of disposing of the unwanted Lancasters. The winter of 1946/47 was very bad and kept the airfield closed as snow-clearing equipment was being used to keep open public roads.

Flying a motley collection of aircraft including Mosquitoes, Spitfires, Wellingtons, Lancasters and Lincolns, the Bomber Command Instructors' School (BCIS) moved in from Finningley on January 22 1947. Its role was the categorisation and training of all instructors for Bomber Command. In July 1947 it was restyled the Bomber Command Instrument Rating and Examining Flight (BCIRE).

During the 'cold war' Scampton was one of the stations made available to the US government and on July 17 1948 30 B-29 Superfortresses of the 28th Bomb Group arrived. The Americans quickly settled in but on October 18 1948 this unit was replaced by the 301st Bomb Group. However, it was only a short stay and by the beginning of 1949, the crisis in Europe had passed and on January 15 the B-29s returned to the USA. The Americans were replaced in February 1949 by the Lancasters and Lincolns of No 230 OCU.

The following years were uneventful. In January 1952 a detachment from Nos 120 and 240 Squadrons arrived with their Shackletons and used the airfield for about six weeks. The Americans arrived back in June 1952 when the 3930th Air Base Squadron was established and throughout October two Fortresses and two Constellations of a US Navy detachment used the station.

By now the training of Lincoln crews had become superfluous and, on May 1 1953, 230 OCU disbanded. During this time BCIRE moved to Binbrook and the

Scampton in June 1976. Hastings TG517 and TG503 on dispersal. These were two of the only four remaining Hastings left in the RAF which were all based at Scampton. The other two were TG505 and TG511.

Bomber Command Bombing School, that was just forming, moved to Lindholme. The American unit disbanded in July 1953 for by now Scampton was already an operational bomber station again, with No 10 Squadron having re-formed as a light bomber squadron with Canberra B.2s on January 15.

In keeping with the expansion of the Canberra force, three more units followed to complete the wing, No 27 on June 15, No 18 on August 1 and No 21 Squadron on September 21. These units moved out in May 1955 for Scampton had been ear-marked for development as a V-bomber base. No 10 moved to Honington, No 18 to Upwood and Nos 21 and 27 to Waddington. On June 1 1955 the station was closed and placed on C & M.

For the next three years work progressed to make the airfield capable of operating the new generation of V-bombers. The old wartime runway pattern was replaced by a single runway 9,000 ft long. Because it was so long more land had to be obtained to the north and east and this entailed diverting the old Roman Road, the A15, to enable the runway to be extended across the original road.

On May 1 Scampton was reactivated as a Class 1 airfield and No 617 Squadron re-formed here, its original home, with Vulcan B.1s. Today, 617 Squadron occupies the same hangar as the original 'Dambusters' and one is constantly reminded of that epic mission by the presence of 'Nigger's' grave which fronts the present day crew rooms. 617 Squadron *had* returned in 1953 but, that was only in spirit during the making of the film *The Dam Busters*.

The next to re-form with Vulcans was No 83 Squadron during October 1960 and, to complete the wing, No 27 on April 1 1961. Throughout this period an extensive building programme had been underway and since the squadrons re-armed with Vulcan B.2s for the Blue Steel role, this meant specialist buildings to handle the weapon system and its fuel.

On July 19 1969, No 83 Squadron was disbanded and in December that year No 230 OCU returned to one of its former homes. In 1972 the Hastings Radar Flight joined the OCU's establishment. Its task was to provide radar training for navigators but, in July 1977, this flight disbanded. The task today of No 230 OCU is to provide flying training for all Vulcan crews of Strike Command. It also provides refresher training.

In March 1972 No 27 Squadron disbanded only to reform here with Vulcan SR.2s on November 1 1973 in the strategic reconnaissance role. When the Near East Bomber Wing disbanded in Cyprus in January 1975, No 35 Squadron returned to the UK and joined the Vulcan Wing at Scampton. During this period from September 1 1972 until January 1 1974 Scampton also housed the Strike Command Bombing School, equipped with Hastings; because of their aircraft the school had the nickname of the 1066 unit!

For many years Scampton was a Vulcan base but in 1979 it was announced that all but one squadron would be disbanded and replaced by Victor tanker squadrons from Marham. Today a Lancaster, sadly not one of the many wartime veterans but one completed at Longbridge in April 1945, stands as gate guardian and a reminder of those wartime days and our proud and glorious past.

Scopwick (Digby), Lincolnshire
See Digby

Skegness, Lincolnshire
122/TF564656. Just N of Skegness between the A158 and A52 roads

In the First World War Skegness opened in August 1914 as an RNAS base, but closed the same month. In the Second World War it was a non-flying unit and in February 1941 opened as No 11 Recruits Centre which disbanded in October 1944 and then closed.

Skellingthorpe, Lincolnshire
121/SK935695. 3 miles W of Lincoln N of the B1190 road

February 20 1944, ops were on, and Wing Commander Reg Stidolph was just starting his Lancaster for the Stuttgart raid. 'I had two engines going when a car came swinging into our dispersal and screeched to a stop. The driver waved to me as he got out and ran to the rear-gunner's turret. I heard faint mutterings over the intercom, then the rear-gunner spoke: "Congratulations Skipper, your wife has just had a baby son!" I thought, "Christ, what a time to tell a man; OK, start number 3 and 4".'

A surprising time to receive such news was in keeping with Skellingthorpe for this was a rather unusual location for an airfield, being situated in an area of gravel pits and woods just outside the boundary of the City of Lincoln. It is reputed that the airfield came into being because two Hampdens crash-landed in the fields and the only way to get them out was to repair them where they were, then build a runway and fly them out. Having built the makeshift runway the airfield was then extended and used for the remainder of the war. However, be this true or not, construction work started early in 1941, and much of the hutted accommodation was dispersed in the woods, particularly to the east of the site, which opened in October 1941 as a satellite for Swinderby in No 5 Group, Bomber Command. At that time Skellingthorpe was a grass airfield with very primitive facilities and was shut in on three sides by heavy woods.

The first users of this primitive airfield were a detachment of No 50 Squadron (code letters 'VN'), which arrived at the end of October from Swinderby while the runways were being built at that station. The remainder of the unit moved in the following month with their elderly Hampden bombers. The squadron converted to the fateful Manchester in April 1942 and there was always tight security around the troublesome aircraft. There were many crashes and the aircraft very easily caught on fire. Only half of the Manchesters were operational at any given time and they were called 'Flying Coffins' by the crews. However, good came out of bad for the Manchester was the forerunner of the Lancaster.

Despite these setbacks No 50 Squadron took part in many major raids, and participated in the thousand bomber raid on Cologne on the night of May 30/31 1942. It is true that No 50 Squadron suffered from the Manchester but, it was in such an aircraft that Flying Officer Leslie Manser gave the station its only Victoria Cross of the war. He was captain and first pilot of a Manchester on this Cologne raid and, while over the target area, the aircraft was hit repeatedly and the rear gunner wounded. The front cabin filled with smoke and the port engine burst into flames. However, Manser held the badly damaged aircraft steady for those few vital seconds and ordered the crew to bail out, knowing it meant certain death for himself. The aircraft plunged to earth and blew up with the gallant captain still on board. He was posthumously awarded the Victoria Cross.

During June 1942 No 50 Squadron returned to Swinderby to facilitate the construction of runways at Skellingthorpe. There were three of these, the main runway starting from the B1190 Lincoln-Doddington road and running in a north-easterly direction towards Lincoln Cathedral. They were the standard war-time pattern and were linked by a perimeter track around which were hard-standings for the aircraft. Because the main runway came right up to the B1190, the road had to be closed when the bombers took off.

By September the runways were again operational and at the end of the month two conversion flights, Nos 97 and 106 Squadrons, arrived but within three weeks they moved to Swinderby and on October 16 1942 No 50 Squadron, having re-equipped with Lancasters, took up residence again and was to remain at the airfield until after the end of the war in Europe. In November 1943 it was joined by No 61 Squadron which also remained at Skellingthorpe until after the war apart from a couple of months in the spring of 1944 when it moved to Coningsby.

Both squadrons played a major part in the bombing offensive. No 50 Squadron put up 12 Lancasters for the low-level dusk raid on Le Creusot in October 1942. In 1943 it took part in the first 'shuttle-bombing' attack and in the Peenemünde raid. In 1944 amongst its many targets were the V-1 storage sites. On the disastrous Nuremberg raid of March 30/31 1944, No 50 Squadron despatched 19 aircraft of which one crashed on take-off and three failed to return. One of these was 'A' Able in which Sergeant J. Dunn was wireless operator, and it was their thirteenth operation. They had just turned on their final leg and at 01.15 hours sighted the target ahead, when suddenly the aircraft gave a sickening lurch. 'I switched back on to the intercom in time to hear the two gunners acknowledge the order to "bale out", and the bomb aimer shouting "I can't get this bloody hatch open". Not waiting to hear any more, I tore off my helmet and clipped on my chute. I scrambled to the rear of the fuselage following the navigator, but the next moment a violent explosion threw me off my feet, and I was trapped, pinned to the inside of the fuselage of a blazing aircraft at 21,000 ft with nearly 12,000 lb of incendiary and high explosive bombs. My limbs were weighted, I seemed too heavy to move even a finger, and the whole world was gyrating madly. Suddenly, I saw a gaping jagged hole, through which the moon shone—the aircraft had broken its back at exactly the point at which I was pinned—its last dying lurch. But in that instant and before I knew what was happening, I was catapulted into the cool clean night air above the Bavarian slopes.'

Of the crew of 'A' Able, the navigator, mid-upper gunner and rear gunner were killed. Sergeant Dunn was taken prisoner of War and held in Stalag Luft 6. He was freed in late April 1945.

When No 61 Squadron arrived at the station during November 1943 it was commanded by Wing Commander R.N. Stidolph, DFC, a very experienced pilot, who remained at the head until April 1944 when he handed over to Wing Commander J.B. Tait, DSO, DFC.

No 61 Squadron was on its home ground at Skellingthorpe for the squadron badge was 'The Lincoln Imp' so it was only appropriate that it should return to fight the war from its home base. Four of the squadron Lancasters became veterans of more than a hundred operations— ED860 with 130, JB138 with 123, EE176 with 122 and LL843 with 118.

Lancaster 'N' Nan, ED860, had completed 130 sorties and crashed on take-off on Saturday, October 28 1944. It had been entrusted to Flight Lieutenant Laurence Pearse and his crew to further the aircraft's total. But, as it thundered down the runway, it suddenly started to swing to port, ran over the flare path, burst a tyre, and at that point the undercarriage collapsed. Then, the port wing broke off and the bomb bay and fuselage was crushed. As the aircraft ground to a halt Flight Sergeant Arthur Perry, the wireless operator, made a lightning dash for the rear escape hatch but, as he scrambled out he was greeted with a lake of 100 octane fuel with a torn-off engine sizzling in the middle of it. After the crew was all out the pilot turned to Flight Sergeant Perry. 'I'm glad you heard my second order, Bill, we would have been in trouble otherwise.' Perry had to admit he had not heard the first order which had been to fire a red Very light, but the pilot had been cool enough to have a rethink and cancel it because of the fire risk.

The City of Lincoln has today adopted the last flying Lancaster, but it is a pity they did not take over one of these for a museum in the city for 61 Squadron was the obvious choice and had the aircraft; instead they acted like the squadron motto, 'Per purum tonantes' (thundering through the clear air).

No 50 Squadron, Skellingthorpe. Sergeant R. Hutton, Flight Engineer on board 'O'-Orange during the Le Creusot Raid of October 29 1942. This photo was taken by a newspaper reporter on board.

At April 1945, No 61 Squadron had 22 Lancasters on strength and the following June it moved to Sturgate. Also in June, No 619 Squadron arrived from Strubby, but disbanded on the 18th of the following month. That same month No 463 Squadron arrived from Waddington as part of 'Tiger Force' to participate in the war against Japan. The squadron had been told in May that it would not be needed, but continued training until September 14 when all flying was then cancelled. On September 25 the unit disbanded.

By early 1946 only very few airfields remained open for flying but for some unknown reason Skellingthorpe was one, being used as a Relief Landing Ground by the Swinderby HCU for some time and remaining open for that purpose until about 1952 when the airfield then closed. The station was also used from 1946 until closing by No 58 MU who salvaged crashed aircraft and also used the site for storage purposes.

A post-war boundary alteration brought the site of the airfield into the City of Lincoln and there was some consideration given to the possibility of re-opening it and developing it into a municipal airport, but again the opportunity was not taken and these plans fell through and the airfield was completely dismantled. The control tower and hangars were demolished and at the northern end there is a housing estate which in a few years will have overrun the airfield leaving few traces of the busy wartime operational bomber station.

South Carlton, Lincolnshire

121/SK965762. Situated just N of Lincoln, E of South Carlton village and the B1398 road

The steep Lincoln Cliff, running parallel to and about a mile west of the old Roman road, Ermine Street, was a favourite location with the planners of World War 1 aerodromes for they could make use of the prevailing south-westerly wind. It was a natural choice even for World War 2 sites, the most famous being Brattleby, later to become Scampton and the home of the 'Dam Busters'.

South Carlton aerodrome was constructed between the Ermine Street and B1398 roads immediately to the north of Hallifirs Wood and was equipped with seven permanent hangars of the 1916 RFC pattern, one of which served as an Aeroplane Repair Shed. In addition there were several temporary hangars of the Bessonneaux type and living accommodation was provided for by rows of wooden huts.

The aerodrome opened in November 1916 with No 45 Reserve Squadron with Farman FB5 aircraft. For the remainder of the war it housed training units, the final one leaving in April 1920 after which it closed. Units and aircraft based at South Carlton were No 61 TS with DH6 and FK8 aircraft and No 46 TDS, made up from 39 TS and 46 TS, with Camels, Dolphins and 504s.

During the post-war period it also acted as the demobilisation base for two squadrons which disbanded as part of the reduction in size of the permanent armed forces. These were No 25 Squadron with de Havilland 9A aircraft from September to December 1919 and No 57 Squadron,

also with DH 9As, which disbanded at South Carlton on December 13 1919.

The station closed in 1920 and the site reverted to agriculture after it was vacated by the RAF. There is no record of any further flying activities since that date and many of the buildings were used by the local farmer. One of the hangars survived in fair condition until about 1975 when the wooden roof collapsed, and several other buildings were still in use in 1979.

Spanhoe (Harringworth, Wakerley), Northamptonshire

141/SP935970. Approximately 8 miles SW of Stamford between the villages of Harringworth, Wakerley and Laxton

This was one of the many airfields built during 1943 and handed over to the Americans as their bomber force increased in England. The old quarry near Harringworth village formed the western boundary and use was made of the heavy woods on the southern and eastern boundaries.

It was a typical wartime bomber airfield and was built to class 'A' specification having a main runway 2,000 yards long, and 50 yards wide with two intersecting runways, each 1,400 yards long, placed at the western side of the airfield. The encircling perimeter track had 50 loop-type hardstandings and, between the perimeter track and the Harringworth—Laxton road on the southern edge of the airfield, were two 'T2' hangars. The technical site was also in this area and the living accommodation, mess and sick quarters were on the south side of the country road, in and around Spanhoe wood, from which the airfield was given its name. But, it was always known as either Wakerley or Harringworth, the latter causing confusion by its similarity to the airfield at Harrington.

The pyrotechnic and bomb store was set in the wooded area to the south-east of the airfield and the northern end housed a 72,000-gallon fuel store with two further 72,000-gallon stores at the quarry end.

On January 1 1944 the station was ready and it was allocated to the 9th ATCC, Substitution Unit, and during the first week the first ground units moved in, namely the 461st Signal Construction Battalion and the 309th Station Company Squadron. Spanhoe officially opened on January 7 as Air Station 493. On February 7 the 315th TCG, made up of only two squadrons, the 34th and 43rd, moved in

Spanhoe in June 1944. Fully equipped 'troops of the air' march in formation towards aircraft of the IXth Air Force Troop Carrier Command. For many, it was to be their last walk. Thought to be Spanhoe even though the aircraft in view is coded 'M2' which is the 438th of the 53rd TCW. The 50th and 53rd Wings did train together so this would not be unusual.

from Welford Park equipped with C-47, C-53 and two Oxford aircraft plus about a dozen Waco CG-4A gliders that were attached to the Group.

During February and March the Group gathered itself into order as aircraft and men were posted in while the build-up continued, and by the beginning of April the 315th had 61 aircraft, mainly C-47s, and 30 CG-4A Waco gliders plus a few Piper L-4As on strength.

The training programme now increased and on April 4 the 818th Medical Air Evacuation Squadron arrived here with 25 female nurses who injected some much-needed warmth into the station for bad weather had made training difficult and the airfield's atmosphere matched the weather. By the end of the month the 315th was brought up to strength and had a full complement of four squadrons, the 34th, 43rd, 309th and 310th.

On May 11 the dress rehearsal got underway when 48 C-47s of the 315th took off from Spanhoe at 22.30 hours. The operation consisted of 432 aircraft of the 50th and 53rd Wings, carrying over 6,000 men of the 101st Airborne Division, and 369 aircraft of the 52nd Wing carrying in each aircraft only a token compliment of two paratroopers of the 82nd Airborne. The reason was that these

men were fully trained and were not to be risked at this late hour. By 04.37 hours all Spanhoe aircraft were back. The mission was not a success and several squadrons did not drop their paratroopers, including those of the 315th.

Everyone at the station could feel the invasion was near and on June 3 they knew it when 864 paratroopers of the 505th Paratroop Infantry Regiment of the 82nd Airborne Division arrived at the station. Spanhoe was bursting at the seams and the men used one of the hangars for sleeping accommodation. On the evening of June 5 the paratroopers started to climb aboard their aircraft. As one of the men waited to board Flying Officer Harper's aircraft of the 43rd Squadron he dropped a grenade which exploded and also detonated several others. Three troopers were killed and 15 others wounded, one being the radio operator of the aircraft.

Minutes later the 48 C-47s took off headed by Colonel McLelland who led the formation. The destination for the 315th was Dropping Zone 'O' which was near Ste-Mère-Église and the Group had a successful drop, with good concentration of paratroopers. By 04.40 hours on June 6 1944, 45 aircraft were back at Spanhoe, two others had made it back into Southern

Spanhoe control tower overgrown and, when photographed in 1979, being used to store hay. A far cry from when the C-47s returned after the D-Day operation.

England and the other was hit over the target area. Twelve aircraft received slight flak damage.

After D-Day the Group did a supply mission and other routine tasks. On July 8 a training mission was planned with the 315th, and 369 Polish paratroopers arrived at the station to take part in operation 'Burden'. At 21.30 hours 33 C-47s took off from Spanhoe and headed for the drop zone at Wittering. During the flight an aircraft of the 309th squadron moved out of formation and collided with one on its starboard side, both crashing near Tinwell, Rutland. Eight crew and 26 paratroopers died. Throughout July the Group was kept very busy and exercises continued into August.

Between the middle of August and the middle of September three major airborne operations had been planned, these being 'Transfigure', 'Linnet' and 'Comet', then called off at the last minute due to the speed with which General George Patton's tanks were moving. However, 'Market Garden' was to be on and, on September 14, 354 paratroopers of the 82nd Airborne moved on to the airfield from their living sites on Braunstone Park.

The 315th were to fly two serials of 45 aircraft, the first of which began its take-off at 10.39 hours on September 17 1944. The second serial started at 11.01 and, along with the main force, took the northern route to their Dropping Zone just north of the River Maas. One aircraft, piloted by Captain Bohanan, was hit by flak and he and four other crew members were killed. The other 89 aircraft dropped their paratroopers and made it back to Spanhoe. Upon their return the groundcrews began to change the American parapack racks to the British

type and next day two serials of 27 aircraft took off with 462 British paratroopers of the 4th Parachute Brigade on board. Their destination was Dropping Zone 'Y' at Ginkel Heath but this time many aircraft were hit and upon return to Spanhoe several pilots complained of lack of fighter support on the final run-in.

Bad weather then held up the flights and 700 Polish paratroopers who had arrived at the airfield were not flown out until the 21st, D + 4, when several of the Group's aircraft were hit by flak. Bad weather prevented operations on the 22nd but on the 23rd, D + 6, 42 aircraft carrying 560 Polish paratroopers and 219 parapacks headed for Arnhem although, by now, the battle was lost. Later the 315th transported 334 British troops and equipment, and after combat operations the Group carried freight to the continent. For the next few weeks the freight missions continued and in November it was thought the 315th would move to a new station at Birch in Essex, but this did not transpire. Then, in March 1945, the 315th took part in operation 'Varsity' during which they lost 19 aircraft with 36 others needing repairs.

By this time the Americans had become well established in the area and 'any gum, chum' had become a favourite saying, but now they were on the move and by April 11 all American units had moved to Amiens Glisy in France.

On May 30 1945 the station was handed back to the Royal Air Force, Maintenance Command, No 40 Group, who used it for the repair and disposal of military vehicles. Flying had ceased and the base was non-operational. On July 8 1945, No 253 MU, whose task was to prepare vehicles to be sold in public auctions, was formed; in March 1946 they had 16,069 in store, a treasure trove for any modern enthusiast—but where have they all gone?

However, by the spring of 1947, 253 MU had departed and the airfield closed down. However, on August 12 1960 a Valiant, XD875 from No 7 Squadron, Wittering, took off at 10.30 on a training flight but suddenly it dived towards Spanhoe airfield and crashed.

Today, part of the western side of the airfield has been eaten away in the quest for iron ore and the few remaining Nissen huts have been eroded by time. The control tower and most of the technical site still remain, but slowly they crumble away.

Spilsby, Lincolnshire

122/TF450650. Just over 2 miles east of Spilsby, north of the B1195 road

This airfield was sited on the southern end of the Lincolnshire Wolds a few miles west of Skegness between the B1195 and A158 (T) roads. Work started in early 1943 and a number of minor roads to the north of Great Steeping were closed and taken over as part of the site. It was constructed as a bomber station with the usual three concrete runways and an encircling perimeter track, but the runways were above average length. They were the standard 150-ft width but the main runway was 7,590 ft long, the second one 6,000 ft and the third 4,290 ft. For some reason the airfield was named after the largest of the market towns to the west and opened in September 1943 as a bomber airfield in No 5 Group.

The first to take up residence were the Lancasters of No 207 Squadron which moved in from Langar during October. They continued operations from here and on D-Day the squadron's Lancasters bombed Caen in support of operation 'Overlord'.

In September of that year the resident unit was joined by No 44 Squadron, also flying Lancasters, and Spilsby became a two-squadron station, both units remaining here until after the war in Europe. The last mission of the war for both units was on April 25 1945 when eight Lancasters of No 44 Squadron and ten Lancasters of No 207 Squadron were despatched to bomb Berchtesgaden.

In July 1945, No 44 Squadron moved to Mepal, Cambridgeshire, and was replaced by No 75 (New Zealand) Squadron from that station. This unit remained until October 15 1945 when it then disbanded,

bringing to an end a distinguished war career. The decorations won by New Zealand personnel of 75 Squadron were one VC, six DSOs, 88 DFCs, four bars to DFCs, two CGMs and 17 DFMs. Because of these squadron honours the Air Ministry suggested that the RNZAF should take over the squadron number plate in memory of their fine war effort.

That same month No 207 Squadron moved to Methwold, Suffolk, and it too had achieved a fine war record—much of it during its two-year stay at Spilsby. The squadron had flown 540 sorties and lost 154 crews. The decorations won were seven DSOs, 115 DFCs and 92 DFMs. With the departure of the last flying unit the station was then taken over by No 2 Armament Practice School which remained until November 1946. By the end of the year the station had closed down and was put on care and maintenance.

For the next few years Spilsby was surplus to requirements and was just another disused airfield. Then, in June 1955, the station reopened and was used by non-flying units of the USAF, stores and maintenance sections for nearby East Kirkby. The Americans remained until 1958 then, with the Korean war over, the units moved out in March.

The station closed immediately the Americans had left and, today, very little remains. The control tower has gone and most of the runways and perimeter track have been demolished. The remaining hangar is used for some industrial purpose, but the few other buildings that remain are in poor condition and are fast disappearing.

Spitalgate (Grantham), Lincolnshire

130/SK940345. E of Grantham adjacent to the A52 road

This aerodrome was first constructed during 1916 on a hilltop site overlooking Grantham. It was equipped with wooden hangars of the 1915 RFC pattern and in November 1916 it opened as a training aerodrome with the arrival of 49 Reserve Squadron with their BE2 aircraft.

Grantham (later to be renamed Spitalgate) remained a training airfield throughout the First World War and it was very much a hit and miss affair in the early years. Throughout 1917 there were many arrivals and changes: during April No 11 RS arrived with BE2s, only to be re-

Nine DH 9as from 39 Squadron, Spital-gate, over Grantham.

named 11 TS in May while the resident unit became 49 TS. In September both units departed and were replaced by three units, 20 TS, 37 TS and 15 TS, flying a variety of aircraft including DH6s, FK3s, Avro 504s, RE8s and BE2s. During August 1918, 20 TS moved out and 15 TS and 37 TS disbanded to form 39 Training Depot Squadron equipped with FK8s, FE2s and Avro 504Ks. The following year this was re-named 39 Training Squadron.

During the post-war period, Grantham remained an active airfield but was used mainly by cadre units. In February 1919, No 70 Squadron moved in with Camel and Snipe aircraft. This unit was followed in August by 29 Squadron and in September by 43 Squadron. By the end of the year both 29 and 43 had disbanded and in January 1920 No 70 Squadron also disbanded and later in the year 39 TS moved out.

During 1920 No 6 Flying Training School was formed here but it never received any aircraft and in May 1921 moved to Manston. By now though the station had received its first day-bomber squadron for, in February, No 39 Squadron had arrived with de Havilland 9As. This squadron was followed a year

later by 100 Squadron which, upon arrival, also re-equipped with DH 9A day-bombers, 'D' flight being equipped with Vickers Vimys. The squadron had just started to re-equip with Fairey Fawns in May 1922 when it moved to Eastchurch in Kent only to return again in July. During the General Strike of 1926 the squadron distributed mail and copies of Winston Churchill's *British Gazette*.

In April 1922, No 3 Flying Training School moved in from Scopwick with an establishment of 504s, F2Bs, Snipes, Atlases and Tutors. The station expanded and for a time it was one of the busiest aerodromes in the UK. Eventually both the day-bomber squadrons left, in January 1928: No 39 Squadron to Bircham Newton and No 100 Squadron to Bicester. Grantham now became solely a training station until the summer of 1937 when No 3 FTS moved out, and it then became an operational airfield in No 5 Group, Bomber Command.

In August 1937, No 113 and 211 Squadrons arrived. Both units were equipped with Hinds and moved to the Middle East in April 1938. They were immediately replaced in September by two Fairey Battle squadrons, Nos 106 and 185. But it was now obvious that the airfield was too small for a bomber station and in October both squadrons moved to Thornaby and the station reverted to a training role with the formation of No 12 FTS that same month.

At the outbreak of war in September 1939, the station strength was 927 personnel and the school was equipped with Harts, Ansons and Audaxes. The aircraft and personnel quickly built up and within two months 12 SFTS had on strength 105 aircraft. In addition to the school's aircraft, the station had also housed No 5 Group Communications Flight since 1938 and this unit was equipped with Tutor, Oxford and Magister aircraft, replaced later by Percival Proctors which were used to ferry the officers from HQ 5 Group at St Vincents to airfields within the Group.

At the beginning of 1940 it was decided to lay out a decoy airfield (K-site) at Folkingham for Grantham, but this was abandoned in 1941. By the summer of 1940, Battles had replaced the biplanes and in August the school was on standby for a possible move to Canada. However, in October the order was cancelled and the training programme increased. By early 1942 the circuit had become so congested that it was decided to re-open the nearby World War 1 aerodrome at Harlaxton, and in April it became available as a relief landing ground as a satellite to Grantham. The personnel had now increased to over 2,500 and its satellite and a large Nissen hutment area had sprung up to accommodate the increase.

That same month, 12 SFTS was renamed 12 (P) AFU and by the middle of 1943 had re-equipped with Blenheim V Bisleys. The major role of the unit was night fighter training and, to complete the programme, No 1536 Beam Approach Training Flight arrived in March 1943. Its role was to give newly qualified night fighter pilots the necessary training in instrument landing.

By November 1943 the grass airfield began to break up under the years of continual use and, because of the volume of traffic at the satellite field, it also was beginning to break-up. By the end of the year the situation had become serious and the aircraft moved to airfields in Cheshire and Lancashire. A few of the station's Blenheims were housed at Balderton. Because of the move by No 5 Group HQ at the end of 1943, the 5 Group Communications Flight moved out during November of that year.

In the early part of 1944, steel tracking was laid and the aircraft quickly returned. By the summer of 1944, Spitalgate, as it was renamed on March 29 1944, had on strength 57 Blenheims, 30 Oxfords and a few Ansons. The original hangars on the western boundary had been supplemented by a brick hangar and further hangarage had been provided by the erection of three Bellmans in the north-west corner of the airfield. But the heyday of the airfield was over and, on February 8 1945, 12 (P) AFU moved to Hixon and Cranage. This unit was replaced the following month by 17

SFTS from Cranwell. In May 1945, 1536 BATF moved out which left only the Oxfords at the airfield. The school continued to use them until 1947 when it was renamed 1 FTS and was re-equipped with Harvards.

Spitalgate continued to be used by the post-war Royal Air Force but its days were numbered. Throughout the war it had remained grass-surfaced with only temporary steel mesh runways. These would not be suitable for the new breed of jet aircraft and the site had limitations. Therefore it was not surprising that, when 1 FTS moved out in February 1948, Spitalgate lost its last flying unit.

Over the next few years the station housed a series of non-flying units, the first of these being the RAF Officer Cadet Training Unit that arrived in March 1948 and remained until March 1954. During this period the airfield was used by the Prentice aircraft of No 7 FTS, Cottesmore, as a RLG. Other units were the Mess Staff School from September 1949 to August 1957. The station was also HQ for No 24 Group, TTC, from March 1954 until it disbanded in August 1957. During this period the station further housed the Royal Air Force School of Education and Central Library 1955-1958. Other units based here in 1959 were the Secretarial Officers' School and HQ 3 Police District, renamed HQ Provost and Security Services.

In 1960, Spitalgate became the WRAF Depot and all airwomen did their basic training here before moving to Hereford in March 1974. Over the past few years the Central Gliding School had used the airfield but in 1975 it moved out to Syerston and the station was then transferred to the Army and used by the Royal Corps of Transport.

A Bristol Blenheim Mark V, AZ959, of No 12 (P) AFU at Spitalgate in 1943/44.

Above *A Piston Provost XF874 and* (above right) *a Varsity WJ941, come into land at Strubby on January 18 and September 18 1961, respectively.*

Strubby, Lincolnshire

122/TF450810. SW of Louth, between the A157 and B1373 roads

Sited a few miles further south of Manby between the villages of Strubby and Woodthorpe, this was a very late arrival. Constructed as a bomber station in No 5 Group, it had the usual three runways, which were 4,300, 6,000 and 4,800 ft long, with an encircling perimeter track and widely dispersed accommodation around the flat countryside.

However, Strubby opened as a Coastal Command station on April 15 1944 and, on May 1, No 280 Squadron arrived with Vickers Warwicks. A most unusual sight for the people of Lincolnshire who had now become accustomed to the twin-engined Wellington and the four-engined Lancaster. Equipped with airborne life-boats, the Warwicks were used in an air-sea rescue role. They did a very important job in rescuing ditched airmen, but their stay was to be very brief.

The status of the station on June 6 1944 was 280 Squadron in No 16 Group. However, on July 1 Nos 144 and 404 Squadrons moved in from Davidstow Moor. Both units were equipped with Beaufighters and they formed the Strubby Strike Wing, on anti-shipping and anti-'E' boat strikes in the North Sea. During September both units moved to Banff and No 280 Squadron went to Langham.

That same month the station was transferred to Bomber Command and took on a more offensive role with the arrival of No 619 Squadron towards the end of the month from Dunholme Lodge. This became the resident unit and remained here during the last few months of the

Below *Strubby in 1979. The control tower and buildings are now deserted, and* (below right) *the Guardroom.*

war. The squadron took part in many of the major raids and on March 3/4 1945, during a raid on the Dortmund-Ems Canal at Ladbergen, Wing Commander S.G. Birch, pilot of Lancaster PD441, 'B' Baker, destroyed a V-1 in flight. The last bombing mission of the war was on April 25 when six Lancasters were despatched to bomb the SS barracks at Berchtesgaden. The last operational mission was on April 25/26 when four Lancasters were despatched to lay mines in Oslo fjord off Horten.

During April the resident unit was joined by 227 Squadron that arrived from Balderton, and together they helped to fly British ex-POWs home from France and Belgium. During June, No 227 Squadron moved to Graveley and No 619 to Skellingthorpe for disbanding. Strubby was now without any flying units and on September 7 1945 the airfield closed. For a time the airfield was used to store Lancasters while their fate was decided. Then, in July 1949, the airfield re-opened as a satellite for Manby. It continued in

this role until September 1972 when Manby then relinquished control and the airfield was closed. During this period a variety of aircraft, including Dominies, Varsitys, Meteors, Vampires and Athenas used the airfield.

The final chapter in this wartime bomber station's story came on March 4 1980 when the airfield's 515 acres (of which 50 are concrete) were put up for auction. Sold in four lots, the airfield made £683,000. The pension fund of Boots the Chemists purchased two of the four lots and one went to Mr Morris Stovin, a neighbouring farmer. A heliport has been established on the east side of the airfield and is run by Conoco which now flies men and equipment to oil rigs in the North Sea from Strubby. The standard World War 2 tower remains intact, but it has been vandalised and its future is uncertain. The two 'T2' and one 'B1' hangars have been retained by the Ministry of Agriculture for grain storage. The estimated five miles of runway are still intact . . . but for how long?

Sturgate today—control tower, fire tender shed and searchlight and tractor shed.

Sturgate, Lincolnshire

121/SK880875. SE of Gainsborough between the villages of Heapham and Upton

Constructed as a No 1 Group, Bomber Command, operational station, Sturgate was one of the last airfields to be built during the Second World War and did not see any operational service for, by the time it was completed, the demand for operational bomber stations had already been met.

Situated in the west of Lincolnshire, it was constructed during 1943-1944. The airfield name was derived from a small hamlet about a mile to the north. Sturgate had the usual three concrete runways, the main one being 2,000 yards long and on an east-west axis with an encircling perimeter track, off which were the normal hardstandings. Two 'T2' hangars and the standard other buildings completed the airfield.

Sturgate came into use during the latter part of 1944 as an Aircrew Training School in No 7 Group, Bomber Command, being known as 71 Base Sub-Station. The school was, in fact, a holding unit for bomber crews awaiting posting to HCUs and they only used the airfield for circuit training. The airfield was also used as a Relief Landing Ground for Blyton until June 1945. The only flying unit based here during the war was 1520 BAT Flight from September 18 1944 to May 30 1945 with Oxford aircraft.

It is ironic that the airfield never housed a four-engined bomber during the war and it was not until after the Oxfords had left that two squadrons of Lancasters did arrive, in June 1945. These were Nos 50 and 61 from Skellingthorpe, but their stay was very brief and they both left for Waddington in January 1946 when Sturgate closed to flying.

From January 1946 the airfield was left to decay, unwanted, until the Korean War brought American units back to Europe and disused airfields all over Britain were designated as reserve USAF airfields, although few were ever activated. However, Sturgate was one of those few and, on July 30 1952, it was allocated to the USAF who brought it back into service and used it from June 1953 to 1964. One unit was 3928 Air Base Group, 7th Air Division, of SAC on rotation. The airfield was also occupied by the 508th Strategic Fighter Wing with Thunder-streak jet fighters.

After the Americans had gone the airfield again closed but this time most of the buildings were dismantled and the site sold by auction. Today, parts of the runways are used by the Lincolnshire Aero Club, preserving the slim aviation link. The control tower is still standing and nearby is the original wartime shed with the lettering 'Crash Fire Station No.1' over the triple doors.

Sutton Bridge (Holbeach), Lincolnshire

131/TF485205. E of King's Lynn, S of the A17 road

An unusual and rather unique site because of its geographic position, Sutton Bridge is just inland from the Wash on the south side of the main A17 with the river Nene along the western boundary. Tucked away in the backwater of the fen country, it derived its name from the bridge that crosses the A17 road. Part of the landing ground was in Norfolk, the domestic site in Lincolnshire and a few other sites in Cambridgeshire.

The site was first used in 1926, when it opened as a temporary armament practice camp for use by fighter squadrons or advanced flying training units of the

Royal Air Force and Fleet Air Arm for bombing and gunnery training during the summer season only. This site was chosen because of its closeness to the Wash which is in turn ideally located for the firing and bombing ranges.

Sutton was used in this way for the next ten years, during which time very few buildings were erected and tents were the only accommodation for both aircraft and airmen, being very cold, even in summertime. During this decade the main aircraft to be seen here were Bulldogs, Siskins and Harts.

In 1936 the airfield was established as a full-time permanent Royal Air Force station and a limited number of married quarters were built. The resident unit was an Armament Training Camp, renamed No 3 Armament Training Station, which carried on in the aforementioned role until the outbreak of war in 1939 when it at once moved to a safer area.

In September 1939 Sutton Bridge, having gained a brief operational role when the Blenheim fighters of No 64 Squadron were here the previous month, was transferred from No 25 Group, Flying Training, to No 11 Group of Fighter Command. It became an assembly point, known as a Fighter Pilot Pool, for newly qualified fighter pilots. The station also saw the formation in October 1939 of two fighter squadrons, Nos 264 and 266, but only the latter received Fairey Battle aircraft as makeshift fighters. The unit began to get some Spitfire Is in January 1940 and in March it moved to Martlesham Heath and took part in the Battle of Britain. No 264 was the first Defiant unit, moving to Martlesham Heath in December to receive them.

On March 9 1940, No 11 Group, Fighter Pilot Pool, formed into No 6 OTU. This was one of several such units forming at this time for the purpose of training newly qualified pilots to fly fighter aircraft in an operational capacity. The aircraft used were Hurricanes, and this was probably the most important role of the airfield for No 6 was one of the few OTUs that supplied pilots to the seriously depleted Hurricane fighter squadrons during the Battle of Britain. The unit had an establishment of 53 Hurricanes, plus several Harvards, Gladiators, Mentors and Masters.

During this time of great activity Sutton Bridge remained a grass-surfaced airfield and temporary accommodation huts had been erected in the middle of the small village on the other side of the bridge. Facilities were primitive and the site was prone to flooding thanks to its close proximity to the river Nene. However, Sutton Bridge did warrant a decoy airfield which was situated at Terrington Marsh a short distance away between the A17 road and the Wash.

In November 1940, in common with other fighter OTUs, No 6 had '50' added to its number, becoming No 56 OTU. This unit moved to Tealing in Scotland during March 1942 but, during its stay at Sutton Bridge, had provided hundreds of fighter pilots with their operational training. Sadly to say, they had a very high accident rate to which the local cemetery bears witness.

A change of role took place in April 1942, when the station reverted to No 25 Group, Flying Training Command, becoming the new home of the Central Gunnery School. The school operated

A Gauntlet being pushed into a Bessoneau hangar at the Armament Training Camp at Sutton Bridge in 1937.

courses for Gunnery Leaders and Pilot Gunnery Instructors with the ranges again being situated in the Wash. A wide variety of aircraft were used but the main types were Wellingtons, Hampdens and Spitfires. The Hawker Henleys of No 1489 Flight provided the target-towing facilities.

In February 1944 the CGS departed for Catfoss in Yorkshire and Sutton Bridge was handed over to No 21 Group, still within Flying Training Command, and Squadron Leader M. Griffiths, AFC, took over in March when the station became a satellite for Newton. On March 29 1944 Sutton Bridge was handed over to Peterborough as a satellite to be placed on a C & M basis since Newton was now back in service. There then followed a period of inactivity until sections of No 7 (P) AFU arrived at the airfield on June 21 1944, operating Oxford aircraft of the AFU based at Peterborough.

This unit continued to train those newly qualified pilots who had been trained either in Canada or other overseas locations until April 1946 when, having been re-titled No 7 SFTS since December 21 1944, it moved to a more permanent station at Kirton-in-Lindsey, and Sutton Bridge closed.

The life-blood of the airfield had gone, its active life, during which it had remained a grass airfield with poor facilities, was over. However, the Royal Air Force continued in occupation for a further ten years, probably due to the presence of the permanent pre-war married quarters. The hangars were retained for storage purposes. During the mid-1950s No 58 MU, engaged in the recovery and salvage of crashed aircraft, used the station for a temporary base, although by this time the grass airfield had already come under the plough. By 1958, No 58 MU had moved out and the Royal Air Force disposed of all the site, except the married quarters. The three 'T' type hangars and other buildings on the technical site were, up to the 1970s, owned by the Potato Marketing Board, but there is no trace of the control tower.

Swinderby, Lincolnshire

121/SK880620. On the A46 midway between Lincoln and Newark

Swinderby was built on Thurlby Moor and Laings, the civil engineers who transformed the 80 fields and woodland during the summer of 1940 into the airfield,

encountered one or two problems. The main one came when digging the foundations and locations for the underground fuel tanks. These filled with water and could not be pumped dry. Laings had tapped an underground river, a problem which they eventually solved by laying an underground pipe and piping the water into a ditch on the north side of Moor Lane. Evidence is still in existence to this day.

At last the airfield was ready, albeit there were no beds, chairs, officers' mess or, indeed, water, except underground. The Station Headquarters, armoury, two hangars and the barrack blocks were not completed until the end of the month. However, on August 17 1940 the first Commanding Officer, Wing Commander E. Lewis, arrived from Bramcote to take command of the station, Lincolnshire's second under No 1 Group. It was the last station to be built to the pre-war building specifications, which included a fountain and fish pond at the front of the officers' mess (although these were never completed!) With Swinderby airfield now open, the heavily camouflaged bomb dump of No 93 MU, sited by Swinderby station, was redesignated Norton Disney.

On August 22 and 23, No 300 Squadron arrived from Bramcote. This consisted of 42 officers, 199 airmen, 12 Fairey Battles and one Anson. Then, on August 28 and 29 No 301 Squadron arrived, with an establishment of 17 Battles and one Anson with their Commanding Officer, 2nd Colonel Roman Rudkowski. Both units were Polish manned and many were war veterans with a personal score to settle with Hitler. The Poles were very friendly and won the hearts and admiration of the locals, they liked the Lincolnshire countryside and, after the war, many who could not return to their own country settled in the county that had become their homeland.

Each squadron now had 16 Battles, ten crews and 180 groundcrew. Their first raid was on September 14 1940 against Boulogne harbour when three crews from each squadron took part and all returned safely. This was the first Polish operational bomber raid from Britain and was the first of many such attacks against invasion shipping assembled in the French Channel ports. The Poles were soon to make a name for themselves and, as if to remind them of the German Stukas dive-bombing their homeland, they had wailing sirens fitted to their Battles. These were made by

Parade outside the Polish hangar at Swinderby. The Polish badge is painted on the doors and inside is an altar.

Robey of Lincoln and were unofficial, but no-one tried to stop them.

On October 13 Swinderby had its first taste of air warfare when the Luftwaffe dropped six bombs, damaging two Battles and injuring one airman. The Group headquarters telephone cable was also hit and in order to keep open communication with headquarters the Post Office at Swinderby village was manned by an RAF operations officer, and the Postmistress received a letter of thanks from the Air Ministry for her part in the war effort.

This was the first of many attacks and although a few high explosive and incendiary bombs landed within the bounds of the airfield, very little damage was done. Because of these early raids Swinderby had a decoy airfield at Bassingham, but this was soon phased out.

Returning from a mission against Boulogne on October 14 1940, the squadron encountered very bad weather and two aircraft crashed. L5499 from 300 Squadron crashed at Watchwood Plantation, near Blidworth, Nottinghamshire, and the three crew were killed. They were Flying Officer Jan Gebicki, pilot, Sergeant Edward Norawa, observer, and Sergeant Tadeusz, air-gunner. All are buried in Southern Cemetery, Westbridgeford, Nottinghamshire. A memorial was later erected 50 yards north of the crash site.

During October and November the squadrons converted to Vickers Wellington Mark 1cs with Pegasus engines and by the end of 1940 each squadron had 16 aircraft. The squadrons had a break

during conversion, but during the period from September 15 to October 18 they made 85 sorties and dropped 45 tons of bombs.

On December 22 1940 three Wellingtons from 300 and three from 301 Squadron attacked the Antwerp refinery and all returned safely. This was again the target on December 28 but this time their other enemy, the weather, turned it into a bad mission. On their return thick freezing fog covered the airfield and one Wellington crashed after hitting a tree. The pilot, Flight Lieutenant S. Kryski, and front gunner Sergeant H. Wegrzyn, were killed.

During January 1941 the night bombing continued on the main industrial targets. On the 22nd of the month the King and Queen visited Swinderby. Because of very heavy rains over the winter months, the Wellingtons got bogged down and the airfield was constantly being made unserviceable throughout the latter part of January and February so some aircraft were deployed to Swinderby's satellite at Winthorpe. Other airfields were also used in order to continue operations, with raids being made on the Ruhr valley, and on February 25 to Cologne. By March Swinderby was operational again and attacks continued on enemy targets which included Berlin on the 23rd, followed by Brest, Kiel and Bremen.

On June 21 a Wellington of No 300 Squadron returning from a raid against Bremen crashed at Roe-Wood Farm, Winkburn, near Southwell, Nottinghamshire. The starboard propeller broke away and by so doing caused the engine to over-

Swinderby—some of the early Poles load up one of their Wellingtons.

heat and burst into flames. The aircraft was too low for the crew to bale out so the pilot tried a crash-landing, but the aircraft struck some trees and immediately burst into flames, killing one member of the crew. Mr and Mrs Broadberry from the nearby farmhouse, ignoring the blazing inferno and exploding ammunition, managed to rescue the other crew members. Some were seriously injured and, thinking these Poles were Germans, the couple arrested them! They became the first to be awarded the British Empire Medal for joint bravery.

With the threat of invasion from France now over the two Polish squadrons moved to Hemswell on July 19 1941 and Swinderby was transferred to No 5 Group, Bomber Command. Today, if one looks in the little church at Norton Disney, one can see two hand-carved plaques that will bring back the wartime memories of the Poles, and, as silent reminders, 19 of the gravestones in the Newark Polish Cemetery are those of airmen from Nos 300 and 301 Squadrons who died while at Swinderby.

The Poles were replaced by No 50 and 455 (RAAF) squadrons. The latter commenced its official existence on June 6 1941 but had no crews, did not get its first Hampden aircraft until a month later, and did not become operational until September. This was the first Australian medium bomber squadron to form in No 5 Group and was under command of Wing Commander J.E. Gyll-Murray. Its

formative months highlighted the many difficulties then facing the RAAF and Bomber Command. No 50 Squadron had arrived from Lindholme on July 18 and on the 20th/21st of the month 11 Hampdens from their squadron attacked Cologne.

Throughout 1940 and 1941 the building programme had continued in order to improve conditions on the station but work had been held up by bad weather and labour shortages. To help the labour problem Italian Prisoners of War started to build a new road to connect the villages of Swinderby and Norton Disney. Swinderby was growing fast and there were now over 100 WAAFs on the station who carried out a variety of duties. Their presence also allowed mixed entertainment.

During November a Hampden pilot of No 50 Squadron made a perfect night landing on the A46 Fosse Way, alongside the airfield. As soon as he realised his mistake he accidentally taxied the aircraft into a ditch. It was one thing to land on the road but another to keep out of the ditch.

On November 26 1941, No 50 Squadron moved to Skellingthorpe while the runways were being built. At the beginning of 1942 Skellingthorpe and Wigsley became satellites of Swinderby and in February No 455 Squadron moved to Wigsley. On June 20 No 50 Squadron moved back to the parent station having

Swinderby in August 1942. Some of 50 Squadron's first Lancasters. In the fore is Lancaster B1 R5689 VN-N which later crashed at Thurlby while returning from a Gardening sortie on September 18/19 1942.

re-equipped with Manchesters. The squadron continued operations but, on October 14, No 50 Squadron flew its last sortie from Swinderby and by the end of the month the unit had returned to Skellingthorpe. October also saw the Conversion Flights of 61, 97, 106 and 207 squadrons at Swinderby formed into 1660 HCU with Manchester, Lancaster and Halifax aircraft and, on November 14 1942, the station ceased to be a front-line bomber station. Skellingthorpe was handed back to Waddington.

On January 2 1943, Manchester L7482 from No 1660 HCU had icing problems, had to be abandoned and crashed at Highfield farm, Metheringham, Lincolnshire. The era of the Lancaster was upon us and the ill-fated Manchester was slowly being replaced.

The air war was now entering a new era with greater demands being placed on the bomber crews. Bomber Command was on the offensive and Swinderby had a large part to play in training the crews. There were many changes and on March 15 RAF Conversion Base Swinderby was re-designated No 51 Base. Its task was to co-ordinate the training of Lancaster crews for No 5 Group. In November 1943, the unit's aircraft were changed from Lancasters to Stirlings.

On June 15 1943, No 2776 Squadron RAF Regiment arrived from Davidstow Moor to add to Swinderby's crowded

conditions. They remained at Swinderby until March 18 1944. As fast as buildings were erected to ease the situation, others were posted in to occupy them instead. The base was terribly overcrowded and by March 1944 had 3,000 aircrew on strength. Naturally there were many facilities, including a cinema which gave two shows per night, six nights a week. There were concerts and dances. A new station church was opened and a post office, along with a new airmen's mess and NAAFI. In April double-tier bunks were brought in, but they added to the discomforts.

As the war continued, so did the workload and with operation 'Overlord' now underway and the Allies in Normandy, demands from No 5 Group were high so during July all leave was cancelled in order to give maximum effort. During this month the base flew a record monthly hours, but the price was paid in August with large sick parades and low serviceability. Changes were in the wind and No 7 Operational Training Group was re-formed in Bomber Command to take charge of the HCUs, Swinderby being transferred to No 7 Group, Bomber Command. On November 3 1944 the base was re-designated No 75 Base and lost Syerston. Stirlings were now to be replaced and by February 1945 all of the three conversion units were fully equipped with Lancasters.

Wellington T10 of 'B' Flight, 201 AFS, at Swinderby in 1948. The Wellington started out the war here in 1939 and was still in service almost a decade later.

Victory was now in sight as the strategic bombing of Germany continued during the long winter nights. Within the space of a few months 'civvy street' was on the cards. June 1945 saw the start of the demobilisation and a 36-hour stand-down at weekends was inaugurated. On September 15 the first post-war 'At Home' was held at Swinderby and approximately 8,000 civilians attended to see the static and air displays. During September No 1660 HCU began disbanding and in October 1945 Swinderby ceased to be a base, becoming an independent station with Winthorpe as its satellite. But, for some unknown reason, No 1660 HCU remained and continued to train Lancaster crews up to November 23 1946 when it then moved to Lindholme.

The European war had ended and although Swinderby had played a major part in the air war in Europe it did not share the fame and glory. Between March 1943 and August 1945 it had trained 3,123 crews and flown 130,568 hours.

On September 20 1945 No 13 Aircraft Modification Unit (AMU) was formed. Its task was to convert Lancasters for operation in the tropics as part of Tiger Force, but with the dropping of the atomic bomb they were never needed. No 13 AMU was disbanded on August 1 1946. The run-down of personnel continued and on December 21 1946 Swinderby was transferred from No 7 Group to No 91 Group, Bomber Command.

No 17 Operational Training Unit arrived at Swinderby equipped with Wellingtons during November 1946. In May 1947, in keeping with the peacetime programme, further administrative changes took place and No 91 Group was transferred from Bomber Command to Flying Training Command to become No 21 Group. At the same time No 17 OTU was re-designated No 201 Advanced Flying School and remained at Swinderby as part of No 21 Group. This was the only flying unit at the airfield until it was joined by the Mosquitoes of No 204 AFS in June 1950. Married quarters were built throughout 1947 and 1948 to house the regular Servicemen and building continued until 1950.

On February 20 1952, No 204 AFS moved to Bassingbourn. During this period No 201 AFS began to re-equip with Varsities as the Wellington was being phased out. On June 1 1954, No 201 AFS became No 11 FTS and on June 1 1955 the unit moved to Thorney Island to become part of No 2 ANS. The unit was replaced by No 8 FTS which arrived from Driffield on July 4 and at the same time Swinderby became part of No 25 Group.

The jet age had arrived at Swinderby for No 8 FTS was equipped with Vampire T II jet trainers and Meteors in addition to Piston Provosts. The Piston Provost Flight was disbanded on October 2 1956 after the 'all-through' experiment was concluded. The object of the experiment was for 'all through' training at one school but it was not a success and the pupils moved to Ternhill to finish their Provost training.

Flying training with the Vampire began on August 25 1955 with 19 pupils on No 101 Course. During the winter months fog interfered with training and during November Master Pilot Evans and his pupil Acting Pilot Officer Jago abandoned their aircraft while in stable inverted spin. They were the first double ejection from the Vampire.

During this period there were many alterations made on the airfield with new taxiways and aprons being built. The wood at the end of runway 06 was felled and the airfield lighting improved. New buildings sprang up including a control tower. During May 1956, the East Midlands Gliding Club moved to the station and remained here until March 1976.

On January 1 1957, re-organisation of Groups within Flying Training Command came into effect and No 8 FTS was transferred to No 23 Group.

In March 1964, No 8 FTS was disbanded and flying at Swinderby ceased. During its life, 8 FTS had not only trained pilots for the RAF but also for the airforces of Ceylon (Sri Lanka) Iraq, Indonesia, Lebanon and Syria. But again the wind of change had blown. On March 20 1964 the station was transferred to Technical Training Command and on June 29 No 7 School of Recruit Training opened. A dramatic change had taken place and Swinderby had a new role to play. No 1 hangar where, almost two decades ago, a VE-Day dance had been held which was attended by 1,500 people, had now been turned into a gymnasium. The medical centre was extended and the engineering workshops converted into a cinema and Church of England church. Even the Vampire that had stood guard

opposite the gates since 1960 was involved in the shakeup and moved to RAF Catterick.

On July 16 1970, No 7 SRT became the RAF School of Recruit Training, the only school of its kind in the Royal Air Force.

Today Swinderby is still an active station and occasional flying does take place. There are many reminders of those wartime days and from Sheepwalk Lane the derelict huts of the WAAF quarters are visible among the undergrowth.

Syerston, Nottinghamshire

129/SK730480. 6 miles SW of Newark-on-Trent and W of the A46 road

An unusual site for an airfield because it was wedged between the main A46 road and the River Trent, Syerston opened on December 1 1940 as an operational bomber station in No 1 Group, Bomber Command, with a satellite airfield at Balderton and a decoy airfield at Kneeton about two miles south-west of the station.

During December, two Polish heavy bomber squadrons, Nos 304 and 305, arrived from Bramcote where they had both recently formed. They were the first occupants and had settled in by the end of the month. Both units started operational flying with their Vickers Wellingtons in April 1941, when on the 25th/26th, No 304 sent two aircraft and No 305 despatched three to bomb the petrol and fuel oil storage tanks at Rotterdam. Both units made many more raids before

Vickers-Slingsby Venture TX2, XZ551, photographed over Syerston by the RAF in January 1980. The bleak winter conditions, with fog closing in, gives some picture of what it was like for the wartime aircrews.

Harvard T2s from Syerston.

moving out to Lindholme, Yorkshire, in July 1941.

Their Majesties King George VI and Queen Elizabeth visited the station on January 27 1941 accompanied by Air Marshal Sir Richard Pierse, CB, DSO, AFC, Commander in Chief, Bomber Command. His Majesty The King made a further visit to the station in November of the same year.

As the Polish squadrons moved out the newly formed No 408 (Goose) Squadron, RCAF, arrived from Lindholme on July 20. The squadron was equipped with Hampdens and its first bombing mission came on August 11/12 1941 when four Hampdens were despatched to bomb the docks at Rotterdam. No 408 Squadron carried out many more bombing attacks against naval and industrial targets before moving to the satellite aerodrome at Balderton on December 8 1941. The station now closed to flying while the runways were constructed in preparation for the four-engined bombers then coming into service. The airfield was constructed to the usual wartime pattern with two runways each 1,430 yards long and joined at a point at the main A46 road and the main runway, 1,900 yards long, running almost east to west. Accommodation was dispersed with many of the aircrew Nissen huts built in the grounds of Flintham Hall.

In May 1942, Syerston re-opened as a heavy bomber station, the first squadron to arrive being No 61 from Woolfox Lodge, Rutland. This unit was equipped with Lancasters and began regular night bombing operations against enemy targets. On May 5, No 61 Conversion Flight arrived from North Luffenham with their Manchesters and Lancasters. That same month No 408 Conversion Flight was formed but this disbanded after a few weeks.

In September 1942, No 106 Squadron arrived with Lancasters from Coningsby and the station was now a two-squadron airfield. The bombing attacks not only continued from the station but also increased.

Both squadrons took part in the successful daylight attack on the Schneider Armament works at Le Creusot when one of 106 Squadron's aircraft was piloted by Wing Commander Guy Gibson, the Commanding Officer of the squadron. Lancaster W4118, ZN 'Y', named 'Admiral Prune', was the aircraft used by Wing Commander Guy Gibson and shared with his 'B' Flight Commander, Squadron Leader Worldridge. The Syerston squadrons took part in many of the major raids, including the first shuttle-bombing raid by Bomber Command, the Battle of Hamburg and the attack on the Peenemunde Air Research and Development station.

During this period, from November 1941 to September 1943, LACW Spooner was a mess waitress in the Sergeants' Mess. It was a busy life for the catering staff since the dining room held 650 and with day and night operations it never

Syerston in August 1941. A Hampden bomber and four-man crew of 'B' Flight, 408 (Goose) Squadron. One crew member, F/O Anthony Watts, was later killed in action on January 17/18 1943 while acting as a spare navigator in a Lancaster crew.

stopped. She well remembers Guy Gibson and his dog Nigger for, when Gibson was on operations, Nigger would return to the Sergeants' Mess for some food and await his master's return, when he would then rush to dispersal to greet him. LACW Spooner remembers them well, 'Such brave young men who always had a laugh and a joke with us knowing all the time they might not be back in the morning.'

As the pace increased so did the casualty rate, which at this time was very high in Bomber Command. But that the courage and leadership was there was shown on the raid on November 3/4 1943 against Düsseldorf. One aircraft, piloted by Flight Lieutenant Reid, had just crossed the Dutch coast when it was attacked by an Me 110. During the fight the pilot's windscreen was shattered by fire and Reid was wounded in the head, shoulders and hands. The aircraft was badly damaged and became difficult to control and the communications systems and compasses were put out of action. Not saying anything about his own injuries, Reid pressed on to the target. But the Lancaster was again attacked and raked from stem to stern by an Fw 190. In this attack the navigator was killed and the wireless operator fatally wounded.

The guns were put out of action and Reid himself was again wounded. He still pressed on to the target, which he reached some fifty minutes later and bombed.

Flight Lieutenant Reid set course for home using the pole star and the moon to guide him. He was now growing weak from loss of blood and the cold was intense. With help from the bomb-aimer and flight engineer he managed to bring the crippled and defenceless Lancaster back home to make a safe landing. For his action that night he won the Victoria Cross.

The Commanding Officer of No 61 Squadron was Wing Commander R. Stidolph, who was also on the Düsseldorf raid and who recalls, 'The citation report was written by the station commander and myself and we both agreed that after the incredible conditions Reid and his crew experienced that night and still continued to target, the Victoria Cross was the only award we could cite him for.'

November 1943 saw both units depart, No 61 to Skellingthorpe and No 106 to Metheringham. Syerston then ceased to be an operational station. These squadrons were replaced the same month by No 1485 Bombing and Gunnery Flight which was equipped with Wellingtons and Martinets, and No 1668 HCU. This latter unit was equipped with 18 Lancasters and on January 15 1944 became No 5 Lancaster Finishing School. During February, No 1690 Bomber Defence Training Flight was formed and was one of several such units for each bomber Group. In March No 1485 B & G Flight disbanded. The follow-

F/O Geidrys and crew with their Wellington Mark 2 of No 305 (Polish) Squadron at Syerston in 1941.

ing July No 1690 BDTF moved out to Scampton.

On October 1 1944, No 1690 BDTF returned from Scampton with their Spitfires and Hurricanes. On October 30, No 56 Base HQ opened at Syerston and remained here until it disbanded in April 1945.

On March 31 1945, No 5 LFS disbanded, the last pupils of the Lancaster Finishing School having passed out the previous month. March also saw the Bomber Command Film Unit Flight arrive. This unit operated Lancasters from here until October 1945.

On April 22 1945, No 49 Squadron moved from Fulbeck to Syerston and once again the airfield became an operational heavy bomber station, albeit very briefly for the first operation by the squadron was the attack on Berchtesgaden on April 25 when ten Lancasters participated, but this proved also to be the last bombing mission of the war from this station.

No 382 MU arrived on July 23 and remained until October 1945. That same month No 1690 BDTF departed. Meanwhile, No 49 Squadron continued with its training as part of 'Tiger Force' but, with the capitulation of Japan, this training ceased and the squadron left during September for Mepal, Cambridgeshire.

On October 20 1945 the station was transferred from No 5 Group Bomber Command, to No 4 Group, Transport Command, and Syerston took on Winthorpe as a satellite. A few days later No 1333 TSCU arrived from Melton Mowbray and Leicester East with

Dakotas and Horsa gliders. During August 1946 the unit was renamed Transport Support Training Unit and during July 1947 moved to North Luffenham.

On December 14 1946, 1331 HCU reformed at Syerston from the Halifax Training Unit at Dishforth. Later, on January 5 1948, it was further disbanded into 240 OCU. On May 10 1946, No 504 Squadron reformed at Syerston with an establishment of Mosquitoes and remained here until April 1947. During November 1947 the airfield passed to the control of No 21 Group Flying Training Command and the role of the station reverted from transport to training.

On January 7 1948, No 22 Flying Training School arrived, its role being to train Royal Naval personnel as pilots, with Tiger Moth and Prentice aircraft. From the end of 1949 to 1955, Tollerton was used as a satellite by No 22 FTS. During May 1955 this unit was replaced by No 1 FTS and, in November 1957, by No 2 FTS. The unit's role was to train RAF pilots on Piston Provost aircraft but in 1958 it changed to Jet Provosts and by early 1960 Syerston had the distinction of being the first station in the world to train student pilots on jet aircraft. By 1962 the unit had the powerful Mk 4 Jet Provost.

On September 20 1958, during the annual Battle of Britain air show, tragedy struck the airfield. Avro Vulcan B1 VX770, being used by Rolls-Royce for engine tests, was giving a display when, during a high-speed run, the aircraft broke up and crashed, killing the crew.

During 1971, No 2 FTS left and the airfield was placed on a care and maintenance basis. For a few years the station lay silent and took on an abandoned look then, in 1976, the airfield re-opened to accommodate the Royal Air Force Central Gliding School, No 644 GS, at this moment occupying only a small part of the station. This is administered by RAF Newton, which also offers limited barrack block accommodation to ATC lads who come on their annual camps. Otherwise Syerston is left very much on a care and maintenance basis.

Today only memories remain of those wartime days. The wartime flight office is now only a pile of rubble and the concrete taxi strips that run alongside the Fosse Way are overgrown, but standing on a piece of that overgrown concrete one can feel the atmosphere that descends and one can see the aircraft in the mind's eye as they cycle to dispersal. Many of the old aircrew Nissen huts are still to be seen in the grounds of Flintham Hall, overgrown and derelict.

Theddlethorpe, Lincolnshire

122/TF480890. N of Mablethorpe just E of the A1031 road

Theddlethorpe opened in 1935 as a bombing and gunnery range. It was here in December 1939 that the Hispano 20 mm cannon was first fired. As soon as Manby became operational it took over Theddlethorpe, which closed in December 1973.

Tollerton (Nottingham), Nottinghamshire

129/SK620360. E of Nottingham, S of the A52 road N of Tollerton village

Sited just north of Tollerton village, the aerodrome was officially opened on June 19 1930 by Sir Sefton Brancker, Minister of Aviation, who was later killed in the R101 crash. The licence for the field had been obtained by Nottingham Corporation on July 27 1929 and it was first leased to National Flying Services who erected a club house and hangar early in 1930 when the membership had reached 40. Before these facilities were available the pilots' times were logged by a ground engineer who had a tent at the edge of the airfield. The facilities, which also included fuel and oil, were housed at the western end of

the site. The landing area was grass-covered and in the south-east corner there was a small wood.

Nottingham Flying Club, which had earlier used the old wartime airfield at Hucknall, moved to Tollerton in September 1931 and occupied part of the hangar for storage. This was the birth of Hucknall Fight and Test Establishment whose first aircraft was a Fairey IIIF followed by a Hawker Horsley torpedo bomber and a Hawker Hart light bomber. The company was successful and soon needed a more permanent base for development and installation of aero engines. Thus, in December 1934, the company became tenants of two hangars at the RAF Station at Hucknall. That same year National Flying Services vacated the field and the lease was adopted by the club's chief flying instructor, Captain L.W. Hall, and his wife. Many alterations were carried out over the next two years.

In 1937 the Civil Air Guard was formed and a school opened with about 50 pupils. A Royal Air Force Volunteer Reserve Training School, No 27 E-RFTS, formed on June 24 1938 and training was carried out on Miles Magisters, Ansons and Hawker Harts.

1938 saw many new developments, with the Training School expanding and a map room, parachute section, canteen, office block, Bellman hangar and a cinema for showing training films being built. On the west side of the site a large factory hangar was erected by Field Aircraft Services Ltd, of Croydon, who were to run a part of their repair and servicing organisation from here.

With the outbreak of war the flying club closed down and with it the Civil Air Guard scheme. No 27 E-RFTS disbanded, the RAFVR staff moved to Burnaston and the airfield was taken over by the Air Ministry for possible use by the Royal Air Force. It was immediately brought into use as a scatter field and used by the Hampdens of Nos 44 and 50 Squadrons from Waddington.

Field Aircraft Services now took over the existing maintenance company and the airfield became a satellite to Newton for training purposes. In early 1941 three runways were laid, two 1,120-yard ones and a third of 1,000 yards. A large 'R' Type hangar was built on the northern perimeter and a Bellman hangar on the apron. There were also many more buildings added, including stores, barracks, link

Above *Lancaster repair and maintenance section at Field Services Ltd, Tollerton, 1945.*
Below *Aerial view of Tollerton (Nottingham) Aerodrome in 1933.*

trainer building, crew rooms and dispersal huts. A communal site was also erected to the west side of the Tollerton road.

From July 1941, No 16 (Polish) SFTS from their parent station at Newton used the airfield with a variety of aircraft until the early part of 1946. Throughout this period Field Aircraft Services had been engaged in the major overhaul and repair of battle-weary aircraft for Bomber Command. the company employed about 700 people and the many aircraft that passed through their works included Dakotas, Hamptons, Halifaxes, Manchesters, Liberators, Bostons and Lancasters, the latter being the most numerous. These were either ferried in by pilots of the Air Transport Auxiliary or brought in by road on Queen Marys. Field's repair unit was the main role of the airfield and they pressed all the new hangars into service for repair shops as erected. Their chief test pilot was Mr N. Rogers, formerly of the Royal Air Force.

After the war the Flying Club was reformed and Blue Line and Trent Valley airlines started operations. The Ministry of Aviation set up offices with the intention of making Tollerton the official airport of Nottingham. Field Aircraft Services, who during the war completed for MAP 1,700 aircraft and 2,000 components, now reversed their wartime role as large numbers of ex-operational Lancasters of No 5 Group were flown in for demolition. They lined the perimeter, nose to tail, their engines silent as if in shame at their reward for a job well done.

During 1949, the small airlines closed down and the Ministry of Aviation then gave up the tenure. The original Flying Club closed but individual private aircraft still continued to use the airfield. Towards the end of the year the Royal Air Force returned and used the airfield as a satellite to Syerston for No 22 FTS. It remained in this role until 1956 when the airfield was de-requisitioned by the Air Ministry. The following year Field Aircraft Services moved their operation to Wymeswold. The Sherwood Flying Club was then formed and was the sole occupier for a

short period. The airfield was finally taken over in 1963 by Truman Aviation Ltd, on a 75-year lease to operate the airfield solely for the needs of private aviation. The following year the company started an air-taxi service. By 1974 helicopters had joined the 35 or so light aircraft at the airfield and were on hire by East Midlands Helicopters.

Today most of the wartime additions have been demolished, only the workshop hangar and the old club hangar remaining. However, the runways and perimeter track are in good condition. Throughout the years many flying displays have been held here, including the King's Cup Air Race, but the future of the site as an airport was limited by its relatively small size. The Grantham Canal forms the northern boundary and to the east there is a river. It is now certain that those jet liners will never scream down the runways, but with Truman Aviation operators of the airport, it looks as if the aviation link will be retained for the future.

Waddington, Lincolnshire

121/SK985645. S of Lincoln, between the A607 and A15 roads

Waddington aerodrome is well sited on the Lincolnshire Heights, just five miles south of Lincoln and within easy view of the Cathedral that was such a welcome sight for so many of the wartime bomber crews as they returned in the twilight hours.

The station opened in November 1916 as a flying training station with 47 Reserve squadron under the control of Northern Group Command at York. During further re-organisation it was redesignated 48

Training Depot Station. On December 1 1917, No 97 Squadron, RFC, formed here as a training unit but in January 1918 moved to Stonehenge. The aircraft used at the station up to the end of the First World War were Maurice Farman Shorthorns, DH4s, DH6s, DH9s, RE8s, Armstrong-Whitworth FK8s and Avro 504s. The station closed in 1919.

Waddington was one of the few World War 1 stations to retain its buildings and airfield during the rundown immediately after the war. Therefore, during the attempt to bring the RAF up to strength, it re-opened in October 1926 as the base of the newly formed No 503 (Bombing) Squadron. This was a cadre unit of the Special Reserve and remained as such until 1st May 1936, when it was converted to an Auxiliary squadron. During this time the unit was equipped with Fairey Fawn light bombers. The squadron was later re-designated No 503 (County of Lincoln) Squadron. In 1929 the squadron was re-equipped with Handley Page Hyderabads and changed its role to a night bomber unit until 1935 when it again reverted to a day bomber unit and re-equipped with Westland Wallaces.

During the mid-1930s a rebuilding programme began to give the station its present appearance. On May 18 1937, No 110 (B) Squadron re-formed here as a bomber unit with an establishment of Hawker Hinds. On May 3 No 50 (B) Squadron was also re-formed with Hinds and on June 7 No 88 (B) Squadron re-formed as a bomber squadron from a nucleus of personnel from No 110 (B) Squadron, also equipped with Hinds. In June 1937 No 44 Squadron arrived at the station having been re-formed at Wyton in March, while in July No 88 Squadron

Waddington—Lancasters in winter, bombing-up.

Hampden at Waddington in July 1939. Note 'Fort' type control tower in background.

moved to Boscombe Down, Wiltshire. Bomber Command was now rapidly expanding and No 44 became in December the first Waddington squadron to receive Blenheim Is. During October 1938, No 503 Squadron moved to Doncaster where it disbanded and reformed as No 616 (South Yorkshire) Squadron. During January 1938, No 110 Squadron re-equipped with Bristol Blenheims and in May 1939 moved to Wattisham, Suffolk.

By the outbreak of war both Nos 44 and 50 Squadrons were re-equipped with Handley Page Hampdens and readied for operations. Almost immediately, at 18.35 hours on September 3 1939, nine Hampdens of No 44 Squadron took off for a reconnaissance over Heligoland Roads. In the years that followed Waddington played its full part as an operational station and its squadrons were at the 'top of the league' in No 5 Group. However, the losses were heavy in the early months and the bombers were forced to operate only at night.

During June 1940, the Fairey Battles of No 142 Squadron (code letters 'QT') arrived at Waddington from Villiers-Faux, France, where they had served with the Advanced Air Striking Force. They remained only a few weeks here and in July moved to Binbrook. July also saw No 50 Squadron move to Hatfield Woodhouse (re-named Lindholme in mid-August 1940).

The Hampden was Bomber Command's front line aircraft for the first 18 months of the war until No 207 Squadron was reformed at Waddington on November 1 1940 with the sole purpose of bringing the new twin-engined Avro Manchester (coded 'EM') into operational service. The joy with the new heavy bomber soon turned to resentment for it was plagued with engine and other troubles. On

February 25 1941, No 97 (B) Squadron reformed in No 5 Group as a heavy bomber squadron equipped with Avro Manchesters (code letters 'OF'), but in March 1941 the unit moved to Coningsby. During November 1941, No 207 Squadron moved to Bottesford. Out of the fateful Manchester came the Lancaster, having been redesigned to take four Rolls-Royce Merlin engines, the first unit to be equipped with the new aircraft being No 44 Squadron. On December 24 1941 the first aircraft arrived, L7537, L7538 and L7541. In September 1941, the squadron's title was officially altered to No 44 (Rhodesia) Squadron in recognition of that country's contribution to the war effort.

On December 19 1941, No 420 (Snowy Owl) Squadron, RCAF, formed at Waddington, the fourth Canadian bomber squadron formed overseas (code letters 'PT'). The squadron was equipped with Handley Page Hampdens whose first operational mission was on January 21/22 1942, when five were despatched to bomb targets at Emden. In August 1942 the squadron moved to Skipton-on-Swale, Yorkshire, and was transferred to No 4 Group, Bomber Command.

During the early Lancaster period a low-level unescorted daylight attack was made, on April 17 1942, by Nos 44 and 97 (Straits Settlement) Squadron from Woodhall Spa. The raid on the MAN Diesel factory at Augsburg was an heroic failure and did little more than let the Germans know that the RAF now had a new four-engined bomber. Inevitably, seven of the 12 Lancasters were shot down, four en route and three during the attack. Squadron Leader J.D. Nettleton of No 44 Squadron was awarded the Victoria Cross. This meant the squadron had the distinction of having two recipients of the VC on the unit at the same time as Wing Commander Learoyd, VC, was the Commanding Officer of No 44 Squadron.

In August 1942, No 9 moved in from Honington and re-equipped with Lancasters. As the pace of the air war increased, so did the many dangers and as, on December 20/21 1942, the Lancasters took off to join the main force for a raid on Duisburg, one from No 9 Squadron and one from No 44 Squadron collided in mid-air over Lincoln and came down in Canwick Road. The aircrews worked hard and took life as it came, day by day, the favourite local pub for the Waddington crews being the 'Horse and Jockey' in the village.

As the pace of the bomber offensive increased No 9 Squadron moved to Bardney during April, then No 44 Squadron moved to Dunholme Lodge in May 1943 while the airfield acquired its three concrete runways. By November 1943 Waddington was again operational and the station re-opened with No 467 (RAAF) Squadron which moved in from Bottesford to what would prove to be its home for the rest of the European war.

On November 23 1943, No 463 (RAAF) Squadron was formed from 'C' Flight of No 467 Squadron, and also remained at Waddington for the duration of the European war. Unit codes were 'JO' and 'PO', later 'JO-E'. The squadron began operations with an attack against Berlin the day after it was formed.

The Aussie squadron took part in all the major raids and was prominent in the bombing offensive. However, it had many setbacks, one disastrous raid being on the night of May 10/11 1944 when the station put up 31 aircraft of the total force of 86 Lancasters in an attack on Lille. Flak was only light but the bomber force was engaged by numerous night fighters and Waddington lost twenty per cent of the crews that took part. But not all was gloom for No 467 Squadron had one of the most famous Lancasters in Bomber Command and, on May 11/12 1944, during a raid against Bourg Leopold in Belgium, Lancaster R5868 'S' Sugar

Lancaster B1, R5868, PO-'S'-Sugar of 467 Squadron at Waddington. Celebrations after P/O T.N. Scholefield and crew returned after their 100th sortie. An event of great psychological importance to ground and air crews who knew only too well that the average life of a bomber was under 30 trips. 'S' Sugar stood until recently at the gates of RAF Scampton but she has now been moved to the RAF Museum where she can be seen today.

logged its 100th sortie. It went on to complete 137 operational sorties, the second highest in Bomber Command, and was selected by the Air Ministry for preservation.

During the second phase of Bomber Command operations in 'Overlord' on June 6 1944, No 5 Group played a major part in attacks against the shore batteries. The Waddington squadron target was the Pointe du Hoe battery on Omaha beach. Wing Commander Kingsford-Smith personally led 14 aircraft from No 463 Squadron, while the 14 aircraft from No 467 Squadron were led by Squadron Leader Deignan. The final pre-invasion raids were carried out in poor visibility and the bombing was inaccurate and failed to silence many of the shore batteries.

The RAF Film Unit was with No 463 Squadron and the film Lancaster took part on the attack on the *Tirpitz* with Nos 9 and 617 Specialist Squadrons, on September 15 1944, and is the only aircraft to claim any success. Flight Lieutenant B. Buckham, DSO, DFC, piloted the special film aircraft. After the attack the bombers returned to Yagodnik, their Russian base, but Buckham set course for Waddington. He flew at sea level most of the time, under terrible weather conditions, to reach base after 14 hours 33 minutes, which was a record for a Lancaster operation.

On March 3/4 1945, after a raid against Ladbergen, the bombers returned to find Luftwaffe intruders attacking the aerodrome, and the bomb dump on fire. Nevertheless all aircraft landed safely.

The last operational mission of the war for both 463 and 467 Squadrons was on April 25/26 1945 when each unit despatched 14 Lancasters to bomb an oil refinery and tankerage at Vallo (Tonsberg). In June No 467 Squadron moved to Metheringham and in July No 463 departed to Skellingthorpe.

After the war Waddington remained as a bomber base and returned to a peacetime training role with the famous 'Dambusters' squadron, No 617, that moved in from Woodhall Spa during June. In January 1946, No 617 Squadron moved to Salbani, India, and was replaced by No 61 Squadron that arrived from Sturgate. The Royal Observer Corps moved their Operations Room to the station, but this later moved into a purpose-built underground ops room on the ex-wartime airfield of Fiskerton.

The Avro Lincoln followed in the footsteps of the wartime Lancaster and, in May 1946, No 61 Squadron re-equipped with this type. During July, No 12 Squadron arrived back from Binbrook and, after re-equipping with Lincolns, returned to Binbrook the following September. During October the Lincolns of No 57 Squadron flew in from Lindholme. From 1947 the squadron was detached at various times to Hemswell, Singapore, Marham and Malta.

In March 1950, the Lincolns of No 100 Squadron arrived, only to depart again in June and in December. By now the Lincoln era was coming to an end and in April 1952 No 57 Squadron moved to Coningsby. In May No 100 Squadron moved to Shallufa, Egypt, but returned the following August. During July 1952 the Lincolns of 49 Squadron arrived. Then, in August 1953, all the squadrons, Nos 49, 61 and 100, moved to Wittering.

The station was put on care and maintenance while the base was brought to Class I airfield standard in readiness for 'V'-bombers. In order to take these aircraft one long runway was needed and this extended over the main A15 Ermine Street, causing the road to be re-routed to curve around the lengthened runway. This was the first change from the standard wartime pattern. The main runway is now 9,000 ft long by 200 ft wide and orientates 210°/030°. The two other runways have been retained but are not used for flying purposes. Also needed were stronger dispersals and taxiways. Specialised buildings were also constructed and at the end of 1956 the electronics and operations blocks were completed.

In June 1954, the Queen gave her approval to the RAF Waddington Station badge, which includes the towers of Lincoln Cathedral standing above the morning mists—a sight forever in the minds of the wartime aircrews. The Lincoln coat-of-arms can be seen on the fin of the aircraft.

On June 1 1955 the station re-opened as a Master Diversion Airfield with Nos 21 and 27 Squadrons from Scampton, both flying Canberras. The Vulcan Mark 1 was introduced in 1955 and, during mid-1956, No 230 OCU conducted Service Trials on the aircraft at Waddington. On June 30 1957, No 21 Squadron disbanded, followed on December 31 1957 by No 27 Squadron. The OCU had by now begun crew training for the Vulcans and on May 21 1957 No 83 Squadron was re-formed as

'Good Luck, Aussies'—station personnel wave off each bomber of 467 Squadron. This is a scene at Waddington in 1944.

the first operational Vulcan squadron in the RAF.

On August 10 1960, No 44 re-formed as a V-force squadron and in October of the same year No 83 moved to Scampton. In June 1961 the OCU departed and No 101 moved in from Finningley that same month. To continue the build-up No 50 Squadron was re-formed as a V-force squadron on August 1 1961. Finally, to complete the Waddington Wing, No 9 Squadron joined the station from Cyprus in January 1975, arriving with Vulcan B2s. Since then the station has been an effective V-force base and, today, Vulcans are still based at the two Lincoln airfields, Scampton and Waddington, although they are due to be phased out.

Over the years the station has seen many changes, but the hangars that were built in the Expansion of the late 1930s are still standing almost half a century later.

On May 8 1975 a further page in the history of the station was written when over 120 Australian ex-members of 463 and 467 Squadron Associations held a reunion at Waddington. During their stay they presented a memorial clock to the station in memory of those members of the two squadrons who flew from Waddington during World War 2 and did not return.

The station's role today continues to be part of the Strike Command deterrent but the future indicates a change to airborne early warning and the Nimrod will become a familiar sight in the skies over Lincolnshire.

Wainfleet, Lincolnshire

122/TF522570. SW of Skegness

Wainfleet opened as a bombing and gunnery range in August 1938 on the site of an old Artillery Range that was first used in the 1890s.

It was the main bombing range for the Dambusters when they were testing the new Stabilising Automatic Bomb Sight. The Lancaster crews of No 5 Group also used this range to practice for operation 'Robinson' and on October 1 1942 carried out a practice bombing run and fanned out over the Wainfleet sands for their plan of attack. On October 17 they repeated the performance with 100 per cent success.

Today it is still in use and is one of the main Air Weapons Ranges used by the Royal Air Force, United States Air Force and many of the NATO air forces.

Wakerley (Spanhoe), Northamptonshire

See Spanhoe

Waltham, Lincolnshire

113/TA280025. S of Grimsby just W of the A16 road

During the 1930s Grimsby had a civil aerodrome which was a large field a few miles south of the town and south-east of the village of Waltham. It was equipped with a clubhouse and two wooden hangars where minor repairs were carried out. It is

An oblique photograph of Waltham taken in April 1980, looking west with Waltham village top right of photograph. Part of the main runway at right of photograph is used as storage for VW cars.

interesting to note that the aerodrome telephone number was Waltham 1. The airfield was used by light aircraft and, in June 1938, No 25 Elementary and Reserve Flying Training School (E & RFTS), operated by the Herts and Essex Aero Club, flying Tiger Moths, Miles Magister and Hind trainers, was established here. The object behind the school was to teach pilots basic flying who then went on in the RAF Flying Training Schools for further flying and service training.

However, the school was disbanded at the outbreak of war in September 1939 and the aerodrome does not appear to have been used any more after having been selected for development into a heavy bomber station which was to be built on the old flying club airfield. Work started in 1940 and involved expansion of the site across the main A16, Louth to Grimsby road, almost to the village of Holton-le-Clay on the eastern boundary. The southern boundary was the country road to Waltham village and the perimeter ran close alongside of it. The sites were to the north of the airfield and the hospital was on the other side of the country road near to Waltham village. Beside the main gates was 'Joe's Café', a familiar haunt for both air and ground crews. The three concrete runways were laid to the standard triangular pattern, the main one being on a north-south axis and roughly parallel to the A16.

Waltham opened in November 1941 and the first to arrive was No 142 Squadron which flew in with Wellington

Mk IIs from Binbrook. This unit remained for just over a year during which time they carried on the strategic night bombing offensive. In December 1942, 13 'tropical-ised' Wellington Mark IIIs plus crews and ground crews were sent to Blida in North Africa. The home echelon moved to the newly opened Kirmington in the latter part of the month, and was replaced that same month by No 100 Squadron which re-formed here on the 15th as a heavy bomber unit equipped with Lancasters (code letters 'HW'). No 100 Squadron, with its skull and cross-bones badge, was to be the operational life-blood of Waltham.

In just under three months the squadron was ready for action and their first operational mission with Bomber Command was on March 4/5 1943 when eight Lancasters were despatched to lay mines in enemy waters. One bomber was missing and another crashed on return to the UK. The first bombing mission was a few nights later, on March 8/9, when six Lancasters took part in a raid on Nuremberg. The squadron made its first of many raids on Berlin on March 27/28 1943. The squadron played a vital role in the bomber offensive and attacked targets all over Germany and the occupied countries of Europe.

On November 25 1943, No 550 Squadron was formed here as a heavy bomber squadron in No 1 Group flying Lancasters Is and IIIs (code letters 'BQ'). They began operations that same month, on the 26/27th, when eight Lancasters

were despatched to bomb Berlin.
However, Waltham was not to be a two-
squadron station and early in the New
Year No 550 Squadron moved a few miles
further north to North Killingholme,
leaving 100 Squadron to continue the
bombing offensive from Waltham.

Sergeant Reg Trueman flew as a rear-
gunner with the 'skull and cross-bones'
squadron, which to him was lucky, and he
successfully completed 30 sorties with the
same crew and aircraft, Lancaster 'G'
George, ND388. The one he will never
forget is the raid on Mailly-le-Camp, on
May 3/4 1944, when Nos 1, 5 and 8
Groups despatched 254 Lancasters and
Mosquitoes. The target was the largest
German military camp in western Europe.
It was a perfect night for night fighters,
being bright moonlight, and the
Luftwaffe wasted no time in engaging the
bomber force. In very fierce fighting no
fewer than 42 bombers were shot down.
Sergeant Trueman recalls that catastrophic
raid:

'We arrived over target before it was
marked properly and were told to circle
and await instructions. This we did along
with 200 or more other aircraft and many
broke radio silence as tempers got strained.
Never in all my raids had I seen so many
of our aircraft shot out of the sky.' The
raid was successful, but it was a high price
to pay.

Between June 16 and 30 Bomber
Command carried out 16 raids on traffic
centres in Eastern France. The Waltham
squadron took part in these and the
heaviest loss was on the last one of the
series against Vierzon on the 30th, when
14 aircraft were shot down from a total
force of 118 Lancasters. Sergeant A.

Above *Waltham control tower in May
1980.* **Below** *The few remaining Nissen
huts at Waltham are just skeletons.*

Palmer was a wireless operator on the
raid. His aircraft was attacked as it left the
target area. It started a corkscrew
manoeuvre and the aircraft rolled over
and fell like a stone. The pilot, Pilot
Officer Jack Rees, wrestled with the
control column, the Lancaster shuddered
violently, flattened out and then climbed
skywards at a most uncomfortable speed.
Squadron Leader Palmer looks back:

'We had fallen from 18,000 to 2,000 ft
in our little escapade but our admiration
for the Lancaster increased with every air
mile, a loop, a screaming dive and a
rocket-like ascent had been taken in her
stride. I thanked God for the vigilance of
the rear-gunner and the expert recovery
action by the Captain.'

The last operational mission of the war

for 100 Squadron was on April 25 1945 when 15 Lancasters bombed Berchtesgaden. During its wartime role, No 100 Squadron dropped more than 17,500 tons of bombs and four of its Lancasters passed the 100-operation mark. They were 'A' Able, ND458, with 123; EE139 'R', named 'Phantom of the Ruhr', with 121 sorties; ND644 'N' Nan, which went missing on its 115th sortie on a raid against Nuremberg on March 16/17 1945; and JB603, 'E' 'Take it Easy', which did over 100.

For Waltham, the war was over when 100 Squadron moved to Elsham Wolds in April 1945. The Lancasters had gone and their departure signalled the death knell for the station. After the war it was used for a short time by No 35 MU for storage purposes.

Since the station closed the site has been used by the occasional light aircraft and glider. In 1980 a 'B1' type hangar has weathered the years at the northern end of the airfield. The control tower was still standing on the western side and on the south-west corner of the airfield a 'T2' hangar and other buildings were still standing. A memorial to the former aircrews of No 100 Squadron is sited in a lay-by on the A16 road which crosses the old No 2 runway.

Wellingore, Lincolnshire

121/SK988545. Situated E of the A607 main Lincoln-to-Grantham road, just S of the village of Wellingore

Ever since the formation of the RFC the Lincoln Escarpment has been regarded as a prime site for aerodromes, early examples north of the city including South Carlton, Brattleby and Harpswell, while to the south were Waddington and Leadenham. About three miles south-east of the latter was Cranwell and when the circuit there started to get congested in the 1930s several large fields were used on the scarp top as forced landing grounds. Two of these were at Temple Bruer and Wellingore. The latter was on Wellingore Heath just south of the village, and was used by Cranwell until June 1940 when it then became a Relief Landing Ground for the fighter station at Digby.

The first arrivals were the Hurricanes of a 46 Squadron detachment and the airfield was also used by fighters of No 29 Squadron with Blenheims and Beaufighters. During December 1940 the Hurricanes of No 402 Squadron, which were based at the parent station, used Wellingore until June 1941. The airfield was then made available to Sawbury as a RLG for the Oxfords of No 11 SFTS that was based there. This was only a short chapter in the airfield's history which lasted from September 29 1941 to October 1941 when the unit departed and the fighter squadrons returned. The first to arrive was No 412 Squadron on October 20, equipped with Spitfires, and this unit remained until April 30 1942 when it moved to Martlesham Heath. Then, in September 1942, No 154 Squadron arrived with Spitfires. During its stay No 81 Squadron with Spitfire Vbs and Vcs made a short two-week stay from October 5 to 29 1942.

Various units continued to use Wellingore, mostly staying only a few weeks. No 288 Squadron arrived during December 1942 with Blenheims but in January 1943 they moved out. The end of March 1943 saw the arrival of No 613 Squadron with their Mustang I aircraft, but on May 29 they also departed. That same day the Canadians returned in the form of No 416 Squadron. This unit remained until June 6 when it then moved to Merston, Sussex, only to return as part of the Canadian Digby Wing on September 19 1943. It remained at Wellingore until October 1 1943 when it then moved to the parent station at Digby.

On December 31 1943, No 439 (Fighter Bomber) Squadron formed here, equipped with Hawker Hurricane Mk IVs (code letters '5V'). This was a Canadian Army Co-Operation Training Squadron that had been transferred overseas in preparation for the Allied invasion of Europe. It moved to Ayr, Scotland, on January 7 1944. On the 12th of the following month No 402 arrived back, but this time with Spitfire Mk Vcs. They were the last fighter squadron to be at Wellingore and, after No 402 Squadron had left on April 29 1944, the airfield ceased fighter operations and reverted to being a Relief Landing Ground for Cranwell up to its closure in 1945.

Throughout its operational life, Wellingore remained a grass-surfaced airfield with very spartan facilities although the field was encircled by a perimeter track and PAB stripping was laid during 1944. The eastern boundary was adjacent to the site of the Ermine Street, a Roman Road long since disused at this point, but most of the buildings were on the western side, one dispersed domestic site being located in a thicket on the far side of the minor road running along the clifftop parallel to the A607 main road.

Today, several shelters and a 'Blister' hangar are still evident and can be clearly seen from the road to the west of the airfield, which was far too small for the modern jet trainers used by post-war Cranwell.

West Common, Lincoln, Lincolnshire

121/SK960720

Lincoln was a great industrial centre but what is not often realised is that when the Great War started it soon became one of the largest aircraft production centres in the world. The City companies were the Ruston Aircraft Factory, later known as Ruston, Proctor and Co Ltd; Robey and Company Ltd; Clayton and Shuttleworth.

The manufacturers needed a site where they could deliver their aeroplanes ready for test flying and acceptance by the RFC. So, a ready-made site was found on the local racecourse on the West Common, and like many other racecourses was pressed into military use. Part of the common was prepared as a landing area and two triangular-roofed, camouflaged sheds were erected as hangarage at the clubhouse corner of the common for the unit, No 4 Aircraft Acceptance Park, which opened in 1915. Two more sheds were put up on the eastern side alongside Alderman's Walk, these later being converted into one large hangar when the gap between them was roofed in. At a later stage in the war five wood-framed, canvas-covered Bessoneau hangars were added to supplement the more permanent structures.

No 4 AAP received Bristol F2b aeroplanes built at Gainsborough by Marshall in addition to a number of different Lincoln-built designs such as the Sopwith Gunbus from Robey, the Handley Page 0/400 built by Clayton & Shuttleworth and the BE2c from Ruston Proctor. Other aeroplanes from outside the county that were tested at No 4 AAP included the DH5, DH6, DH9, Sopwith Cuckoo and Blackburn Kangaroo.

The facilities were never very satisfactory, particularly when the HP 0/400 bombers started to fly in from a makeshift airstrip adjoining the Clayton & Shuttleworth works in east Lincoln, so an alternative site was sought. Eventually it was decided to develop Robey's Aerodrome at Bracebridge Heath, just southeast of Lincoln, and new, permanent brick-built hangars were constructed there to accept No 4 AAP.

However, the transfer was not completed until 1919. The sheds were dismantled after the war and the West Common site was soon cleared of all buildings. The two original sheds were sold to local garage owners in Lincoln, Gilbert in Pelham Street and Stock in Lucy Tower Street. Both survived as motor workshops until a few years ago and today nothing exists on the West Common site to reveal Lincoln's aviation past. The short-sighted council did not take the trouble and even the famous racecourse has now closed.

Wickenby, Lincolnshire

121/TF095805. NE of Lincoln, N of the A158, and on the B1399 road

The airfield is situated immediately to the south-east of the village of Wickenby and is one of the numberous heavy bomber airfields that sprang up almost overnight. The land was owned by Mr Bowser; one morning some surveyors called to say his land might be used for an airfield and, by 3 pm in the afternoon, bulldozers were at work clearing the site! The airfield

Aerial photograph of Wickenby taken just after the war when the road was re-opened across the airfield.

Lancaster B1 ME758, PH-N, of No 12 Squadron, being awarded a DSO and DFC by Wing Commander Mike Stockdale on completion of her 106th sortie. 'N'-Nan (or Nuts) completed 108 sorties and was struck off charge in October 1945.

conformed to the standard pattern with three concrete runways and domestic sites widely dispersed round the district, particularly east of the airfield towards the hamlet of Holton. The contractors were McAlpine and the work force was 80 per cent Irish. In the course of constructing the airfield a minor road which crossed the centre of the site was closed and another to the west of the airfield was crossed by the taxi track to some dispersed hardstandings. The tower was inside the perimeter track on the eastern side of the field with a 'T2' hangar on the northern side and a 'B1' in the south-west corner. Wickenby was considered important enough to have a decoy airfield which was built at Rand, just over a mile south of the actual airfield.

Wickenby was quickly pressed into service and opened in September 1942 in No 1 Group, Bomber Command, being occupied the same month by No 12 Squadron (coded 'PH') flying Wellington IIs and IIIs. This unit was to remain at Wickenby until after the end of the war. During the winter of 1942/43 it converted to Lancasters and played a large part in the bomber offensive. One aircraft, Lancaster I ME758 'N' Nuts flew 108

missions and emerged as the squadron's champion. On November 7 1943 Wickenby became a two squadron station with the formation of No 626 Squadron (code letters 'UM'), equipped with Lancasters from a nucleus provided by 'C' Flight of No 12 Squadron. The following month Wickenby became 14 Base Sub-Station parented by Ludford Magna and formed part of No 1 Group.

No 626 Squadron took part in many major raids on enemy targets and also in the use of heavy strategic bombers in front line ground operations. One such mission was during the Caen deadlock in 1944 when the target was an area two miles and a half by one mile to the north of Caen with the bombline 6,000 yards ahead of the foremost British troops. Flight Sergeant Eric Haslett, the engineer in a 626 Squadron Lancaster, on the raid:

'This was a daylight operation and should have been an easy one. Our target was immediately south of Caen and we were to bomb only on 'smoke markers', the object being to avoid hitting our own troops. There was a vast concentration of bombers and as we approached the coast the Germans let up a huge amount of "flak"—I have never seen so much before—one could almost step out and walk on it. We were hit by the flak many times and a small piece came through the fuselage on my side—starboard—passed by me, went through the navigator's legs, through the radio operator's legs and it was found afterwards in the radio operator's upholstery. There were our fighters but they were way in the distance—quite naturally! Despite the flak we bombed on target and made it back to Wickenby.'

On the fateful Nuremberg raid on March 30/31 1944, 626 Squadron sent 16 aircraft and all returned. Now, almost 12 months later, and with the war almost over, the target was again Nuremberg, and the dangers were just as great. The following is a report, 'K' Report No 1G/K19, of the raid, completed at the time, and gives a general picture of a bombing mission and the stress bomber crews worked under.

'Lancaster Mk I PD207 (Y Type) 12/W took off from Wickenby at 17.06 hours on March 16 1945, for a bombing mission to Nuremberg, being briefed to attack at 21.30 hours and carrying the following crews, the Captain being on his 13th sortie in his first Tour:-

'Captain. J.29015 F/O Wallace, James Lester. Canadian. Navigator. J.40793 F/O Harrison, Douglas McLean. Canadian. W/OP. 2205541 F/SGT Smith, George Tyson. Eng. F/ENG. 3021727 Sgt Tracey, William. Eng. A/B. J.40940 F/O Broocke, William Rufus. Canadian. M.U.G. R.366134 F/SGT

Adams, Douglas Edmund. Canadian. R/G. R.272882 F/SGT Hardick, Raymond Earl. Canadian.

'A normal take off was made at 17.06 hours and the aircraft set course and had proceeded as far as 4849/0939E (flying at 14,000 ft) above 5/10ths cloud with good visibility, Window being dropped at ordered rates, when a white fighter flare ignited at 21.11 hours 300 yds ahead. The flare was avoided and the aircraft continued on course, no indication being given on Fishpond of the presence of another aircraft.

'At 21.24 hours an Me 410 was sighted visually 100 yds away on the port beam and level with our aircraft at 14,000 ft. No engagement took place and the E/A broke away. At 21.25 hours an Me 410 again appeared and manoeuvred to attack from just below on the port quarter, (position 4917N 1015E). A Fishpond warning was not received as the Navigator was making an H2S check at the time. Corkscrew, port, was called for by the M.U.G. and neither aircraft opened fire, the E/A being lost to sight.

'Our aircraft had just finished its evasive action when the E/A opened fire with cannon from astern and below at 21.28 hours in the Nuremberg area. 14,000 ft, no cloud with good visibility, striking the rear turret and starboard inner engine causing an immediate fire, before the E/A broke away. Fire was not returned as the Rear Gunner was injured and the E/A was below the Lancaster, and hidden from the M.U.G. During this

No 626 Squadron at Wickenby. Taken soon after it was formed in November 1943.

Wickenby control tower today, with very little change from its wartime days.

attack the R/G received his injuries and the M.U.G. instructed the Captain in weaving evasive action. The W/OP went back to the R/G and rendered first aid, applying a tourniquet to his injured leg.

'The S/I engine was feathered, extinguishing the fire, and the aircraft commenced its run into the target. Control was difficult as the elevator trimmers had been damaged and the aircraft was in a shallow dive. S/Ls were seeking the Lancaster and the Captain decided to bomb immediately the bombs released at 21.29 hours from 12,000 ft, believed one mile short of the target. On the bomb doors being closed the aircraft was coned by several S/Ls and immediately hit by H/F setting the P/O engine on fire and causing extensive damage to the undersurfaces of the main plane's fuselage and bomb bay. The P/O was feathered and the run through the target completed on two engines.

'The Flight Engineer reported the S/O coolant temperature to be 110/120 degrees at 21.32 hours, and the Captain, believing he would lose a third engine and have to bale his crew out, asked the Navigator to give him a course for Switzerland. The original homeward course, however, was flown as the Wireless Operator who had been giving first aid to the R/G informed the Captain of his condition and he decided to get his gunner to an Allied Hospital as quckly as possible.

'WT Contact was established with Base at 22.43 hours, the W/OP giving details of the aircraft's predicament and their intention of trying to reach Juvincourt. Navigation was carried out on DR with the aircraft losing height at 50 ft per minute on a maximum IAS of 125 mph until coming into range of the Saar GEE chain when the aircraft's position was fixed as 4852N/0750E at 23.08 hours. Course was immediately set for Juvincourt and the IFF switched to distress code.

'The Battle Area was cleared at 22.30 hrs while the aircraft was flying in 10/10ths cloud at 4/5,000 ft, and Mayday watch contact attempted on Channel D from 23.35 hours onwards. Other channels were also used and single reds fired through breaks in the cloud. One SBC of 150 × 4 lb that had hung up over the target was jettisoned safe by H type jettison switch at 4918N/0410E from 4,000 ft at 00.23 hours. Mayday contact was made at 00.25 hours with A 62 control while the aircraft was in the Reims area, the condition of the aircraft and crew being given with a request for an emergency landing. A 62 control informed the Captain that their lighting was at the moment U/S and his RT strength was fading. The Lancaster was orbited at 4,000 ft and reds fired at minute intervals. These were seen by A 62 and the aircraft homed by RT.

'A double row of flarepath lights was observed without circuit funnels or glide path indication lighting. A QDM of 240° was passed and the aircraft prepared to land with the crew in their allocated crash positions, the injured R/G being supported by the B/A who had been with him since 21.34 hours. The undercarriage was lowered by the Flight Engineer using emergency air and the aircraft came in. Speed control was made difficult by the two US engines and lack of glide path indicators. The aircraft on final check touched down approximately 2/3rds the way along the 1,600 yd runway, and brake pressure being negligible, over-ran and straddled a railway cutting removing the entire railway signal system. The Captain and Bomb Aimer received slight facial injuries but the remainder of the crew were unhurt.

'The crew were removed from the aircraft by the American Air Force, and given First Aid, the Rear Gunner being conveyed to 178 US General Hospital at Reims, suffering from a large wound and fractures in his right leg, and splinters in

12 Squadron, Wickenby, in April 1945.

his left leg sustained during the fighter attacks.

'The crew and their equipment were taken to Reims for interrogation and after ascertaining on the following morning, March 17 1945, that a mobile RAE unit had stripped their aircraft of all equipment, left for Juvincourt. On March 18 1945, they returned from Juvincourt to Wickenby ferrying back a Lancaster belonging to No 101 Squadron which had been awaiting collection. Our aircraft 12/W is category E.'

Following its final bombing mission on April 25 1945 when 14 Lancasters bombed Berchtesgaden, the squadron took part in operation 'Manna', helped to repatriate British ex-POWs back to good old Blighty and bring British troops home from Italy.

Flight Lieutenant Tom Wardle was bombing leader of 626 Squadron and had been lucky to survive 42 operational missions. On April 29 1945 at 12.10 hours he took off in Lancaster D2-NG247, as bomb-aimer, but this time with four blocks of 1,254 lbs of supplies for the starving Dutch people. As they passed over Delft, the Dutch were out in force, on the roofs of the houses, clinging to chimney stacks, and always waving— towels, flags, sheets or scarves. Sheets and flags were spread out on roof tops, possibly away from the gaze of the occupying troops. They flew lower and waggled their wings to acknowledge the heart-warming display by the ordinary people—on this mission they could certainly be sure that the 'natives were

friendly'. Wardle was able to pick out a German patrol of about a dozen soldiers, marching with rifles slung along one of the main streets of Delft, but they did not appear to be taking much notice of the reaction of the people around them, and they were not fired on in any way.

Their drop zone was the local football pitch and the tiny grandstand was crammed to capacity with waving, cheering spectators, all behaving as though they had just witnessed the winning goal in a Cup Final, and seemingly quite oblivious of the fact that an overshoot by any of the aircraft could quite easily deposit a couple of tons of provisions in their laps. Flight Lieutenant Wardle:

'The disregard for their own safety in order to show us their appreciation affected me strongly, and left an indelible impression on my mind. I waved back through the Perspex nose of the aircraft after doing my "bombing" run, and was relieved to hear from the rear gunner over the intercom that our load had landed "smack in the middle of the target".' They touched down back at Wickenby after two hours and fifty minutes.

On September 24 1945, No 12 Squadron moved out to the permanent station at Binbrook and on October 14 No 626 Squadron disbanded, having spent its entire life at Wickenby.

After the departure of the heavy bombers, No 109 Squadron arrived during October 1945 with Mosquito XVIs but on November 27 1945 they departed and the airfield closed to flying. No 92 MU then took over and the airfield was used for the storage of bombs until 1956 when the unit moved to Faldingworth. The airfield was then sold and most of the site reverted to agriculture.

In 1963 a group of enthusiasts formed Lincs Air Touring Group to operate a Proctor light aircraft from Wickenby. Years of disuse had caused the runways to deteriorate and the group had to start their flying activities from a section of perimeter track while the runways were cleared of rubble and repaired.

The title was changed to Wickenby Flying Club in 1971 and the following year, when the site was up for sale, they were able to buy the northern part of it including the tower, a 'T2' hangar and parts of the runways. The 'B1' was still standing in 1978 apparently in use as a store by the local farmer.

Wigsley, Nottinghamshire

121/SK855695. W of Lincoln, between the villages of Wigsley and Spalford

Wigsley opened in February 1942 as a satellite for Swinderby in No 5 Group, Bomber Command. The main runway cut across the Wigsley road and part of Wigsley Wood was used in the airfield layout. On February 8 1942 the first unit to arrive was No 455 (RAAF) Squadron equipped with Handley Page Hampdens. The duties of these inexperienced crews were attacks on French ports or on Nickel raids over Lille and Paris. This unit took up extensive minelaying sorties which was to be their main role.

The Australians were just beginning to settle into the operational routine when, on April 19 1942, No 455 was withdrawn from the line. On the 26th of the month Wing Commander Lindeman moved 455 Squadron to Leuchars in Scotland to form a torpedo-strike squadron within Coastal Command. In May 1942 the first Lancaster Conversion Unit was formed with eight Lancasters and eight Manchesters into No 1654 HCU of No 5 Group (code letters 'JF' and 'UG'). The aircraft arrived from Swinderby in June 1942. No 1654 was responsible for accepting personnel from OTUs and then, after four-engined familiarisation and training, turning them out as complete crews for the squadrons of No 5 Group.

On March 15 1943 Swinderby became No 51 Base and Wigsley became a sub-station but this made no difference to conditions, which remained primitive. During 1943 there were many crashes: on January 26, Lancaster R5772; on April 15, Manchester L7294, which crashed as it approached the airfield; on May 17, Lancaster L7591, which crashed on take-off and Lancaster L7294 which stalled and burnt out. Manchester L7596 also overshot the runway.

In November 1943 the unit converted to Stirling IIIs so that all available Lancasters could return to operational units. On November 3 1944, the station was changed to No 75 Base in No 7 Group and the unit continued with its training programme.

With the war over, No 1654 HCU moved to Woolfox Lodge and on September 20 1945, No 28 Aircrew Holding Unit was formed, only to disband the following year. The airfield remained open as a satellite for Swinderby and was used for routine flying exercises. On July 1 1958 Swinderby stopped using the airfield as a relief landing ground and Wigsley was finally de-requisitioned.

Today the airfield has resumed its agricultural role and the control tower now houses bales of straw and stands gaunt against the elements as a stark reminder of its bleak wartime days. The few remaining huts are so overgrown with bushes it is hard to imagine that it was ever an airfield, such is the rapid reclamation by man and nature.

Winthorpe, Nottinghamshire

121/SK825565. NE of Newark between the villages of Winthorpe and Coddington

Winthorpe officially opened as a satellite for Swinderby in September 1940 but the two Polish Squadrons housed at the parent station did not move in until October. The squadrons used the airfield as a dispersal with three Fairey Battles from each of No 300 and 301 Squadrons. Training continued from both airfields and on October 29, No 300 Squadron lost another crew when Battle L5356 crashed at Sutton-on-Trent while on a training flight.

By October 1940 the Polish bomber squadrons were told they would be re-equipped with Vickers Wellington Ics and, on the 18th, the first Wellington arrived, flown by Pilot Officer Janas. During the period from September 15 to October 18 1940, Nos 300 and 301 Squadrons carried out 85 sorties and dropped over 45 tons of bombs with their Battle aircraft.

On November 14 1940 the Luftwaffe paid Winthorpe a visit. The airman on

Aerial view of Newark Air Museum on Winthorpe Airfield, taken in 1978, before moving to new site. From left to right the three large aircraft are a Varsity, Shackleton and Hastings.

duty looked into the sky and saw what he thought was a parachutist but which was in fact a landmine. Shouting to his mate they flung themselves into a ditch as it blew up their hut. It left a crater 39 ft across and 20 ft deep, and is thought to be the first parachute mine to fall in England. No damage was done to aircraft or men.

1941 started with an attack on Bremen on the night of January 1/2 but, when the squadron returned the weather had deteriorated. With a snow blizzard blowing and visibility down to a few yards, the first Wellington, R1006, crashed on landing, fortunately with no casualties. The other aircraft were then diverted to other airfields. Two crashed at Waddington with only a rear gunner surviving from both crews.

The airfield continued to be used for training, particularly when Swinderby was rendered unserviceable by heavy rain that bogged down the Wellingtons.

On November 27 1941, control of Winthorpe passed to Ossington and on February 7 1942 Winthorpe became a second satellite for Syerston. No 455 Squadron, which was based at Swinderby and later Wigsley, used Winthorpe as a dispersal for some of their Hampdens during the latter part of 1941 and early 1942. After their departure the airfield was closed for runway construction and there was no further activity for the rest of the year.

The runways were of the standard pattern with the main one being 2,000 yards long and the two intersecting ones 1,430 yards each. But the airfield was used as little as possible, for unfortunately the usual take-off direction on the main runway was over Ransome & Marles' roller bearing factory, which was on important war work. The risk was considered very great that a fully laden bomber might crash into the factory with devastating consequences. It was a pity this was not thought about before the runways were laid.

On October 15 1942, Winthorpe was returned to the control of Swinderby as a second satellite and on the last day of the year received its own unit, No 1661 Heavy Conversion Unit, of No 5 Group. This was formed at Skellingthorpe on October 7 1942 by Squadron Leader Nettleton from Nos 9, 44 and 49 Bomber Squadron Conversion Flights.

On arriving at Winthorpe No 1661 HCU were operating eight Manchesters and ten Lancasters (coded 'GP' and 'KB'). The unit's first Commanding Officer, Group Captain E.S. Butler, OBE, arrived on February 1 1943. In March, Winthorpe became a sub-station of Swinderby Base Station. Crashes were frequent, including a Manchester on May 19 1943 and eight Lancasters, one of which was burnt out and another which crashed at Balderton.

Group Captain N.C. Pleasance was the next Commanding Officer of Winthorpe, and took over on August 1 1943. He was succeeded on December 7 by Group Captain E.L.S. Ward, DFC. In the autumn, 16 Halifaxes arrived to replace the Manchesters but by November they in turn were replaced by 37 Stirling IIIs. In January 1944 all the Lancasters departed because of the need for this type in operational squadrons of Bomber Command which were converting from Stirlings under the Ladder Plan.

The changeover to the new Officers' Mess took place at this time and the Old Mess at Coddington Hall was turned over entirely to sleeping accommodation for officers while the Station Headquarters moved to the new Station Office Block.

Winthorpe now ceased to be a satellite of Swinderby and became a Station Headquarters. Group Captain J.H. Woodin was appointed Commanding Officer on April 27 1944. On May 26, Stirling LJ558 swung on landing and crashed into the station workshops. Fortunately none of the crew were seriously injured, but on August 27 Pilot Officer Round, RNZAF, and his crew were not as lucky when their Stirling, LK616, crashed and burst into flames at Hawton, near Newark. The only survivor was Sergeant Solly, air gunner.

During 1944 a large number of Horsas and some Hamilcar gliders were in storage at Winthorpe in readiness for operation 'Market Garden'. The station church was completed by July and dedicated by the Rt Rev The Lord Bishop of Southwell. Then, on November 3 1944, control of No 1661 HCU was transferred from No 5 Group to No 7 Group and No 51 Base Headquarters was renumbered No 75 Base Headquarters.

At the end of 1944 and the beginning of 1945, Lancaster Is and IIIs replaced the Stirlings as the equipment of the conversion unit. This changeover would result in crews being able to proceed in future directly to their squadrons. The last Stirling crew completed training on February 4 1945.

No 1661 HCU now had an establishment of 32 Lancasters and by March the unit was engaged in automatic gun laying training, which involved fighter affiliation, and subsequently a number of Hurricanes and Spitfires arrived. During this period three Lancasters crashed, at Langford on March 24, at Oxton on April 16 and at Winthorpe on May 25 1945.

Squadron Leader R.O. Rose was appointed Station Commander on August 13. With the termination of the war in Europe the activities of No 1661 Heavy Conversion Unit had come to an end, and

training ceased on August 8 1945. The Lancasters were despatched to other units during August and No 1661 HCU was disbanded on September 10. Ten days later, RAF Station Winthorpe transferred from Bomber to Transport Command, and in October was reduced to a care and maintenance basis, once again becoming a satellite to Swinderby. No 75 Base Headquarters disbanded on October 1 1945 and on the 20th of the month Winthorpe became a satellite of Syerston in No 4 Group, Transport Command. No 1333 Transport Support Training Unit, which was based at Syerston and operating Halifaxes, Dakotas, Oxfords and Horsa gliders (coded 'CM' and 'ZR'), used Winthorpe as a Dropping Zone until July 1947. No 1331 Heavy Transport Conversion Unit, also based at Syerston and operating Halifax aircraft, used Winthorpe during 1947. In this period a number of Royal Army Service Corps troops were billeted here.

Winthorpe was later transferred to Maintenance Command and in February 1953 the Central Servicing Development Establishment arrived from Wittering. No aircraft were operated by this unit, which moved to Swanton Morley in January 1958.

In 1956 Winthorpe was transferred to Home Command and, although during this period it was allocated to the USAF as a hospital, it was never occupied and control reverted to MOD on June 30 1958. The following month Swinderby took over the parenting responsibilities before its eventual closure and in July 1959 Winthorpe was reduced to inactive status.

A faithful satellite during the war years, it is today the home of the Newark and Nottinghamshire Showground and the runways are used for parking. One piece of runway is still in fair condition and used from time to time by light aircraft. Also, the Ministry of Transport operates a Heavy Vehicle Testing Station on part of the runway and the airfield maintains its link with the past through the Newark Air Museum that is also based here.

Woodhall Spa, Lincolnshire

122/TF210615. 2 miles S of Woodhall Spa just W of B1192 road

Situated midway between Woodhall Spa and Tattershall Thorpe in the flat countryside of south Lincolnshire, this was a perfect site for a heavy bomber station, albeit a little close to Coningsby just a few miles to the south. Construction work started early in 1941, at which time much of the site was heavily wooded. Use was made of this factor, particularly on the northern perimeter where Ostler's Plantation provided natural cover. The airfield had three concrete runways which were laid out in the standard pattern with the main one running from Ostler's Plantation right up to the B1192 road. The technical site was on the southern side of the airfield.

Woodhall Spa opened in February 1942 in No 5 Group, Bomber Command, as a satellite for Coningsby. The first unit to move in was No 97 Squadron from Coningsby, on March 1 1942, so that the parent station could start running down in preparation for having concrete runways built. No 97 Squadron, equipped with Lancaster Mks I and III, remained at Woodhall Spa until April 17 1943, during which time it took part in the historic low-level daylight attack on Augsburg in conjunction with No 44 Squadron; the 1,000-bomber raids on Cologne, Essen and Bremen; the dusk raid on Le Creusot, during which a total force of 94 Lancasters took part and bombed the target every four seconds; and Bomber Command's first daylight attack on Italy, the target being Milan. A very hectic 12 months for the unit before it moved to Bourn and joined No 8 (PFF) Group.

No 97 Squadron was replaced by 619 that formed here on April 18 1943 as a heavy bomber squadron equipped with Lancasters Mk I and III (code letters

'PG'). This unit also took part in many major raids before moving to Coningsby on January 10 1944.

During January, No 617 Squadron (the famous 'Dambusters') moved to Woodhall Spa. It would remain here until the end of the war and, again, play a major role, possibly its greatest. The move to Woodhall Spa was to give the unit better security since it could only house a single squadron. The Petwood Hotel was commandeered in the village, but as this was some three miles from the station it did have its drawbacks. It was from this Lincolnshire station that Wing Commander Leonard Cheshire, now Group Captain Cheshire, VC, DSO, DFC, RAF Rt'd, and Wing Commander 'Micky' Martin, DSO and Bar, DFC and 2 Bars, AFC, continued their target marking experiments. Martin tried divebombing his Lancaster at a target and it worked—this was now to be the drill for releasing markers.

Inside the station it was all very hush-hush and the Lincolnshire locals thought Woodhall Spa was just another bomber station, but these were special crews. They trained hard and gained a high reputation for accurate low level marking and bombing of specific targets. The two Mosquitoes loaned to the squadron proved so successful that Air Chief Marshal Hon Sir Ralph Cochrane, drove down to see Air Marshal Harris for four extra Mossies and, shortly afterwards, on April 15 1944, No 627 Squadron arrived at Woodhall Spa equipped with Mosquito

Petwood Hotel, Woodhall Spa, 1944. Officers' Mess of the famous 'Dam Busters', 617 Squadron. Many country hotels and large houses were requisitioned for RAF use.

IV aircraft. This was a squadron from Bennett's Pathfinder Force and its transfer was a challenge since Bennett did not think 617 Squadron could improve on the Pathfinders, but he did not reckon with a perfectionist like Cheshire.

The most remarkable operation undertaken by 617 Squadron was in operation 'Taxable', a task for which it had trained night and day for the past month. 16 Lancasters, in two groups of eight, pulled off one of the best bluffs of the war; the simulation of a large 'ghost' convoy of ships. Each aircraft had a 12-man crew—an extra pilot, an extra navigator and three men with stop-watches to drop the bundles of Window. Meticulous timing was necessary for, if one Lancaster had been 50 feet out in height, or four seconds out in ETA timing, the ghost convoy would have looked suspect.

At 23.00 hours the first eight Lancasters took off from Woodhall Spa and flew at exactly 200 mph over all the little ships, following the drill to perfection, hour after hour. Around 03.00 hours the second wave took over in a changeover which needed split-second timing. When the last Lancaster turned for home, before the light was good enough for the Germans to see that they had been tricked, the crews knew they had done a good job as the radar-predicted fire opened up on the ghost armada with their 12-in shells.

In August 1944, the C-in-C sent for Cheshire who arrived to learn that he had been awarded the VC, which is usually conferred for a single act of heroism. In Cheshire's case it was awarded in effect for four years of courage and for target marking.

Guy Gibson was less fortunate. After the Dams raid he had been withdrawn from front-line operations, but he always wanted to return and volunteered to act as Master Bomber in a Mosquito of No 627 Squadron on a raid against Rheydt, Germany, on September 19/20 1944. Sadly, he came down in flames on his return journey and his aircraft crashed in Holland, killing both himself and his navigator.

No 617 Squadron was first to drop one of the Barnes Wallis six-tonners, code-named 'Tallboy', which were used on the Saumur railway tunnel in northern France. Further attacks were made on dams and, on March 14 1945, Squadron Leader C.C. Calder, in Lancaster PD112

'S' Sugar, dropped the first of the 22,000 lb 'Grand Slam' bombs to wreck the Bielefeld railway viaduct in Germany.

By April 1945 the strength of the station was No 617 Squadron with 25 Lancasters plus one Mosquito, and No 627, the only non-Lancaster squadron in 5 Group, with 27 Mosquitoes. The last operation by 617 Squadron was on April 25 1945 against Berchtesgaden. On June 18 No 617 Squadron moved to Waddington, and on October 1 No 627 was re-numbered 109 Squadron and equipped with Mosquito Mk IXs and XVIs; but they were no longer needed, now the job was done, and pulled out before the end of October. The airfield then closed to flying but the site was retained for defence purposes. As part of the 1957 White Paper missile programme, part of the former airfield was reactivated in 1959 to enable No 112 Squadron to be based here. This unit was equipped with 16 Bloodhound missiles and remained at Woodhall Spa until 1965. The site was then used as an out-station for engine testing and part of the former airfield, including a 'T2' hangar and supporting buildings, was retained to provide facilities for Coningsby.

At June 1980 the units at Woodhall Spa are the Police Dog Flight, Supply Squadron Hangar—Storage, Engine Test Facility and the Propulsion and Rectification Section. The role of the latter unit is to strip and repair engines, then to test and return them to the parent station at Coningsby.

Woolfox Lodge,
Leicestershire (Rutland)
130/SK960130. Approximately 6 miles NW of Stamford, adjacent to the A1 S of Stretton junction

Woolfox Lodge was one of several airfields sited adjacent to the main A1 and was on the east side just south of the Stretton junction. It was rushed into service in a very basic state on December 13 as a RLG for Cottesmore some five miles to the north-west. The Hampdens and Wellingtons of No 14 OTU used the airfield until August 1941.

In October, the station was transferred to No 5 Group, Bomber Command, as a satellite for North Luffenham, and No 61 Squadron moved in that same month. The unit was equipped with Manchesters and began to convert to Lancasters in April 1942, but the following month it moved to Syerston, Nottinghamshire.

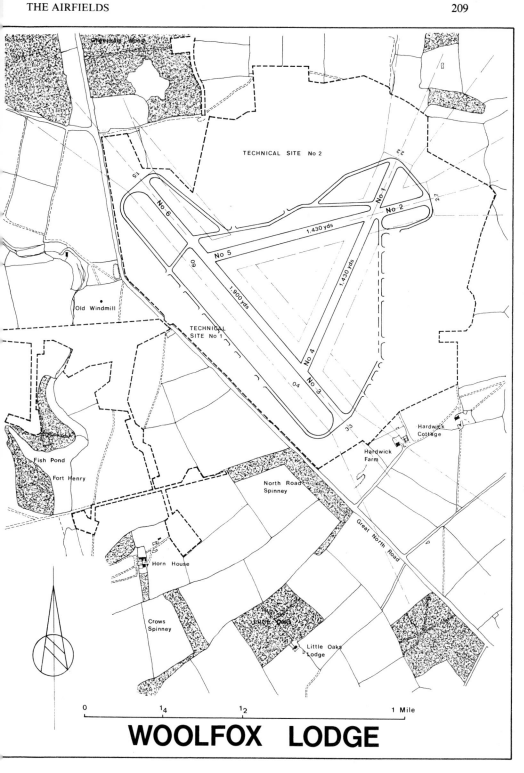

Croxton Wood

TECHNICAL SITE No 2

No 6

No 5

No 1

No 2

1,430 yds

1,430 yds

1,900 yds

04

No 3

No 4

60

Old Windmill

TECHNICAL SITE No 1

Fish Pond

Fort Henry

North Road Spinney

Hardwick Farm

Hardwick Cottage

33

Horn House

Crows Spinney

Little Oaks

Little Oaks Lodge

Great North Road

0   ¼   ½   1 Mile

WOOLFOX LODGE

Stirling of No 1651 HCU seen here at Woolfox Lodge.

Then, in June, the role of the parent station changed to operational training and Woolfox Lodge was taken over by No 1429 (Czechoslovak) Operational Training Flight that moved in from East Wretham on July 1 1942. The Commanding Officer was Squadron Leader Breitcetl and the unit was equipped with Wellington aircraft. No 1429 (Czech) OT Flight carried out normal training but by August 31 1942 it had departed for Church Broughton and 93 Group.

The airfield then closed for the construction of concrete runways and a general 'facelift' on October 18 1942. Station records show that two 'Q' sites were operated by this station, one at Pickworth and the other at Swinstead. An entry at March 1944 gives mention to these sites and records that both had been unserviceable for some time due to trouble with the generators and that steps were immediately taken to put these into operation, but that they were not yet serviceable. From the scant official evidence available I am certain that the only one the station could have had was at Pickworth. Swinstead is on Lord Ancaster's estate and it was certainly not there. In any case, Swayfield was only a mile or so away, and this was where Cottesmore had a decoy.

On June 1 1943 the airfield re-opened and was now complete with three concrete runways and an encircling perimeter track. The main runway, 33-15, was 5,700 ft long and almost parallel to the A1 road. The two intersecting runways were 4,200 ft long each. Hangarage consisted of four 'T2' type and one 'B1' type, and Woolfox had the usual dispersed accommodation and hardstandings. During the first week of June No 1665 Heavy Conversion Unit (code letters 'NY' and 'OG'), arrived from Waterbeach with Stirling I and III

aircraft and, on June 7 1943, Woolfox Lodge became a parent and independent station under No 3 Group. During the first few weeks No 1665 HCU had many crashes. On July 4 Stirling G/BF339 swung on take-off and crashed, as did V/BK621 on the 24th and K/BF444 on the 27th. On the 25th, Stirling C/EF35 landed out of control and crashed. To round off the month, J/EF337 swung on landing and crashed. The crash crews were kept very busy. No 1665 HCU moved on January 29 1944 to Tilstock.

With the departure of the conversion unit the airfield was signalled unserviceable in view of the incomplete state of the Drem lighting. Work started on sodium funnels on two runways and plugs for a portable sodium flarepath, but records do not show if this work was fully completed.

During the autumn of 1943, 32 Horsa gliders arrived at the airfield and were held in dispersed storage. These were maintained by a detachment of No 2 HGMU from Snailwell. The gliders were moved to their operational bases in March 1944. That same month the Stirlings (coded 'HA') of No 218 (Gold Coast) Squadron arrived. The unit continued operations, most of which were minelaying, with the Stirlings and, during the summer months, began to have them replaced by Lancasters. The strength and type of aircraft for No 218 Squadron at the end of July 1944 was ten Stirling Mk IIIs, six Lancaster Mk Is and three Mk IIIs.

With the arrival of the Lancaster, however, the operational life of the station was coming to an end and, following the departure of the few remaining crews of No 218 Squadron early in August, Woolfox Lodge ceased to be an operational station. The airfield was then used for a few weeks by one flight of No 3 LFS from Feltwell. The last operation from Woolfox Lodge had been on August 2 1944 when six aircraft of No

218 Squadron took part in a daylight raid on a V-1 Launching Site at Mont Candon, south of Dieppe. All aircraft returned safely to base by 19.57 hours. By August 7 the remaining crews of No 218 Squadron had left Woolfox Lodge for Methwold.

The following day the station was back in action when 19 Lancasters of No 90 Squadron (from Tuddenham) landed here between 01.13 and 02.07 hours. They had been on a bombing raid south of Caen and were diverted to Woolfox Lodge on account of bad visibility at Tuddenham. All aircraft returned to their base the same morning.

During the month of August No 3 LFS carried out training, which consisted of circuits and bumps, at the airfield and they returned to Feltwell on the 28th. The station was then reduced to a care and maintenance basis. At the same time tar spraying of runways and perimeter tracks was carried out and a new MT shed and yard were completed before the airfield was transferred to the USAAF IXth Air Force on September 1 1944 to become USAAF Station 478.

During September and into October the station was under the administration of the 9th TCCSU and the 62nd Station Complement Squadron. No flying units were based here and, on October 20 1944, the station was handed back to the Royal Air Force under the control of No 7 Group, Bomber Command, as a sub-station to North Luffenham. From November 10 1944 until it disbanded on July 13 1945 Woolfox Lodge accommodated No 1651 HCU flying a variety of aircraft, including Stirling Mk IIIs, Lancaster Mk Is and IIIs (of which it had 32 on strength in January 1945), Oxford Is, Hurricane IIcs and Beaufighter NF VIs. During 1945, No 1654 HCU arrived from Wigsley with Lancaster Mk Is and IIIs but on September 1 1945 this unit also disbanded.

On August 1 1945 the station was transferred from Bomber Command and again placed on a care and maintenance basis under the control of HQ Maintenance Command and was then used for several years by 259 MU. During this period, part of the station was used as a German POW camp.

The airfield then became a care and maintenance unit in Flying Training Command in September 1948 and was used as a RLG by No 7 FTS, Cottesmore, for their Harvard T 2B and Balliol T 2 aircraft from May 1951 until it was reduced to an inactive status in April 1954, and closed to flying. From February 1960, as part of 151 Wing, HQ North Luffenham, it accommodated No 62 (SAM) Squadron until this unit disbanded on September 30 1964 when the station was once again reduced to C & M. It was made an inactive station on January 6 1965 and was finally disposed of on November 4 1966.

An unusual shot of a 218 Squadron Stirling from Woolfox Lodge. It is not known why it does not have any code letters.

Today, the hangars have gone but some perimeter track and two runways, albeit moss covered, still remain. At the date of my visit in June 1980 a few buildings on the old technical site remained but they had almost disappeared as a result of shrubs such as hazel, bramble and silver birch. The other remains are a few Nissen huts and the control tower which was lived in until a year or so ago. It is also easy to make out the former Bloodhound SAM compound which defended Cottesmore.

Worksop, Nottinghamshire

120/SK625815. Between Worksop and the A1 road

One of the small number of airfields in Nottinghamshire, Worksop was built in a rather wooded area near the hamlet of Scofton, and the airfield was often called by that name by the local population.

In July 1942 the Air Ministry requisitioned farm and woodland in the Scofton area for an airfield. It was taken a stage further when land clearing started. Then, during 1943, building commenced by contractors Wimpey and Carmichael. The airfield followed the standard pattern, having three paved runways, the main one running almost due east-west, with the accommodation widely dispersed around the surrounding countryside. It was intended to be a satellite for Finningley, replacing Bircotes which only had a grass surface, and opened in that capacity on November 7 1943.

On November 8 the familiar RAF windsock was hoisted into place and on the 11th the first occupants, No 18 OTU, moved in from Finningley on the closure of that station for construction of tarmac runways. The unit had a wide variety of aircraft, such as Wellingtons, Martinets, Oxfords and Tomahawks which were used for fighter affiliation, and remained until May 1944 when part of the OTU returned to Finningley leaving 'B' Flight at Worksop. The airfield was also used as a Relief Landing Ground for No 86 OTU Gamston for a few weeks in the autumn of 1944.

No 18 OTU 'B' Flight finally left Worksop at the beginning of 1945 and its successor at Finningley, Bomber Command Instructors' School, with Wellington aircraft, continued to use the airfield until 1946. In 1945-46 several small units, including the Bomber Command Night Vision Training School

and the RAF Central Vision Training School, were based at Worksop. In November 1946 Worksop ceased to be a satellite of Finningley and was transferred to Flying Training Command. The station continued under that formation until finally, on June 7 1948, the RAF Central Vision Training School moved out and the airfield closed.

August 11 1952 was the day that marked the beginning of a new chapter in the life of RAF Worksop, when No 211 Advanced Flying School formed here with an establishment of Meteor T7s and F8s. Because of the Korean War the airfield had reopened after the necessary repair works had been carried out and it was to enjoy a further period of activity.

The AFS was divided into three squadrons with No 1 flying the F8s and Nos 2 and 3 the T7s. On June 1 1954 No 211 AFS was renamed No 211 Flying Training School and remained at Worksop until it was disbanded on June 9 1956, to re-emerge as No 4 Flying Training School equipped with Vampire T 11s and Provost T1s. Three squadrons were still retained, with No 1 flying Meteor Mk 7s and 8s, and numbers 2 and 3 Vampires.

On May 23 1955 No 616 South Yorkshire Auxiliary Squadron arrived at Worksop while Finningley was inactive for reconstruction as a V-bomber base. The unit's green and grey camouflaged Meteors, with yellow and green squadron markings, were a sharp contrast to the silver and orange training aircraft at the station. But, despite all the hard training, Worksop was to be the last base of this famous Auxiliary unit, which had achieved the distinction of being the first unit in the world to fly Meteor jet fighters operationally in 1944.

During 1955, No 616 went on summer camp to Celle, in West Germany, and in 1956 to Tangmere—their old wartime base where, with different aircraft and pilots, they had flown 15 years earlier with Douglas Bader's famous Tangmere Wing. This was to be their last summer camp, and on March 10 1957, No 616 Squadron, Royal Auxiliary Air Force, was disbanded at RAF Worksop. The station still functioned with No 4 Flying Training School until June 9 1958 when this unit was disbanded and the airfield closed and was put under care and maintenance. On December 8 1960 the site was de-requisitioned and RAF Worksop was

Above *No 504 Squadron Meteors on dispersal at Wymeswold in 1950.* **Below** *Control tower at Wymeswold in 1979.*

finally still after a glorious career of training aircrews during war and peace.

Today only the main all-weather runway remains, used occasionally for testing car brakes. The other two runways, the hangars, buildings and control tower have long since gone. The bustle of camp life has vanished and never again will Worksop be the home for busy training units, or play host to weary bomber crews who, on returning from hazardous operations, had found their own home bases fogbound and had to seek out other airfields, Worksop obliging on many occasions.

Wymeswold, Leicestershire

129/SK585225. A few miles E of Lough-borough between the villages of Hoton and Wymeswold

This airfield was constructed to the standard wartime pattern with three paved runways, the main one running almost east to west and parallel to the minor road connecting Hoton and Wymeswold, after which the airfield was named, being the largest of the villages.

The airfield is bordered on all sides by roads, the B675 to the west, B676 to the south, the Burton-on-Wolds to Wymes-wold minor road to the east and the northern boundary, the Hoton to Wymes-

wold road. Most of the accommodation was dispersed on the east of the airfield and the flight building to the west near Hoton village.

The airfield officially opened on May 16 1942 as part of No 7 Group, Bomber Command, and was concerned solely with the training of aircrew, first bomber crews for Bomber Command during the first two years, and then for Transport Command.

The first unit to use the base was No 28 OTU which was equipped mainly with Wellingtons, but Lancasters, Halifaxes and Stirlings were to be seen at Wymeswold. Many hundreds of aircrews were trained at this station, among whom was Squadron Leader David Penman who was awarded the Distinguished Service Order for his part in the epic low level Augsberg raid. Also, in the historic 1,000-bomber raids, senior aircrew from Wymeswold made up the numbers for it was a case of every available man and aircraft.

On June 6 1944, No 28 OTU was under 93 Group as a mixed unit with Wellington IIIs and Xs, Hurricanes and Martinets. The role of training bomber crews continued until mid-October 1944 when, with Fortress Europe now breached and the Allies gaining ground daily, the complexion of the war altered. There was no longer the overwhelming need for bomber crews, and the emphasis was now for air transport for the forces overseas.

Thus, on October 15 1944, Wymeswold

Above *An end to an era. Wymeswold in February 1977. This shows the main entrance and Guardroom.* **Below** *'T2' hangar and water tower at Wymeswold in 1979.*

passed to the control of No 44 Group, Transport Command, and became No 108 OTU whose task was to train highly qualified bomber crews for the less hazardous transport role. Gone were the bombers from the Wymeswold countryside and in their place came the Dakota III aircraft, the workhorses, that would be used for troops and supplies.

In August 1945, No 108 OTU became No 1382 Transport Support Conversion Unit, still using Dakota III and IV aircraft but now in No 4 Group, Transport Command. This unit remained until December 10 1947 when it then moved to North Luffenham and the airfield closed down.

In February 1949 the airfield re-opened and, on May 3, No 504 Auxiliary Squadron arrived with Spitfire 22s. In November of that year it became the first Auxiliary squadron to be re-equipped with Meteor IV aircraft, later VIIIs. In the following year Wymeswold was transferred to No 12 Group of Fighter Command. At the beginning of July 1954, No 7107 Reserve Flight was formed and towards the end of the month was joined by No 1969 AOP Flight equipped with Auster Mk VI aircraft and piloted by Royal Artillery Officers, but maintained by Royal Air Force crews.

From August 1955-1957, three regular squadrons used the station, although for only short periods. They were No 56 Squadron with Meteors, then Hunters; No 257 (Burma) Squadron equipped with Hawker Hunter 2s; and No 263 (Norway) Squadron, also equipped with Hawker Hunters, which at that time were the latest transonic front-line fighters of the Royal Air Force.

After the station closed in 1957, Field Aircraft Services moved in from Tollerton and were engaged in major overhauls on Viscounts. In 1968 the company moved to the East Midlands Airport. Many aerodrome buildings are now used by various industrial organisations and some of the larger huts are used by local farmers as store sheds. Today the deserted control tower stands bleak and forlorn. The dispersal flight office is overgrown, but the hangars, water tower and guard-room are there as reminders of Wymeswold's Royal Air Force past.

Index of units referred to in the text